Passing It On–
A Memoir

By Yuri Nakahara Kochiyama
UCLA Asian American Studies Center Spring 1998 Scholar-in-Residence

Edited by Marjorie Lee,

Akemi Kochiyama-Sardinha, and

Audee Kochiyama-Holman

UCLA Asian American Studies Center Press

Fourth printing (digital reprint 2017)

Library of Congress Catalog Card Number 2004100253

ISBN 0-934052-37-9 (softcover)

ISBN 0-934052-38-7 (hardcover)

COPYEDITING BY Brandy Liên Worrall

GRAPHIC DESIGN/PRODUCTION BY Mary Uyematsu Kao

COVER DESIGN BY Mary Uyematsu Kao

SENIOR EDITING BY Russell C. Leong, UCLA ASIAN AMERICAN STUDIES CENTER PRESS

All photographs and images in this publication are courtesy of the Yuri Kochiyama Collection, Special Collections, University of California, Los Angeles or are by courtesy of Kochiyama family.

Cover photographs—
Frontcover: Yuri with two activists speaking at a movement event, New York, circa 1970s.
Backcover: Yuri at the 125th Street Subway Station, New York City's Harlem, circa 1980s.

UCLA Asian American Studies Center Press
3230 Campbell Hall, Box 951546
Los Angeles, CA 90095-1546

Printed in the United States.

Billy

Yuri and Bill

Aichi

Passing It On

. . .is dedicated to
my late husband, Bill Kochiyama;
my two children, Billy and Aichi
who passed away prematurely;
my surviving children,
Audee, Eddie, Jimmy, and Tommy,
and their spouses,
Herb, Pam, Alison, and Julie;
my two oldest grandchildren,
Zulu and Akemi,
and their spouses, Masai and Marc;
my younger grandchildren,
Herbie III, Ryan, Traci, Maya,
Christopher, Aliya, and Kahlil;
& my great-grandchildren,
Kai, Leilani, Kenji, and Malia.
I feel there is no way
I can thank you enough
for all you mean to me and
have done for me.

Herbie, Audee, and Herb

Marc, Akemi, Leilani and Malia
(CLOCKWISE FROM TOP LEFT)

Masai, Kai, Zulu and Kenji

Pam and Eddie with Sachi

Ryan, Traci, Christopher, Julie and
Tommy (CLOCKWISE FROM TOP LEFT)

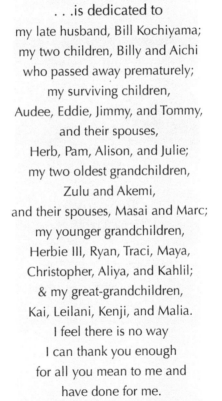

Maya, Jimmy, Aliya, Alison and Kahlil

(FROM LEFT) Grace Lee Boggs, Yuri and Nobuko Miyamoto attending
a student conference on the Asian American Movement at UCLA, May 1998.

Table of Contents

Acknowledgments

My "Scholar-in-Residence" appointment in 1998 was made possible by generous resources provided through the UCLA's Japanese American Studies Endowed Chair and the Nikkei Remembrance Fund. The Endowment and Fund, created by the generosity of the Japanese American alumni and friends of the university, paved the way for the collective effort of many people who helped me begin writing my memoirs. I will be forever grateful that they gave me this unusual opportunity.

Some people have encouraged me to write my memoirs, and I thank them all for their interest in me. Though my life does not seem particularly special, I hope I can make this a worthwhile reading to the "grands" and "greatgrands." Many people have inspired me; so many events have opened my eyes and my mind. My family has always been my home base (base of operation) and kept me grounded from going off into space. Their patience and understanding have allowed me to be independent.

For the general direction of my adult life, I credit my husband Bill, who has always been a major part of my life. We always did things together, and he supported me even if he did not always agree with me. I wish he were with me now, so that we could be writing this together. He was the real journalist in the family. I think, though, he has been and still is right now advising and directing me from wherever he is.

I am also grateful to every member of the K family—their spouses, children, and pets (Frida, Sachi, and Rocky), who are an integral part of our family. My Los Angeles family—Jimmy and Alison, and Tommy and Julie— let me stay at their homes on weekends and provided overall care for me throughout my UCLA appointment. I looked forward to interacting with the grand-children—Maya, Aliya, Kahlil, Ryan, Traci, and Christopher. Family members in the Northern California area—Audee and Herb Holman, and Eddie Kochiyama and Pam Wu—initially showed a curious interest of what I was doing, as well as my grown grandchildren in New York—Zulu Williams and his wife Masai, and Akemi Kochiyama-Sardinha and her husband Marc Sardinha. Writing about myself proved to be quite an undertaking, and my first completed draft provoked considerable dialogue among my children.

After completing the first of what would be many drafts, I received valuable assistance from Audee and Akemi, who played especially critical roles in guiding me and communicating the concerns of the K family. They sacrificed much of their time in the midst of demanding family, career, and academic obligations. They helped me proof, rewrite, and fill in some of the gaps to my personal and political life with their own reflections.

University members who opened the door for me were Don Nakanishi, Director of the Asian American Studies Center; Glenn Omatsu, former associate editor; Mary Kao, production designer who transformed the manuscript into a book; Professor Valerie Matsumoto and the late Professor Yuji Ichioka, who provided me with books to read; and Raul Ebio, who provided computer assistance. I especially want to thank Russell Leong and Brandy Liên Worrall, the Center's Publications editors, who provided technical guidance and brought the manuscript to publication.

There were also Center staff and students who volunteered to give me much-needed and dependable transportation to school: Judy Soo Hoo, Malcolm Kao, Leslie Ito, and Nancy Kim. I also enjoyed the warm relationship of Center staff: Sefa Aina, Meg Thornton, and Cathy Castor. To all those who helped make my Los Angeles residence memorable and the many, many revisions to my manuscript possible—a BIG thanks!

When I first arrived at UCLA, Renee Tajima-Peña and Armando Peña provided me with a computer I could use away from campus. The lovely house owned by the Niwa family at which I resided was arranged through Rev. Mark Nakagawa of West Los Angeles United Methodist Church, who gave the Center the contact for UCLA to rent suitable accommodations for me. I am thankful to Asayo Sakemi and Leona Daley, who were kind and helpful to me as next-door neighbors.

I am also so grateful to Mr. Arthur Tobier, who, years ago in the early 1980s, interviewed me for the Community Documentation Workshop's oral histories series on people who worked and lived in New York City. Out of his efforts, my oral history was published and has actually been a valuable reference for me regarding so many things that happened a long time ago and since forgotten.

My main supporter who kept me going throughout this long process was Marji Lee, UCLA Asian American Studies Center's librarian. Assigned with the daunting task of supervising and monitoring my progress and day-to-day needs in 1998, Marji provided me with many suggestions and advice even when I just wanted to quit. Without her continuous encouragement, coaching, and reminders to keep focused, the editing of drafts and the final manuscript to publish this memoir would never have been completed. I thank her and all her colleagues at UCLA for making possible this opportunity to pass it on.

There was a two-year period I was not in touch with Marji. I was shocked to find out that she was fighting cancer. During her treatment, she even made an effort, with the help of her family, to attend my big eightieth birthday party here in Oakland. She lost her hair and was totally bald. I will not forget Marji's determination to help me finish my memoir even after her treatment was completed, after having gone through such a critical and dangerous affliction. Her selflessness made this book possible.

For any others unnamed and whose assistance, small or large, was extended, please accept my humble thanks. I cannot remember or name you all, but you know who you are and what you have done for me.

Photograph by Marji Lee

Yuri returning to UCLA's Campbell Hall after giving a lecture in Professor Valerie Matsumoto's Asian American Studies class, Spring 1998.

Yuri, Angela Davis and Akemi Kochiyama-Sardinha, October 1997.
Angela Davis moderated the African/Asian Round Table at San Francisco State University.

Foreword

By Akemi Kochiyama-Sardinha

In helping Yuri edit what would become her memoir, my Aunt Audee and I faced two obstacles. For one, we realized how difficult it was for my grandmother to talk about herself, so throughout the book she often reverts to playing an advocacy role for the causes she supports rather than conveying her personal insights and life experiences. The other difficulty is that because she speaks in a more rhetorical manner when addressing certain issues or events, she reflects a political viewpoint that might not be accessible to the average reader. Because my grandmother is who she is, all of us who played an editorial role agreed that while we could make occasional edits and changes, we could not change Yuri's voice, passion, issues, or people to highlight.

As her second oldest grandchild, I have found that being a member of Yuri Kochiyama's family has its advantages and disadvantages. On the one hand, you receive all the benefits of her character as a living example of what it means to be compassionate, courageous, selfless, principled, and committed. On the other hand, living with someone like Yuri is often as frustrating as it is rewarding and can be downright maddening at times.

For people like my grandmother who grew up during the Depression, experienced the mass incarceration of Japanese Americans into concentration camps during World War II, and became transformed by the social movements of the 1960s, life's priorities are organized differently. Thus, things like values and principles, movements, demonstrations, petitions, court hearings, community concerns, and so forth take greater precedence over the everyday situations that concern the rest of us mere mortals. Basic activities like eating, sleeping, and spending quality time with the family can often take a back seat when lives are hanging in the balance, leaflets have to be mailed, rallies have to be organized, meetings have to be attended, and speeches have to be written. These were—and still are—the priorities that have occupied my grandmother's life for as long as I can remember.

I grew up in Harlem very close to Grandma Yuri and Grandpa Bill for most of my life and was not entirely aware of how unusual a life they led until I became an adult. All the house guests, activists, organizers, artists, and characters who converged in their home every week of every month of every year of their lives was, to me, how everybody lived—or so I thought. Like all of Yuri's children, I was trained probably as soon as I could walk and talk to be a coat-checker, table-setter, hostess, and cook (for home gatherings), and collator, leaflet distributor, and demonstrator (for political events). Although those types of duties and responsibilities at such a young age might not sound like much fun, those experiences, probably more than any other in my life so far, shaped the person I am today. Thus, for me, as it probably is for most of our family as well as the many others who have become a part of Yuri's extended family, the culture of her life has been infectious.

Now that I am an adult and have the benefit of perspective and reflection, I can see how living the type of life Yuri has chosen to lead has had its rewards and benefits, as well as great sacrifices for her and her immediate family. Because I lost both of my parents just a few years before my grandfather Bill passed away, and because by that time most of our family had migrated to the West Coast, Yuri and I became especially dependent on each other for the period of years that preceded her own move out west. It was during this time that I got to know my grandmother as a public person and what it really takes to do what she has been doing her whole life. I traveled with her to out-of-town speaking engagements, helped edit her speeches, chauffeured her to and from political events and meetings, cooked for her, and helped do her mailings, which, under Yuri's supervision, is a tedious, demanding, and serious task. An alternately enlightening, exasperating, and awesome experience, getting to know my grandmother in this way has given me a unique perspective on her life, politics, and personality.

What strikes me most about this memoir is what it does not say. From my perspective, some of the most important moments, accomplishments, and events in her life are not described in her own memoir. There are so many stories I wish she had told and political ideas and philosophies I wish she had shared here because I know that she has said and done a lot more than is captured in these pages. More importantly, though, I believe that were they told, these stories would serve both to explain her personal and political evolution more clearly, as well as demonstrate the depth of her sensitivity and commitment to humanity at the most basic levels.

For example, Yuri does not talk about her involvement in the Puerto Rican Independence movement and the fact that she participated in the takeover of the Statue of Liberty in 1977. As a result of her involvement in this bold act—which Yuri takes great pride in—she was arrested along with several Puerto Rican and movement activists. I will never forget the shock of seeing my grandmother on the evening news in handcuffs being escorted into a police paddy wagon.

Also absent is any description of the redress and reparations movement for Japanese Americans in which both my grandmother and grandfather Bill played a crucial part. One of the few that achieved success in that Japanese Americans ultimately won reparations for their unjust incarceration during World War II, this movement was an important and significant struggle (and victory) not only for Japanese Americans, but also for other groups still fighting for reparations.

An equally important yet little known fact about my grandmother that she neglects to share here is her passionate commitment to community service and volunteerism. While growing up in San Pedro, Yuri volunteered for numerous organizations serving children and families in her hometown. I think many would be impressed to know that her dedication to helping people did not get completely usurped by her political involvement as an adult. In addition to all of her movement activities, Yuri still found the time to volunteer at soup kitchens and homeless shelters in numerous New York City churches and taught English conversation classes to international students at Riverside Church in Harlem for most of the 1980s through the mid-1990s.

I also wish Yuri had written about how she met Malcolm X and how this meeting, his political philosophy, and their friendship would ultimately affect her life. While she does talk extensively about Malcolm's exceptional character and his significance to the movement, she does not describe her personal interactions with him, her involvement with his Organization of

African American Unity, nor her presence at his assassination at the Audubon Ballroom on February 21, 1965. This is a day I am certain she will never forget and one that has prompted her faithful participation in nearly every Malcolm X annual pilgrimage up until 1999 (when she left New York and resettled in California). Without question, Malcolm X was and still is the single most influential person in Yuri's political development. As she often says, Malcolm was her "political awakening."

However, this is her memoir, not mine. If I have grown to understand anything about Yuri—through the course of our lives together and the often challenging process of working with her on writing her own memoir—it is that she has a very unique and specific approach to living and understanding life. It is one from which she cannot be swayed. Although I may not have agreed with some of the struggles and individuals she chose to represent in her memoir, I do respect and understand her resolve. Neither a politician nor political theorist, Yuri is an activist in the purest of senses. Consequently, she is passionate about and acts on behalf of anyone or any group that she perceives as fighting for liberation and freedom from oppression.

While my grandmother's memoir is undoubtedly full of paradoxes, contradictions, and odd silences, her commitment to humanity and social justice is and has always been unambiguous and unconditional. She has participated in a wide range of political, cultural, and community movements, activities, and struggles (too many for her to have even recalled) and has been inspired by a diversity of artists, writers, poets, political activists, leaders and organizers. Thus, in my view, there are several specific themes that have consistently dominated Yuri's life. These are her sincere love for humanity, her commitment to friendship, and her unswerving conviction on the power and importance of coalition-building across culture, race, class, and gender.

Anyone who has ever met Yuri knows that she cares deeply about people and how we treat each other. While this may seem like a simple and common human trait to some, I would argue that Yuri's commitment to respecting each individual person and defending each person's right to liberty, freedom, and justice are the bedrock of her personal and political consciousness. It is from this foundation that her passion and unwavering commitment to the struggle for the rights of political prisoners and of all oppressed people grows. It is her love of humanity that has inspired her to dedicate practically every waking moment of her life to the struggle, and it is this inspiration that makes her resilient, strong, and tireless.

It is also from this same place that her commitment to family, to community, and to friendship grows. Anyone who knows Yuri knows that she has a lot of friends. In fact, I don't think I have ever met anyone who has more friends. A good listener and avid letter writer, Yuri has an amazing capacity to offer support to and keep in touch with countless friends across distance and time. From high school acquaintances to political comrades and prisoners, to the numerous students she has met throughout her many years on the college-speaker circuit, Yuri manages to stay in contact with almost everyone she has ever met. Sending postcards, letters, holiday greetings, flyers, announcements and petitions to all of these folks as well as to anyone and everyone who writes to her is one of the primary reasons why she gets so little sleep.

As a child I spent many evenings sleeping over at my grandparents' apartment in the Manhattanville Projects. One of my most distinct memories from back then is saying goodnight to Yuri who would always be sitting amidst a sea of envelopes, stamps, and stacks and stacks of papers at the kitchen table when I was getting ready for bed. When I would ask her what she was doing, she would usually tell me that she was writing to people in prison and that it was very important to write to them because in their loneliness and isolation behind the wall, human correspondence was vitally important to their survival. Even when I would creep out of bed in the early morning hours to peek at her, she would still be in the kitchen writing.

I rarely saw my grandmother sleep in those days, and very little has changed about her since then. While it may drive those of us who are closest to her crazy (especially around the holiday season when she spends many sleepless nights coordinating, composing, addressing and mailing hundreds of pieces of correspondence), staying in touch with her friends in this manner is one of her biggest priorities.

Finally, Yuri's dedication to coalition-building is central to everything she is and does. Anyone who has ever been a guest at Yuri's home in Harlem or at a political event she has organized, can attest to the fact that Yuri's personal relationships and political alliances cross all socially constructed boundaries. As a student of cultural anthropology, I am constantly reminded that the emphasis on "multi-culturalism" and "diversity" is a fairly recent and important "politically correct" trend in education, the political arena, and popular media. What strikes me most about this phenomenon in relation to my grandmother is that multiculturalism and diversity have always been a critical part of her personal and political philosophy and thus the culture of my family and our wider community. Although I usually describe myself (geographically and culturally) as a "Harlemite" when I think of the "community" in which I was raised—the community in which Yuri and Bill raised us all—I think of a community that included Asian Americans, African Americans, Native Americans, Latinos, and people of widely disparate social and economic backgrounds, religious affiliations, and sexual orientations. Yuri's ability to encourage, inspire, and motivate a broad range of communities to struggle in unity and to build coalitions is her greatest strength and legacy.

Recently, Yuri traveled to New York City in order to attend the gala opening of a national exhibit in which she was one of twenty-five people (aged fifty to 100) who were honored for their contributions to the Harlem community. It was the first time she had been to New York since she left back in 1999. During this brief visit, she was also honored at an event at St. Mary's Church on 126th Street. It was hastily organized and informally hosted by a number of her friends and a coalition of different Asian American, African American, Latino, anti-war, and Harlem community organizations. I arrived at the event late, hoping to pick up my grandmother and get back to my nearby home (where she was staying) in time to finish cooking dinner and to get my infant daughter ready for bed. Two hours later, I was still waiting for Yuri, watching in amazement as numerous representatives from various national and local political, cultural, and community organizations got up one after another to talk about how Yuri had served as an inspiration to them personally as well as to their various causes and struggles.

At first, I was somewhat overwhelmed and embarrassed even by the sheer magnitude of praise being bestowed upon my grandmother. Then, as I surveyed the jam-packed pews and aisles of St. Mary's Church, I began to realize that this gathering was one of the most racially, ethnically, economically, and culturally diverse crowds I had ever seen.

The more I think about this experience in relation to Yuri's personal and political life, I realize that her greatest power lies in her extraordinary ability to bring people together in this way. By encouraging people to coalesce and unite around experiences of oppression, exploitation, and discrimination, she has helped not only to forge friendships and ties among individuals and communities but also to strengthen the movement in general. It is this ability and this vision, in my opinion, that represents her most profound contribution to the struggle.

This is my grandmother's memoir. It expresses the primary values and themes that have guided and directed her life, and it describes some of the struggles, movements, moments, and people that have most significantly inspired her to become the person that she is today.

AKEMI KOCHIYAMA-SARDINHA
Harlem, New York
March 2003

Courtesy of the Kochiyama Family

The Kochiyama family (CIRCA 1980s).
(STANDING, FROM LEFT) Aichi, Akemi, Jimmy, Audee, Tommy, Zulu, Eddie; (SEATED) Bill and Yuri.

Yuri at the Jerome, Arkansas
internment camp, 1943.

Preface

I am calling this book *Passing It On*, as I would like to pass on some of my memories to my family. Even if some of my interests are not of special concern to them now, perhaps they will be someday. I am grateful just for them being there—their kindness, sharing, caring and enormous amount of love, patience, and tolerance shown to me through the years. We were an ordinary family that showed that "family life" is not gracious living. But despite the regular squabbles, our family life has been full of the unexpected, the fun times, and the togetherness when needed.

The book is primarily written for my younger grandchildren, Ryan, Traci, Christopher, Maya, Aliya, and Kahlil; my great-grandchildren, Kai, Kenji, Leilani, and Malia; and others who may follow after *Passing It On* is published. I would like them to know about their great-grandparents, grandparents, and uncles and aunts who preceded them.

I would also like them to become acquainted with some Japanese American, Asian American, Latino, American Indian, and Black American history, so that they will be able to make connections with some important movements that took place and in which their parents and relatives participated.

This book is, more or less, a memoir, rather than a regular sort of autobiography. While I write about bits and pieces of my life and my family's life, I also found myself wanting to tell the young ones about many people and events that intervened and also enriched my family. My memoir begins with several chapters on our family, then branches out into other topics. There are also chapters that may not have any significant meaning to my grandchildren when they first read this book, but in time perhaps they will see some connections. Then, I write on a sundry number of family memories and topics that were and still are important to me. I talk about our family Christmas newspaper and the family's own movement newspaper; about

Asian and Asian American political prisoners, as well as Black and white political prisoners; about meeting Malcolm X; about my trips to Cuba and Peru; about the Asian American movement; and about the Third World movement in general.

There is also a chapter about the "Kochiyama Bears," or the "K-Bears." This is not a bear collection story, but rather about my new "family" after the children began flying the coop. The names of most everyone who presented us with a bear is listed—at least, as many as I can remember. I think it is more important to remember those who gave us the bears than the bears themselves, as each bear is special because of the giver.

Lastly, in the appendices are some other memories I want to pass on so that they remain part of my family's legacy. I hope my family will treasure them as I have.

I began writing my personal memoir while at UCLA in 1998, at the age of seventy-seven. Then, my eldest three grandchildren—Zulu, Akemi, and Herb III—were age thirty, twenty-seven, and nineteen, respectively. The younger grands were Ryan, eleven; Traci, nine; Maya, seven; Christopher, five; Aliya, five; and Kahlil, two. I had only one great-grandchild at the time, Kai, one. Now, five years later, I am proud to add three more great-grands to the Kochiyama family roster: Leilani, two; Kenji, one; and Malia, just born in early March 2003. Children from my extended family are Neruda Williams, seventeen, and three goddaughters: Debby Nako, Janice Robinson, and Yuri Torres. Each one of them, I am sure, will make his or her own biography and history in this ever-changing world.

For years, I wanted to leave something for my grands, not knowing what age they would be by the time I finished or if they would even be interested in what I would write. I'm only hoping that someday they will pick up this book.

In closing, I would like to say a few things to my grands. First and foremost, you do not have to live up to or emulate the lives of any of your predecessors. But at the very least, you should know about them. You will have your own life, interests, and ideas of what you want or do not want in life. Do what you enjoy doing. Be honest with yourself and others. Don't think of satisfying anyone: your elders, peers, government, religion, or children who will come after you. Develop meaningful ideals, and become conscious of others, their existence, and their lives.

Just remember that what you put on your pedestal will be your main influence in your life. I am hoping you place love for your family, friends, and humanity; service to your community; concern for human rights, justice, and human dignity on your pedestal. And please show appreciation to friends, old and new. The precious, intangible gems like happiness, satisfaction, self-respect, and pride—they are the thanks to the people who come into your life. Life is not what *you* alone make it. Life is the input of everyone who touched your life and every experience that entered it. We are all a part of one another.

YURI KOCHIYAMA
Oakland, California
March 2003

Courtesy of the Kochiyama Family

Granddaughter Akemi and Marc Sardinha's wedding, 2000.
Akemi and Marc standing directly behind Yuri. (BACK ROW, FROM LEFT) Pam Wu & Eddie; Kai, Masai & Zulu; (FORMING A VERTICAL LINE ON THE LEFT SIDE OF YURI) Jimmy, Alison, Aliya & Kahlil; (BACK ROW ON RIGHT) Tommy and Herb; (MIDDLE ROW) Ryan, Julie, Audee; and (FRONT ROW) Maya, Tracy and Christopher.

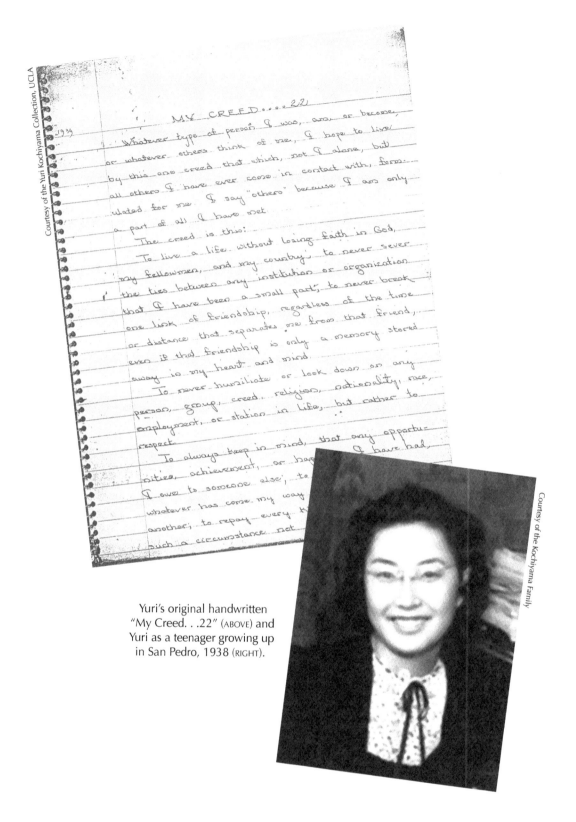

1939

MY CREED....22

Whatever type of person I was, am, or become,
or whatever others think of me, I hope to live
by this one creed that which, not I alone, but
all others I have ever come in contact with, formulated for me. I say "others" because I am only
a part of all I have met.

The creed is this:

To live a life without losing faith in God,
my fellowmen, and my country; to never sever
the ties between any institution or organization
that I have been a small part; to never break
one link of friendship, regardless of the time
or distance that separates me from that friend,
even if that friendship is only a memory stored
away in my heart and mind.

To never humiliate or look down on any
person, group, creed, religion, nationality, race,
employment, or station in life, but rather to
respect.

To always keep in mind, that any opportunities, achievement, or hap... I have had,
I owe to someone else, to...
whatever has come my way...
another; to repay every t...
such a circumstance not...

Yuri's original handwritten
"My Creed. . .22" (ABOVE) and
Yuri as a teenager growing up
in San Pedro, 1938 (RIGHT).

Introduction

I was born Mary Yuriko Nakahara on May 19, 1921, and raised in San Pedro, California, a predominantly white working-class neighborhood. Aside from my twin brother Pete, I also had an older brother, Arthur, whom we called "Art." My parents were Issei (first-generation Japanese) so our home life was traditional in that we spoke Japanese and ate Japanese food and were expected to behave as proper Japanese children. Outside our home, though, I was very much an "all-American" girl. As a teenager and young adult, I volunteered at the YWCA, the Girls Scouts, and the Homer Toberman Settlement House that served the Mexican community in San Pedro. I taught arts and crafts, tennis, first aid to teenagers at the Red Cross, and Sunday School at my local Presbyterian Church.

The day Pearl Harbor was bombed—December 7, 1941—changed all of our lives. Every American, of whatever background, was affected. Before the war, I was seeing America with American eyes. What happened to Japanese Americans after Pearl Harbor made me see the world and America with entirely new eyes—Japanese American eyes. In many ways, this marked the beginning of my political awakening and development.

What follows are my memories, reflections, and beliefs about some of the major events of my life, people I have encountered, and movements I have supported and been involved in. Although I focus mainly on the many people I have encountered, befriended, and learned from since I left San Pedro, my political convictions had already taken root while growing up in my hometown. I must admit that my passion and zeal to address human and social injustices were already taking shape within me as a young girl.

As much as I enjoyed growing up in a friendly cosmopolitan small town, I needed to leave it and grow up, open myself to new ideas, meet new people, learn from life's experiences. My provincial mentality and apolitical ideas needed to change and develop. I needed to leave San Pedro in order to enlarge my worldview, so that the people and encounters I speak of could become the primary sources from which my political ideas and philosophy have grown.

My family found something I wrote long ago as a teenager. While my religious and political beliefs have changed quite a bit since 1939, my basic personal values and philosophy of life have remained the same.

"My Creed. . .22"

What type of person I was, am, or become, or whatever others think of me, I hope to live by this one creed that which, not I alone, but all others I have ever come in contact with, formulated for me. I say "others" because I am only a part of all I have met.

The creed is this:

To live a life without losing faith in God, my fellowmen, and my country; to never sever the ties between any institution or organization that I have been a small part; to never break one link of friendship, regardless of the time or distance that separates me from that friend, even if that friendship is only a memory stored away in my heart and mind.

To never humiliate or look down on any person, group, creed, religion, nationality, race, employment, or station in life, but rather to respect.

To always keep in mind, that any opportunities, achievement, or happiness I have had, I owe to someone else; to be grateful for whatever has come my way through the aid of another, to repay every kindness, but should such a circumstance not arise, to pass it on to someone else.

To love everyone; to never know the meaning of hate, or have one enemy. (An enemy, to me, is only created in one's mind). Should another dislike me or hate me because of some of my weaknesses, my actions, or what I have said, or how I have felt, or through prejudice, I will accept it without resentment, but all the while I will do all in my personality to better my ways and make myself acceptable.

To stay on the same "side of the track" as whoever I am with, but still live within the limits of my own ideals. Regardless of whether my actions seem wrong in the eyes of society, I will do that which I am doing as long as I am not infringing on the happiness of another, hurting another, and as long as I can look at myself without feeling ashamed.

To never harbor a feeling that someone has been unfair to me, but rather to feel in such a case, that I deserved it; to take every disappointment, disillusion, sorrow, and grief as a part of life; to never expect another to be indebted to help me, but should I be able to help anyone, to be grateful that I could be of use.

To give the advantage, but never to ask for it; to be strict with myself, but not with others; to be humble enough to stoop to any degree as long as it is in service for another.

This creed, that people and experience have made for me, I will sincerely try to keep, for if I fail even one portion of it, and although it will be unknown to them, I will be failing not only myself, but those who are the living part of this creed.

And this creed, I call "twenty-two." It is my philosophy of life.

Dear Heavenly Father—Help me *live* it.

MARY NAKAHARA

1939 (age 18)

Yuri speaking at anti-war demonstration and rally in Central Park (CIRCA 1968).

Editor's Note

I only wanted to dash out of the hotel elevator and help a petite Asian American woman who was having problems getting into her room with one of those newfangled magnetic card keys. We had both just arrived to attend the 10th National Conference of the Association for Asian American Studies held in 1993 at Cornell University in Ithaca, NY.

This fortuitous encounter with human rights and political activist Yuri Nakahara Kochiyama ushered me into her amazing life, the Kochiyama homestead in Harlem, her personal library collection that she would donate to UCLA, and this challenging writing project.

When I told her my name and that I was a UCLA academic research librarian, Yuri responded, "Oh, that's great! Do you think UCLA would want any of my junk?" She explained her personal library was so cluttered that her kids called it the "Horror Room." Yuri was relieved to know her materials would be carefully preserved and that generations to come would be able to access materials easily.

The Asian American Studies Center is privileged to receive and process Yuri's generous gift, which when completed will be transferred to the Manuscripts Division of the Department of Special Collections of the Library at UCLA. The Library's Department of Special Collections will ensure preservational storage, retrieval, and access to UCLA and non-UCLA students, community, and researchers.

Many of the items and photographs appearing in Yuri's autobiography have come from this Special Collection, and they were central to enhancing richness, depth, and humanity to Yuri's activist life. More importantly, I hope that the Kochiyama clan will feel they have benefited first and foremost from their mom's/grandma's important decision to gift her materials to UCLA.

▲ ▲ ▲

It was during my second Special Collections trip to Harlem in 1997 that the idea of Yuri writing something for family came up. As Yuri and I spent long hours and days together deliberating over what to donate to UCLA, we also began to talk at length on the significance of collecting photographs, old letters, and even the Kochiyama family newsletter. It was then that Yuri shared with me her personal dream to write something for her grandkids; to "pass on" important memories to them. It became very clear to me that, if possible, our Center should find some opportunity to make Yuri's dream a reality.

In addition to working as an archivist, I also had the challenging role as 'cheerleader' to Yuri through-out the writing and development of her memoir. It was necessary to remind and assure Yuri that she indeed had important things to pass onto her family. The collaborative efforts with the Kochiyama family were also essential. Co-editors Akemi Kochiyama-Sardinha and Audee Kochiyama-Holman were indispensable with fact-checking, filling in some of Yuri's memory gaps, and editorial direction. The K-Family warmly welcomed me into their lives, and I genuinely hope they have not been disappointed.

The last stages involving production were very demanding and could not have been undertaken successfully without my Reading Room staff's assistance, and especially the experienced technical and graphic direction of Mary Uyematsu Kao. From the placement and layout out of the photographic selections to the tweaking of text style, Mary was able to design a book that captured Yuri's heart and soul. *Passing It On* is a warm, inviting collection of memories, thoughts, and ideals for all the Kochiyamas.

My life has been permanently etched with Yuri's passionate quest for social justice and human dignity, and I hope all readers are likewise inspired.

Marjorie Lee
Editor
January 25, 2004

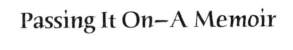
Passing It On–A Memoir

Seiichi Nakahara and Tsuya Sawaguchi's wedding picture, 1917.

My Parents

My mother Tsuya Sawaguchi came from Fukushima-ken, and my father Seiichi Nakahara came from Iwata-ken. These provinces were next to each other and located somewhere north of Tokyo, Japan. Mom attended Tsuda Women's College in Tokyo and after graduation taught college-level English there. Pop's father was the school principal where she taught.

Pop was the youngest child of a retired samurai. Pop's father was born in Wakayama-ken and was left fatherless and poor when still quite young. Among the many jobs he had to support himself through school, he delivered fish for a peddler.

Pop came to America in his late teens, around 1907, before World War I. He first picked oranges at an orchard in Los Angeles, and later worked at a fish cannery on Terminal Island. Together with his two brothers-in-law, Mr. Toyama and Mr. Kondo, Pop started the Pacific Coast Fish Market. The Market sold fresh fish products, meat, fruits, and vegetables to three Japanese passenger liners as well as to the U.S. Navy, and it became a successful wholesale fish company. The business went so well, he was able to go back to Japan to get married by family arrangement. His father, a principal of a school, selected one of the teachers of the school to be his son's bride. Thus, Mom was not the usual "picture bride" of that period when Issei men and women usually exchanged pictures and then made their decisions for their future lives. Mom was more like the women who were married by *baishaku nin* (marriage brokers). Mom and Pop's marriage seemed as close to a love-marriage as could be possible, although there was the traditional go-between. They were so well matched.

Their marriage took place sometime during World War I in 1917. Then Mom immigrated to the U.S. with Pop. It was a period when thousands of Japanese women were joining their Issei husbands in America. They decided to settle in San Pedro, a seaport town in California not far from Los Angeles. They were located just across the bay from Terminal Island, where a colony of Japanese fishermen and fish cannery people lived. Many wives, and later their children, worked in the canneries. Other Japanese lived in the Palos Verdes Hill area, which back in the pre-war era consisted of tomato farms. Outside the house we were very American; inside we were very Japanese.

The lives of the fishermen and the farmers were much harsher than those of the Japanese in San Pedro proper. We lived a rather staid, comfortable life in a white working-class neighborhood. Our neighbors were Europeans of many backgrounds, predominantly Slovenians and Italians, who were also in the fishing industry. We enjoyed their neighborliness. The parents, being immigrants like the Japanese, did not speak English well either, so we did not feel embarrassed at our Issei parents' language shortcomings. San Pedro seemed void of racism, so while attending school, we did not seem to experience discrimination. Mom did not have to work as did many Issei mothers on Terminal Island and the hill.

By 1918, the year after Mom arrived, my brother Arthur was born on December 23. Art graduated from San Pedro High School, attended Compton College, and graduated from UC Berkeley in 1940. My twin brother Pete and I were born three years later on May 19, 1921. Those days, all the Japanese children in San Pedro were brought into the world through one midwife, Mrs. Tanaka, or Tanaka-no-Obasan. No Nisei (second-generation Japanese Americans born in the U.S.) children of Issei ever went to the hospital. I doubt if Asians would have been accepted in a white American hospital. We just accepted such reality without thinking that it was because of racist institutionalized policies.

Mom was always doing her chores as a housewife. She taught some Japanese language skills to young Nisei and was always available to Pop, whose health was not too strong due to lung problems. In fact, there was a period when he spent time in a sanitarium treating those afflicted with tuberculosis. Art also had asthma while very young.

The bombing of Pearl Harbor changed the life of every American, including myself, my family, and others of Japanese ancestry. The ensuing mass hysteria and fear, and our eventual incarceration, shattered the American dream of Japanese Americans forever. Just days before the bombing of Pearl Harbor in early December 1941, our family was eagerly awaiting a special visit from

The Nakahara family at their San Pedro home, circa 1924.
Tsuya (LEFT) and Seiichi (RIGHT) with children Yuri, Pete and Arthur.

Pop's friend, Admiral Nomura, who would be flying into Los Angeles from San Francisco on business. Pop had a great dinner planned for his friend, and the Admiral was expecting to sample *samma* fish, a special Japanese delicacy. But plans suddenly changed, and the Admiral had to fly directly to Washington, DC. Before boarding the plane, Admiral Nomura sent Pop a telegram that said, "Sorry, cannot meet you for dinner. Regret unable to eat *samma*." Pop was very disappointed that his friend could not try his *samma*, but little did we all know how this innocent telegram would cause so much turmoil.

Within the first few days that followed the bombing of Pearl Harbor, the FBI intercepted the telegram and determined that the word *"samma"* was suspiciously treasonous. Because Pop owned a short-wave radio and outdoor antenna to keep in contact with Japanese mariners, he further aroused the FBI's suspicions. We later learned that the FBI had rented a house directly across the street from our home—at 893 West Eleventh Street—specifically to spy on Pop and plan his arrest.

December 7, 1941 fell on a Sunday, so I was teaching Sunday School that day, as I had done for years. After driving home all the kids I picked up to go to church, I returned home by late morning. It just so happened that an hour before I got home, Pop returned from the hospital where he had undergone treatment for diabetes and a stomach ulcer. Within the hour, three FBI agents knocked on our door. They identified themselves and asked me if "Mr. Seichi Nakahara" lived there. I said, "Yes, that's my father." They wanted to know where he was, so I told them (Pop was resting in the back), and without saying another word, they rushed in! Although he had just come home from the hospital and was very weak, the FBI pulled him out of bed and apprehended him.

Everything happened within a matter of two or three minutes. I was the only one home, in complete shock, and did not know what to do. They told Pop to put on his bathrobe and slippers, and they took him away. I didn't have a chance to say anything to Pop. As they hustled him from the house to the car, the FBI refused to tell me why or where they were taking Pop.

Mom was down the block at my aunt and uncle's at the time, so I immediately called her. She rushed home and started making phone calls. We didn't know anything for days. Then a lawyer called back to say he located Pop; he was at the Federal Penitentiary on Terminal Island. Mom visited Pop to give him his diabetes medication, but the officials refused to administer the medicine to Pop or even grant Mom visitation rights. Because he was never given any of his medications, Pop became so sick that they had to transfer him to a hospital. He was placed in a large room with wounded seamen from Wake Island, and Mom feared for Pop's life because they were extremely hostile to him. They placed a sheet around his bed that read, "Prisoner of War." Mom begged the authorities to give him a private room, but she was ignored.

The FBI denied all family members access to Pop, but because my brother Pete had just been drafted by the Army and was waiting orders, the FBI allowed him a brief visit. However, since Pop's health was failing due to lack of medical attention, he did not recognize Pete when he walked into the interro-gation room where Pop sat. In uniform, Pete identified himself, but Pop, a little delirious, accused Pete—in Japanese—of being an interrogator imperson-ating his son.

We believe Pop was detained and tortured throughout his entire interrogation. Because the FBI was unsuccessful at substantiating their suspicions, and because they probably realized his deteriorating health condition was becoming terminal, they released Pop. He was brought home in an ambulance several weeks later. He could no longer talk, and we did not know if he could see, hear, or recognize anyone. His body had become emaciated, and his mind deteriorated dramatically. Lifeless without dignity, he died on January 21, 1942, just a few days after his release. He was only fifty-six years old.

Unfortunately, no Asians, Blacks, or Latinos that I knew of were allowed to be buried in any cemetery in San Pedro before World War II. Instead, all were buried in East Los Angeles at Evergreen Cemetery. Some time after the war ended, Green Hills Cemetery in the Rolling Hills of San Pedro allowed Asians to be buried there, perhaps because so many Japanese American soldiers had died. When the policy changed and Asians could be buried there (the first was a dentist, Dr. Arthur Takii), Mom had Pop's body moved to San Pedro's Rolling Hills. She also bought a plot for herself next to Pop. In 1993, when my husband Bill passed away, I brought not only his urn, but also Billy's (my eldest son) from New York to the same cemetery so that it would be easier for my children to visit them.

Years later, we learned that the FBI had Pop under surveillance for many years prior to WWII. This was shocking to us because we had always been such patriotic Americans. I will never forget what happened to Pop. I saw what the American government did to him with my very own eyes. As I reflect back on that traumatic event, I see the parallel between the way African Americans were treated in the segregated South and the way Japanese Amer-icans were evacuated and relocated en masse to remote internment camps across the U.S. In each instance there were senseless degradation, brutality, and hatred wrought by fear and ignorance caused by racism. So I remain passionately committed to doing whatever I can and saying whatever I must to eliminate racist assumptions and ideas.

The Nakahara family in their San Pedro home, 1938.
(From left) Arthur, Seiichi, Peter (standing), Yuri, and Tsuya.

Growing Up Fast:
Childhood, War, and Camp

My Childhood

So what was I like when I was young? In our Spanish-style house with a cactus garden, I was sheltered, lived comfortably and safely, religious, provincial, and apolitical in thought.

During much of my adolescent through teenage years, I volunteered in many organizations to work with children, teaching arts and crafts, first aid, photography, the Bible, and even tennis. I volunteered with the Girl Reserves, Girl Scouts, Blue Birds, my local church, and at playgrounds. Looking back through the years, thinking of people and events that shaped my life, I know how much I have been blessed, because of the kind of people and events that have impacted me as I grew older. I realize how much of a transformation I have gone through over the many years.

As a Nisei, I was an American by birth. Because we Nisei were born in America, we automatically became American citizens as did other Asian ethnics, and as such, were actually the first generation of Japanese accepted as Americans. We called ourselves Japanese Americans, differentiated from our parents who are Issei, because American immigration laws forbade Issei from becoming naturalized American citizens. When I was young, I did not know that my parents would never be able to become Americans.

While we lived in San Pedro, most of the Japanese lived across the bay on Terminal Island, which was a fishing village. Other Japanese who were not fishing lived in the San Pedro Hills doing farming, gardening, owning grocery stores, or running fruit and vegetable stands. Pop and some of his relatives co-owned a fish market, so we lived in town where our lives were much easier and more comfortable. I always held deep admiration for the Japanese who lived in the "hills" or on the Island. Their lives were harsh, and they worked very hard. I felt a tinge of guilt that by living in closer proximity to the white world, I might be considered a "banana" (a movement term for someone yellow, or Asian, on the outside in appearance, but "white," or mainstream Caucasian, on the inside in thinking).

When I was eleven years old, I discovered how much I loved sports when Los Angeles hosted the Olympics in 1932. I was in heaven when I found out that Japan's Track and Field Olympic Team was assigned to stay in San Pedro. Since the athletic field was practically across from the street where our family and the only other Japanese family (my uncle and aunt's family!) in the neighborhood lived, the Team would come over afterwards and spend time with us sitting on our lawn. My mother and aunt would serve iced tea and cold lemonade, and between what little Japanese I knew and what little English the Team members knew, we all enjoyed these times learning about each other. From then on, I really got into sports.

As a teenager I loved reading and writing poetry, riding bikes, and hiking, but I began to really be involved in sports and journalism even more. I went to all the San Pedro High School athletic events (football, basketball, baseball, gymnastics, track, and tennis), and I enjoyed cheering for my school and my friends. Jim Goss, the editor of the local newspaper, the *San Pedro News Pilot*, allowed me to cover high school sports as a non-paid reporter.

I did other things, too, especially if my mother wanted me to, such as take piano lessons. Japanese parents wanted their daughters to play the piano or violin, but I wasn't musically inclined. Instead, I found myself becoming passionately interested in poetry and religion, which were connected for me. I found reading poetry to be very inspirational, especially by those whom most people didn't even know. Back then, I read everything I could find by Edgar A. Guest, and later on, it was Kahlil Gibran.

I was also strangely drawn to the Christian faith at a very young age, thinking that it encouraged love and brotherhood, justice and peace—all the things public education and churches exposed us to. I didn't know about the enslavement of Africans, the genocide of Native American Indians, and the robbery of Mexican lands. I didn't know about race and class conflicts, imperialism, and colonialism. I didn't know about people being stigmatized and marginalized. I was pretty naïve and ignorant about reality and truth, but when WWII came, I really started learning about reality, the distortions of "truth," and that church just didn't have all the answers to my complicated questions.

Poetry and religion fueled my heart and convictions in the most powerful way. Of course, I didn't "dig" everything the Bible said, and I didn't understand why God couldn't be more compassionate and understanding of people's frailties (see Exodus). But I was deeply inspired by the human compassion expressed in the Bible's message of love, mercy, and forgiveness in the Ten Commandments, 23rd Psalm, Beatitudes, and Corinthians.

When I was fifteen, I started working summers at a tomato cannery in Harbor City, only a few miles away from San Pedro. I would hitchhike to the cannery with my best friend, Vivian Martinez. She was Hispanic, and the two of us must have been the youngest workers there—and maybe a bit too young to understand all that was happening. That was the same year the union started to organize the cannery, and people didn't take us aside to explain why they were overturning tomato trucks or why the bosses' families were targets. I remember seeing some union organizers grab a seven-year-old kid, who was the son of the cannery owner, and watching the kid overcome with fear and screaming. I was really shocked at the tactics used rather than at the conditions the union was fighting against. My sympathies went to whomever was being brutalized.

I also thought it was brutal for the cannery owners to make us stay in our work areas even if we cut our fingers. We just had to keep working. The tomatoes came through in buckets on a conveyor belt, and if we left our positions, someone else grabbed it. People were desperate for jobs in the 1930s. Even the unions didn't care that much about people of color because they didn't let the Japanese, Mexicans, or Blacks become members.

Japanese Americans could not find jobs except in Japantown and Chinatown. Having to work in a vegetable stand or doing domestic work, it seemed impossible for any of us to get a regular job. When I finished Compton Junior College, I was one of the only Japanese Americans who worked in San Pedro. I heard it was the first time that a five-and-dime store hired a Japanese person. Woolworth's hired me when three other stores wouldn't even let me fill out an application.

Being a 1930s teenager who was not socially or politically aware, I was not conscious of the economic downhill slide of the 1930s, which brought on the nationwide depression. Also, although being Japanese, I did not know that Japan had transgressed into China and viciously brought on the Nanjing massacre. I hardly realized that war was imminent at the beginning of the 1940s, that Europe was already embroiled in a World War, and that Germany was rolling across Europe. I was too busy with my volunteer activities and attending college. I majored in journalism and minored in art at Compton Junior College. Shortly after completing my program in 1941, I attended a special training program with the Los Angeles Presbytery to prepare for special work in child education. I finished that before World War II began.

World War II and Internment

The day Pearl Harbor was bombed was like an explosion had ripped through the Japanese American community. The government immediately apprehended community leaders, Buddhists, Japanese schoolteachers, fishermen, and businessmen. As I described in the previous chapter, Pop was one of the people apprehended as a suspected spy. The FBI was suspicious of why there was a radio antenna built right outside our home, even though it was more for show than anything else.

On February 19, 1942, President Franklin Roosevelt signed the Executive Order 9066 ordering the removal of all Japanese Americans—and anyone with more than one-sixteenth Japanese blood—from "strategic areas," including California, Oregon, Washington, and parts of Arizona. Anti-Japanese sentiment surged during World War II, and my family, along with 120,000 others of Japanese ancestry—70 percent of whom were American-born citizens and the remaining 30 percent Japanese immigrants who had been denied the possibility of citizenship—were forcibly removed from their homes and imprisoned in internment camps.

In April of that year, after Pop passed away and all the Japanese people on Terminal Island were removed, we were sent to Assembly Centers since the relocation camps were not built yet. These Centers were mostly on fairgrounds and racetracks. My family was billeted in horse stalls at the Santa Anita Racetrack. The smell of the manure made many Issei sick. In the sparse space the Nikkei (those of Japanese heritage in the U.S.) made their quarters as livable as possible. Carton boxes were made into tables, chairs, and bureaus. The creativity of the Japanese people was admirable. Also, with the help of Sears and Roebuck and Montgomery Ward, purchases of materials for curtains were made for the lone window in the "black houses" and for curtains to provide privacy in the latrines.

While at the Santa Anita Assembly Center, I continued to teach Sunday school for the younger, mostly junior high-aged Nisei schoolgirls. While waiting to be relocated to the internment camps, I wanted to do something to help the war effort and our boys in the service—especially when I found out that several of my students had brothers in the military. I thought it would be a good idea to write to them. The group called itself the "Crusaders." We became more active, and my class began to grow in size as the older teenage girls whose brothers were in the Army wanted to join the Crusaders.

We soon exchanged thousands of letters with soldiers overseas. At first, we just sent penny postcards to Nisei soldiers stationed overseas in hopes of keeping their spirits high. Our lists of soldiers to write grew longer, and even when we were split up to be transferred to different camps, we all promised to continue the work of the Crusaders wherever we were. I was assigned to Jerome, Arkansas, where our Crusaders group developed a Nisei soldiers list of 1,300 names. We gradually received a lot of support, especially from the 232nd Engineers (part of the 442nd) soldiers who started sending money to us from the front lines! We then changed from postcards to regular paper and envelopes that only required two-cent stamps.

Courtesy of the Yuri Kochiyama Collection, UCLA

The Junior Junior Crusaders at Jerome AK internment camp, welcoming Nisei GI's visiting from Fort Harrison, Indiana (circa 1944). Photograph taken by one of the Fort Harrison Nisei soldiers.

Courtesy of the Yuri Kochiyama Collection, UCLA

Yuri's mom (KNEELING, SECOND FROM RIGHT) with Senior Crusaders. Jerome, Arkansas internment camp, circa 1944.

Mom, my oldest brother Art, who graduated Phi Beta Kappa from UC Berkeley, and I were eventually incarcerated at Jerome. It was a dismal swampland surrounded by a forest. Art tried to enlist in the service but was disqualified due to medical problems. It was probably good, since he could take care of Mom and me. My twin brother Pete initially tried to enlist into the Marine Corps and Navy, but they refused to take him because he was Japanese.

Under the draft law, the Army took him and stationed him at Fort MacArthur in San Pedro. Because he could speak, read, and write Japanese, Pete was sent to camp in Monterey to take some tests. He was then sent to the Military Intelligence Language School at Camp Savage, Minnesota. While there, he defied mail regulations and sent out letters to President Franklin Roosevelt, Secretary of War Henry Stimson, and Secretary of State Cordell Hull protesting the racism he witnessed during training. He was really shocked to receive responses, assuring him that the Army was truly democratic and commending the Nisei soldiers for their eagerness to serve in combat.

Pete's first assignment as a translator took him overseas with the Sixth Australian Division at Indooroopilly, Australia, to interrogate Japanese prisoners of war. Pete was then transferred to the Sixth Army at Leyte and Luzon Islands to translate captured enemy documents and broadcast surrender appeals to Japanese troops.

As a young woman seeing the diligence and conscientiousness of the Nikkei under such difficult conditions, I became proud of the Issei and Nisei. I learned that the Japanese were a hardy lot. I came to know my own people

14   YURI KOCHIYAMA—Passing It On

and liked what I saw and learned. I began to discover my own identity. Since my childhood had been comfortable, I had not experienced the financial and physical hardships compared to many Nisei in the farming and fishing communities of Palos Verdes Hill and Terminal Island. I realized that until the outbreak of the war, I had been looking at the world through rose-tinted glasses. Since then, I have admired the "Hill" and "Island" Nikkei. They all did well after the war, although they had to start all over again from scratch in different fields of work.

By October of that same year, ten concentration camps had been constructed in the deserts, mountains, swamplands, and salt flats of America, where more than 120,000 Japanese Americans and people of Japanese descent were interned. That was a life-shattering period for us all, but one good thing came out of this for me: that's where I met Bill Kochiyama! He was the handsomest Nisei I had ever met, but I felt a little intimidated. Here I was—a small-town Sunday school-teaching provincial from California, and then there was this self-assured New Yorker who exuded such energy and confidence. While the all-Japanese American combat team was in training at Camp Shelby, Mississippi, Bill would join some of his 442nd buddies to make trips to Jerome and visit friends and family of friends. (Actually, Bill, who was interned at Topaz, came before enlisting into the Army.) I guess it must have been love at first sight for me because after seeing him on only three quick visits, I knew I was deeply in love with him. It was a common wartime romance, including courtship through mail, but I was fortunate ours had a happy ending. So many of my girlfriends had their hopes shattered with notices that the ones they were waiting for were killed in action.

Just before he was to leave with his unit in April 1944, he asked me to come to Hattiesburg, Mississippi to marry him. All the paperwork had been completed; my mom had given her approval and even

Yuri at Jerome, Arkansas internment camp, October 1943.

Photograph by Yoshio Inouye

managed to get approval to go to Mississippi to witness my wedding. But on the morning of the wedding day, the captain of Bill's outfit received a telegram from Bill's father stating, "I cannot permit this marriage. I don't even know who she is." It was a matter of pride, that this was his only son, and he wanted to be certain that Bill was marrying the right kind of person. I was stunned and hurt; I hardly knew how to tell my mom. She took the news stoically but knew how I felt, and her empathy was heartwarming. My mom went back to camp, and I don't know how she explained the situation to her friends and neighbors. She never told me.

We promised to wait for each other until after the war and Bill's discharge. Until then, the chaplain very kindly offered me a job at the Japanese American "Aloha" USO so I would not have to return to Jerome camp to face curious neighbors. Because Japanese Americans, Latinos, and Blacks were not welcomed in white USOs, the Aloha USO was started with the help from Hung Wai Ching, a Chinese American from Honolulu. Appointed to the Council on Interracial Unity's Morale Division, a liaison group of civilians and the military, Ching helped to prevent the detention of Japanese in Hawaii or have them released. He also succeeded in convincing Army intelligence not to fill its daily quota of arrests on the Islands. He really went to bat for Japanese Americans on the Mainland as well as those in Hawaii.

At Hattiesburg, I found a very cheap place to live on my own for $10 a week. It was challenging but very liberating. First, I was

Courtesy of the Yuri Kochiyama Collection, UCLA

Yuri with twin brother Pete, 1942. Yuri was in the Women's Ambulance and Defense Corps of America, which preceded the Women's Army Corps.

on my own, and second, it challenged my thinking. I knew I was beginning to change my thinking, and I welcomed more changes. How little I understood about anything in life, and until that time was I indoctrinated with status quo mainstream American ideas, but I now knew it was time to go on my own and think for myself.

I worked at the USO for almost two years, and my main job was to take care of the wives of the Nikkei soldiers, find them housing, arrange weekly luncheons and activities, and anything else to help them settle and feel at home. The Aloha USO served not only the Japanese Americans but also the Chinese American soldiers. During that time, I also visited injured Japanese American soldiers in fourteen different hospitals in twelve different states, mostly in the South.

Yuri at Hattiesburg, Mississippi in September 1944.

J.P. Cox Studio, Hattiesburg, Mississippi

I eventually lived in Earl Finch's house with other Japanese Americans— Kei and Tok Ishikawa family and Yuri and Bones Taono. Mr. Finch was a Mississippi rancher and businessman who became an outcast by white Americans because he went out of his way to help the Nisei soldiers who were stationed in Hattiesburg during World War II. When other Americans turned their backs on the Nisei, he made them feel at home. He earned the nicknames "Godfather" by the Nisei soldiers and "Jap-lover" by his own people. We named our first son Billy after Mr. Finch. He became William Earl Kochiyama.

Mr. Finch befriended Japanese American soldiers in many ways; he was a one-man USO. He would take them to the fancy hotels in New York, treat them to dinner, and get them tickets to Broadway shows. For those who had gotten wounded and physically disabled, he would provide prostheses for the amputees. I remember he also went to the trouble of getting seeing-eye

Yuri with mom, Tsuya Nakahara,
in Hattiesburg, Mississippi 1944.

dogs for those who lost their sight. Sanji Kimoto of Bill's Company K was one of them.

Mr. Finch asked if I would go to Minnesota to see how the Japanese American soldiers were doing and what might be needed there. I tried to set up a service program for Nisei GI's, in addition to doing part-time domestic work, working in a laundry, and waitressing. I was in Minneapolis for six months before the war ended in Japan in August 1945. On that V-Day, Nisei civilians were calling each other not to go outside, but rather to stay safe and celebrate inside.

After Jerome and Back to San Pedro

When the war ended, I went back to Rohwer Camp in McGehee, Arkansas to pick up Mom. She was transferred there when Jerome closed in early 1945 when the number of internees had dwindled because they either found work outside or went to school. By the time I reached Rohwer, the camp consisted mainly of the elderly and mothers with very young children. My mom wanted all the family to come to Rohwer, so that's what we all did except for Pete, who was serving the U.S. Army Military Intelligence Service with the Australian 7th in the Pacific. Because he was an attorney, he was asked after the war to go to Japan to work on the Tribunal, which tried all the Japanese generals. At that time, he met and married Aiko Umino of Seattle, who went back to Japan after the war to find her brother and work with the Tribunal as well.

My older brother Art returned to Rohwer with his fiancée Chiyo Ogata, and married there in October (they lived across from my mother and brother in Jerome). Chiyo's family and relatives (Kondos, Imazus, Ogatas, and Toyamas) all returned together to California. After that, we made our return together by train to the West Coast, heading south through Texas. We were both excited and anxious to return, uncertain how we would be received and if there would be animosity toward us.

Although the war was over, the feeling against the Japanese was still strong, particularly in the West Coast. We were lucky because our next-door neighbors welcomed us home and helped us resettle. In fact, the Stevens family took very good care of our house while we were gone. Other families returned home only to discover their farms burned down or homes lost.

Once I got back to California at the end of October 1945, I started looking for a job right away, but it was really difficult because I was Japanese. Before the war, I periodically used the name "Mary Wong" in order to get jobs. Now all employers required identification to apply for jobs. Since I was waiting for Bill to come home, I looked only for waitress jobs so I could take off as soon as I needed. I must have tried every single restaurant in San Pedro, but no one would hire me. Finally, I went to what I remember Walter Winchell said was the roughest place in America: San Pedro's "Skid Row." There, they were willing to take chances on hiring a Japanese American, but I never lasted too long (from a couple of hours to maybe a whole night, working night shifts) before I would get identified as a "Jap" and cause a ruckus. My bosses were afraid of losing business or seeing violence, so they would let me go. Because the war was just over and people regarded us as Japanese and not Americans, we were still treated as enemies.

I worked from six o'clock in the evening until three or four o'clock in the morning, if I was lucky. Every time a few people would start complaining, "Is that a Jap?" the boss would say, "Sorry, I can't keep you. You're hurting my business." I waitressed from one restaurant to

Courtesy of the Yuri Kochiyama Collection, UCLA

Yuri's cousin Seishin (LEFT), also a GI, and brother Pete (RIGHT) at the Jerome, Arkansas Internment Camp.

another, sometimes working only a few hours until I would get the "beat it" sign from the boss. Some nice owners would let me stay until I got a cup of coffee thrown at me, at which time the boss would then tell me, "You'd better go, for your own sake."

These were pretty rough places, but I liked this area because I got to see old friends and classmates. After being away for nearly four years, it felt like a reunion for me. Many girls from my Sunday school class or in Girl Scouts who were thirteen or fourteen were now eighteen, and I would now see them going to bars in these areas. Some were as embarrassed to see me as I was embarrassed to see them—in, of all places, "Skid Row."

I also met former San Pedro High School athletes and classmates who came back from the war; they welcomed me warmly. Three Native American Indian brothers were especially kind to me. They would come and wait for me until 3:00 a.m. or whenever my shift was to end, just to escort me home. I found the "roughest" guys to be the nicest guys, which is why this saying is true: "In men whom men condemn as ill, I find so much of goodness still."

On New Year's Day 1946, Bill was honorably discharged from the Army and returned to New York. I tried to save enough money as quickly as I could to get a one-way bus ticket to New York. Finally I did, and I took a bus from Los Angeles to New York City in early January 1946. It was my first experience with a real winter, and it was a long, cold bus ride. I got so cold that I got sick along the way, but I finally arrived in New York City on January 23, 1946. It warmed my heart to know Bill and I would finally be together.

As Nisei we were as a whole inhibited, shy, and not overtly proud of our heritage and nationality before the war. Much of it was curtailed by racism, but we did not understand our behavior at that time. We bent over backwards, wanting so much to be accepted by white America that we denied our Asian ethnicity—especially our Japanese ethnicity.

Even before the war, very few Nisei were finding work in their chosen fields even after finishing college. One of the young local Nisei men who graduated *magna cum laude* from a Midwest college came home only to continue working at a vegetable stand. However, years later, after moving to New York, he became recognized for his writing skills and became one of the editors of *Sports Illustrated*. Following his stint at Compton Junior College,

Pete went on to UC Berkeley, where he did well. Art, a Phi Beta Kappa at UC Berkeley, was trying to help close out Pop's fish market. But war was just around the corner, and their futures would be put on hold.

Yuri and her mom, 1945. With the help of neighbors, Yuri and her mom were able to return to their San Pedro home (893 W. 11TH STREET) after the war.

The Nisei story is varied, and much has already been lost. But thanks to the many projects by Asian American Studies departments and programs on college campuses across the country, some of the "untold stories" are being recaptured or re-excavated. I have included a story that Bill wrote for a presentation, a more personal and poignant side to father/grandfather Bill. It's in Appendix 1, along with a song whose words I rewrote to capture the essence and spirit of the redress and reparations movement of Japanese Americans (see Appendix 3).

I feel that the Nisei, through their perseverance, optimism, and *gaman* ("endurance through hardship"), were able to overcome the racism, inequality, and stigmatism that prevailed through the pre-war and post-war hostilities. The war and internment experience affected both Issei and Nisei, and ironically both shared the same experiences. Thus, social and economic class, occupational, and religious differences had no bearing or relevance in our camp communities during the war. War and internment brought us together as one. I think we can feel proud of how the Nikkei came through those difficult war years.

Bill with his mom (CIRCA 1924).
The only known picture of Bill's mother. FATHER'S HANDWRITING
ON BACK OF PHOTOGRAPH READS "Masayoshi and his mother."

A Tribute to My Bill

I could not have ever imagined life without Bill, so I cannot imagine my memoir without including some valuable memories about him. We had a wonderful marriage that lasted nearly fifty years until his death in October 1993. Let me begin with some history about his family and background before describing his important contributions.

Yutaka Kochiyama

Bill had a very unique, challenging childhood, but his father, Yutaka Kochiyama, also had an extraordinary one, as he was the youngest of a family of twelve children. Yutaka's father, a doctor, had eleven children with his first wife. When she passed away, he married his wife's youngest sister. It was not unusual in Japan to select another woman from the same family in order to keep the family together. So it was this youngest sister, now his father's second wife, who bore him his last and youngest child, Yutaka.

Being the youngest and from a different mother than his siblings, Yutaka felt like an outsider. He apparently was determined to choose his own destiny and left Japan while he was still a teenager. He came to the U.S. not by the usual route crossing the Pacific as most Issei did. Coming across the Atlantic right after World War I, he made his way through England where he lived for six months.

Although coming from a family of means, Yutaka had no easy time when he arrived in the U.S. as a young, inexperienced foreigner. He also did not know any English or anything about American culture. Although for a brief while he clung to a dream of attending medical school and becoming a physician like his father in Japan, that was hardly his destiny.

Not too much is known of his early years in the U.S., but what is known is that Yutaka eventually made his way to Washington, DC, married a Japanese national woman thought to be the daughter of a Japanese diplomat, and had three children. Of the three, only Masayoshi (Bill's given Japanese name), the middle child, survived. The other two, a sister and brother—Fumiko and Tadashi, respectively three years older and two years younger than Bill—died during a post-World War I flu epidemic.

Whatever happened to Bill's mother is not clear, and he could not remember anything about her. His father had cut out pictures of her face, so he did not even know what his mother looked like. His father told him that his mother died when he was a young child, so Bill never pursued the matter further. But family friends told Bill while he was growing up that his mother was a beautiful woman.

The family moved to New York, where some Issei remembered Yutaka and his wife together in New York caring for a child—no doubt it was Bill. Like hundreds of Issei of his time on the East Coast, Yutaka immediately found himself in the only job that seemed readily available: a domestic worker. He worked for several wealthy employers in New Jersey and New York.

Because he always had to live in the home of his employer, Yutaka could not provide a home for his son. In 1928, after considering various homes, he decided that the best place for his son was Sheltering Arms, a progressive Episcopal orphanage in New York City that cared for children of single parents.

Bill's father, Yutaka Kochiyama, feeding hummingbirds (CIRCA 1966).

It was located near 126th and Broadway, across the street from the Manhattanville Houses, coincidentally where Bill and I moved with our six children in 1960. Back then, the area between Columbia University, Barnard College, Riverside Church, and City College was more white than Black.

Yutaka did the best he could under

the circumstances to be an active, loving father in Bill's life. On Tuesday afternoons—the only day he had off work—Yutaka came to Sheltering Arms, loaded with fruits, candies, and toys. Yutaka's closest friend, Harry Yano, whom our children came to know as "Uncle Harry," would also visit, bearing similar gifts. Back then, Uncle Harry and other close friends of Yutaka were all young Issei men employed as domestic workers like himself, and they eventually organized a group called the Young Men's Association (YMA).

Bill visited his father in Japan (CIRCA 1973).

Because of pride, Dad (as I affectionately called Bill's father) made us promise years ago when I first married his son never to reveal to friends the kind of work he did. Although many Japanese were in domestic work, Dad felt that the Nikkei might look down on him. Only very close Issei friends would ever know. To me, Dad was one of the finest men—very gentle, refined, and idealistic. He was also meticulous about his clothes. It was said that people on the street used to think he was some kind of foreign diplomat. He strangely seemed very western, in fact, British: a "gentleman of the old school," always polite and genteel in his mannerisms. His Japanese roots, however, traced him back to Yamaguchi-ken, Japan, known for its many military leaders. However, Dad had no such military inclination.

Before we started our family, Bill and I visited Dad on Sundays at his Park Avenue address where he would cook delicious dinners. We always used the servant quarters from the back to get into his apartment. His cooking was regular American style, and he was an excellent cook; he made not only roasts and broiled dishes but also fancy desserts. In the tiny space that was his room, one could touch both walls with eagle-spread hands. Beside his bed, only a drawer and a bureau occupied the space. Overhead, under the bed, and squished in-between were Dad's paintings, clothes (very few, but well cared for), knick-knacks, toiletries, and often a dried apple core would roll out from somewhere.

Bill's father, Yutaka Kochiyama, at ninety years old in his home garden, Yamaguchi-ken, Japan.

Sharing this tiny quarter was his pet hummingbird Peter, who was placed in a cage above the bathtub. Peter was his closest companion, a creature he had nurtured from birth. Peter would often sit on his arm as he fed him. It was an incredible sight to see this Issei man who had such rapport with hummingbirds. He could actually call them to him. When Dad worked in Long Island during the summers, he would concoct special food for hummingbirds, and these tiny birds would fly in to receive. Even the Audubon Society said they had never seen anyone else achieve this kind of closeness with these tiny, constantly flittering, elusive birds. Scientists, bird-lovers, the Audubon Society, and the National Geographic Society considered Dad an authority on hummingbirds.

Around 1967, Dad's employer passed away, and the family decided to let him leave and gave him a generous retirement gift—enough money to return to Japan. They saw that he was aging and wanted him to enjoy his retirement years back in his native country. Dad was around seventy, and by 1968, he had become the last surviving member of the Kochiyama family.

Dad was happy to return, although he had been away for more than fifty years, never having the opportunity or funds to go home for even a visit. He was like the legendary Urashima Taro who goes home after he has reached old age, and his family and neighborhood friends have nearly all passed away. Dad's whole life in America consisted of working in New York and New Jersey as a domestic worker, which was demanding and arduous. Yet

Dad was an exceptionally diligent, devoted house-worker, who stayed with this last family for over thirty years.

Masayoshi William Kochiyama

Bill was born Masayoshi William Kochiyama, in Washington, DC on May 10, 1921—just nine days before me. His early years must have been tragic, having lost his mother, brother, and sister in the first three years of his life. His most vivid and fondest memories were his early years while growing up at Sheltering Arms, where Bill was surrounded by very loving "brothers and sisters." Always at the center of attention, Bill's popularity often thrust him into positions of leadership.

His Sheltering Arms brothers and sisters called him "Masa." Until 1943, Bill went by his Japanese name, Masayoshi, the only name he knew at the time. It was not until he volunteered into the Army in World War II that his father told him he had an American name, William. He immediately dropped Masayoshi and became "Bill."

Bill was the only Asian American in a "family" of 120 white children—sixty boys and sixty girls. He grew up thinking he was white. He lived institution style, but because the woman at the head of Sheltering Arms, Ms. Helen Day, was very progressive, she allowed boys and girls to live in the same building. They all got along well as siblings. When his father visited him every Tuesday, he always brought Bill something to eat or treated him to a meal at a nearby restaurant, usually the Chinese restaurant called Wing Hing, on 125th and Broadway.

Bill by a lake, mid-1920s.

Courtesy of the Yuri Kochiyama Collection, UCLA

The first time he told me he had 120 brothers and sisters, I thought he was a big exaggerator. But after I married him and began meeting his brothers and sisters throughout the years, I realized he was telling me the truth. They were primarily of French, Italian, German, and English background. He was very popular among his family because he was handsome, athletic, stylish, smart, nice, and was a good dancer. He was especially popular with the girls. Sheltering Arms was truly his home throughout his teenage years until 1939. He loved it there, and his brothers and sisters held him in high esteem.

Bill graduated in 1939 from one of the roughest schools in New York City, Haaren High School, located in Hell's Kitchen. He said he felt no endearment to that school and just eked his way through. In 1940, Bill went to California with Eddie Singleton, his best buddy from Sheltering Arms. Eddie went to California to join the California Conservation Camps, a program developed by President Franklin Roosevelt during the harsh economic slump of the 1930s. Bill went also to just look around and see what California was like.

Bill found California to be vastly different from New York. He claimed he never felt such racism as he found in California. He couldn't find a job or a place to stay, and the war hadn't even started yet. He had very little experience with Japanese people and didn't know the language at all. He did, however, find "buddies," Nisei who enjoyed the same kind of pastimes: wine, women, and hitting the nightspots. He found a job in a Japanese laundry where they also provided him with a place to stay. He ate Japanese food he had hardly seen before—country-style Japanese food, *okazu*—and saw strange things like homemade wooden bathtubs called *taru*, into which Issei would climb and immerse themselves to bathe. He worked hard for

Courtesy of the Yuri Kochiyama Collection, UCLA

Bill/Masayoshi with his "brothers" at Sheltering Arms (CIRCA 1929).

Bill with "That Old Gang of Mine" at Sheltering Arms (CIRCA 1939).

Emil Pellenberg Studio, New York

meager wages and became a part of the laundry crew. California was where he began meeting Issei and Nisei—and became a "Japanese American." This was all just a few months before the war broke out, when becoming Japanese American would change his whole life.

Bill's War Experience and the 442nd

On May 6, 1942, just four days before his twenty-first birthday, Bill was herded along with 8,000 Nikkei from the San Francisco Bay area to the Tanforan Assembly Center, formerly a racetrack in San Bruno, California. He went reluctantly, a stranger among his own people. He was one of the few men who had no family, and therefore he was assigned to the "Bachelor's Quarter." With no family obligations or responsibility, he was able to live quite independently. During that time, he also volunteered to do seasonal work in an apple orchard in Utah.

He lived in horse stalls for four months until transferred by train to the permanent mass detention camp in Topaz, where he spent one year before enlisting into the service. Located in the middle of a desert and surrounded by barbed-wire fences with searchlights and guard towers at each corner, the camp was patrolled by armed sentries of the U.S. Army.

The talk of the camp was whether young Nisei men should volunteer to fight for this country and serve overseas. Bill was among those who chose to do so. He was one of the mainland Nisei "Yes-Yes" boys to volunteer and join the 442nd Regimental Combat Team, which became the most highly decorated unit in the history of the U.S. military.

He was permitted to leave the camp and go home to New York to see his father before being sent for Army training. It was then that his father told him he had an American name, William, which he shortened to Bill. He loved that simple, one-syllable, easy-to-say, common American name. He never reverted or referred to his Japanese name again.

erpé, Nice, France

Bill in uniform, France 1944.

Armed now with a new name and identification, Bill happily went to his boot camp destination, Camp Shelby, Mississippi, his training ground to become an infantryman. This camp was forming the all-Japanese American Combat Team, the 442nd Regiment. They were sent to Europe, following in the footsteps of the vanguard 100th Infantry from Hawaii, who immediately began winning a reputation as valiant fighters. Bill was assigned to Company K, a rifle outfit in the Second Battalion.

It had equal numbers of Hawaiian as well as mainland members. The Islanders proudly called themselves "Buddhaheads" and nicknamed the mainlanders "Kotonks," meaning "empty heads," like the sound of a coconut. The mainlanders did not seem to mind the name and almost without questioning accepted the nickname. Despite fights and disputes—some lightweight, some

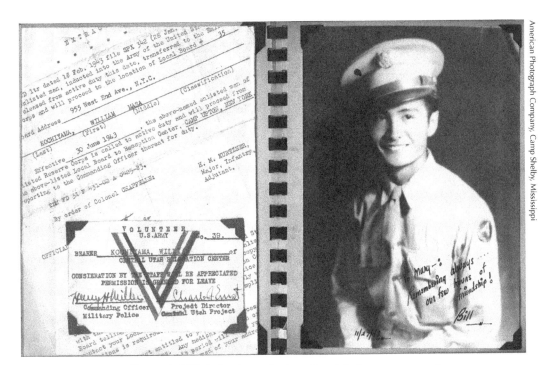

GI Bill (RIGHT); Bill's induction order to active duty (LEFT BACKGROUND) and Volunteer Army Enlisted Reserve card authorizing leave from the Central Utah Relocation Center. From Yuri's scrapbook "My Bill."

serious—the 442nd Combat Team members built a rapport with each other and readied themselves for the life-and-death battles in Italy and France. Actual combat experiences solidified the camaraderie among the Buddhaheads and Kotonks as they experienced equal casualties and grew to respect each other for their courage.

Within a year-and-a-half, the 442nd racked up an incredible number of medals and recognition. They became known as the Purple Heart Regiment because of the number of casualties sustained in combat, and they returned home as the most distinguished and outstanding army unit of its size in the history of the U.S. Army. Its most celebrated accomplishment was the rescuing of the "Lost Battalion" of 200 Texans in the Vosges Mountains of France, but for that achievement, the 442nd lost a man for every yard they advanced; over 1,000 were killed or wounded in this rescue.

Some who were wounded refused to leave the battlefield and stayed to fight until they were eventually killed. The 442nd's casualty of wounded was 308 percent, unheard of in the annals of wartime records, where most units lost some 10 or 20 percent. Some people questioned the 308 percent, but the

TAKEN IN GENOA, ITALY:
AN ITALIAN PARTISAN AND I

SHORTLY AFTER LIBERATION

Bill with an Italian partisan, Genoa, Italy.

reason for the high percentage is because so many Buddhaheads and Kotonks were hit as many as five different times and kept returning to fight. The number of amputees was also exorbitant. But all Nisei, whether in the mainland or Hawaii, were aware that the future for Nikkei would be paid by the heavy sacrifice of our Nisei of World War II.

There were also extraordinary feats of our Military Intelligence servicemen who served in the South Pacific, accompanying Marine assault groups, interrogating captured Japanese who were forced out of caves, dropping propaganda leaflets behind enemy lines, and participating in other dangerous tasks. Japanese American MIS men were shot at, mistaken for the Japanese, and sometimes not picked up as American wounded because of their physical likeness to the enemy.

Bill was lucky to come back alive and in one piece. He returned to the U.S. on Christmas Day, 1945, was honorably discharged on New Year's Day, 1946, and then returned home to New York.

May the Sansei, Yonsei and Gosei (third-, fourth-, and fifth-generation Nikkei) remember these Nisei soldiers who were sent to concentration camps yet chose to volunteer to fight for their country. They were the ones who opened the door for the rest of us. Some 35,000 Nisei chose to serve America in World War II and did so in some wartime capacity. Japanese American women also served as nurses and in military intelligence. Also, totally unknown are the few Nisei women who were in the Women's Ambulance and Defense Corps of America just before the war. As one of that small number, I would like to mention three others who were in the San Pedro chapter: Frances Ishun of Terminal Island, Lily Takahashi of Wilmington, and Mary Kubota of Palos Verdes Hill. However, we were asked to leave because of our ancestry.

The Bravery of the No-No Boys

The story of the Nisei in wartime would not be complete without the lesser known stories of Nisei dubbed "the No-No boys." These are the young men who would have gladly fought for the U.S. but felt that something was remiss when their country incarcerated their families in prison camps and yet could ask their young men to fight for the U.S. wherever ordered. The No-No boys became ostracized by the Japanese American majority who felt they were being anti-American at a very serious time.

Bill staunchly supported the No-No Boys because of the circumstances of that time. He saw the struggle of the No-No's as a struggle against the U.S. government's denial of the civil rights of their Japanese parents. He believed the No-No's would have fought if their parents could have been freed. He felt the No-No's objectives for the future of Japanese America were similar to those who promptly committed their allegiance to the U.S. without question by going immediately overseas to fight and die. Bill's hope had been that the two factions, the Yes-Yes's and the No-No's, could come together in mutual understanding and respect, as they continued on with their lives.

The No-No boys' rationale was more than understandable. They felt that their own rights were violated. As one No-No boy clarified, "I think democracy is sharing of equal rights and responsibilities, but when rights and responsibilities are denied by incarceration, I don't think it would be fair to ask those of us with families in prison camp, to go out and fight for the country that imprisoned them."

These young men felt there were other ways to show their loyalty to the U.S., even in wartime, by fighting for constitutional rights. Some of these men were sent to Leavenworth Prison; others to Tule Lake Camp. Some were sent to the Army's special 1800th Engineering General Service Battalion, a group of Japanese American, Italian American, and German American No-No's who fixed roads, bridges, and highways. After the war, each soldier went through a special military hearing to determine discharge status (honorable, without honor, dishonorable). Many of them received "blue" discharges (without honor). But in 1985, thirty-one members of the 1800th who received "blue" discharges filed a class action suit against the military to have their discharges without honor overturned and honorable discharges granted. Thanks to the persistent service of Attorney Hyman Bravin, who represented the thirty-one Japanese American soldiers in the initial military hearings after the war and represented them again at a board re-hearing, all thirty-one No-No boys had their military records changed to reflect honorable discharge status.

Many Nisei, however, still persist in seeing the No-No boys as those who hindered the efforts of those who fought and died in winning recognition for the future of Nikkei. But in my opinion, they were resisters of conscience who felt they needed to protest the internment and stand on constitutional grounds against the state. They chose another path to fight for the same objectives during the war. Many Nisei, including my husband and I, have often felt it took as much—or more—courage to fight this nonviolent war against racism and discrimination in the home front as going off to battle overseas.

Now there is a strong enough reconciliation among the Nisei to bring both sides to a satisfactory resolution. I think both sides have tried hard to listen to each other, and there have been galvanizing efforts for those who fought overseas enemies and on the home front to come to respect each other.

Bill and Yuri's wedding day,
February 9, 1946, New York City.

Life with My Bill

In reflecting on my life with Bill, I recall again way back when I was waiting patiently for him after the war. Once that day came for his official discharge, I couldn't wait to leave California and meet him in New York. But he felt bad that since he just got out, his future was uncertain and could not promise me anything. I sent him a telegram that said, "Don't worry about apartment, job, etc. . . . Future with you is no risk. It'll be adventure, happiness, love. Will be grateful always. Anxious to be yours. Mary." And I have been and always will be grateful to my Bill.

No words could describe the sorrow in my heart when Bill passed away on October 25, 1993. Some of our grandchildren were just infants or toddlers when he died. Our grandson, Christopher Kochiyama, was given the middle name, Masayoshi, after Bill. We are so glad that his father and mother, Tommy and Julie, gave Christopher this name because shortly after he was born, Bill passed away.

The frontpage of Yuri's scrapbook "My Bill."

Many people, from faraway places as well as in New York, came to Bill's memorial service. This gathering testified to the number of people who were touched or influenced by Bill's life and persona in some way. Those who could not attend expressed their condolences in other ways. All of them avalanched our family with love through phone calls, cards, telegrams, flowers, visits, food, and most of all, their warm, nourishing friendship. His journey, like that of everyone, had been interlaced with good times and bad, moments of sorrow, anxieties and disappointments, but also with satisfaction, joy, and triumph.

In closing this chapter, I would like to provide excerpts of a tribute I shared at a special memorial for him on October 30, 1993, at the church of St. Paul and St. Andrew in New York City. It captures how significant Bill was in my life and in the life of his children:

Life in New York with Bill was a great learning experience. He opened new doors for me—to jazz, theater, a bit of New York nightlife, the Yankees, the Dodgers, the Knicks, and to meeting some of his 120 brothers and sisters from Sheltering Arms. Then there were his college years at Long Island University when the first two of our children arrived.

As our family increased, his interest changed to activities in the Japanese and Asian communities. He helped to organize the 442nd Veterans Association; joined the Niko Niko club, supported the atom-bombed Hiroshima Maidens, played in two Asian American softball leagues; and was advisor to the Nisei Sino Service Organization.

As a father, he took interest in whatever the children were doing. He was excited when Audee (then fifteen) and Billy (eighteen) went off to Mississippi to help with voting rights in the summer of '64. He was solidly behind Eddie when he was suspended from school for his anti-Vietnam War activities in junior high school; also when Eddie was dismissed from his graduating class when he went to the People's Republic of China. He was proud of Jimmy and Tommy's independence in being able to start a new life in California while still teenagers. He was also proud of Aichi's taiko skill and her caring for others.

As a husband, he was phenomenal in sharing the workload at home, whether cooking or doing the housework. He did not feel that there should

"Godfather" Earl Finch takes Bill, Yuri and friends out on the town.

Yuri's brothers and their wives.
(FROM LEFT) Pete, Aiko, Yuri, Bill, Chiyo and Art.

be gender borders around work. He believed in the maxim, "Marriage is that relation between man and woman in which the independence is equal, the dependence is mutual, and the obligation reciprocal."

In the words of Pete, Bill truly had an "enthusiasm for life and a deep sense of gratitude for the wondrous gift of life." Yes, Bill knew the meaning of life and the sharing of love. He lived and loved fully; he felt deeply and experienced widely. And we who are still alive must remember to live fully, deeply, and widely.

Yuri and Bill in their first years together in New York
(CIRCA 1946). From Yuri's scrapbook "My Bill."

After the War:
Marriage, Parenthood, and New York

Only two weeks after arriving in New York City to be with Bill, we got married on February 9, 1946, at one of the Riverside Church chapels; Reverend Akamatsu officiated. Bill's father, who initially stopped our wedding in 1942, attended the small wedding. There was just a handful of people there because it was too far away for my family in California to attend. I can only remember four other people, one of whom was my close friend since childhood who I asked to be my Matron of Honor, Monica Miya (she herself had recently gotten married and settled in New York with her husband). There were also Bill's best friend, Ken Hayashi, who was his Best Man, and Bones and Yuri Taono, with whom I worked in Mississippi.

Newlywed and newly resettled, Bill and I found ourselves living in rooms to rent, moving almost monthly. All the rooms were rat holes: dark, dank, and cockroach infested places you wouldn't even dare to cook or eat food. There were no private toilets or baths; everything was "shared." We used to take our towel and soap and ask friends if we could "shower up" at their apartments.

Before I came to New York, I had never met many Black people, as there were not many living in San Pedro. My first encounter with Blacks was in early 1946, soon after my arrival to New York City. My first job was with Chock Full O' Nuts, a New York City restaurant chain that primarily hired Blacks. Anyone living in New York during the 1940s, 1950s, and 1960s would be familiar with "Chockies," as it was endearingly called. They were located all over Manhattan in busy areas—34th Street, 42nd Street, 72nd Street, etc. I worked at the 23rd Street restaurant near Park Avenue.

Bill's dad Yutaka, Billy, Yuri, and Bill (CIRCA 1948).

All the Chockies restaurants were known for their cleanliness and good service. They were also praised for their delicious wheat doughnuts (which were only seven cents), as well as their hot dogs and cheese-nut sandwiches which were an unbelievable twelve cents each. I found out that two of the men who worked there also trained during WWII at Camp Shelby, Mississippi, where Bill trained. I told them that I used to work at a USO in Hattiesburg but recalled that no Black soldiers came to our USO, and I wondered why. They asked, "Where was the USO?" When I said, "222 Pine," they said, "Well, no wonder. . .No Black soldiers, even in uniform, could walk any major street in Southern towns."

I knew that the South was racist, but I had no idea that life was so unfair and discriminatory for Blacks, that even Black soldiers in uniform would be derogated in such a manner. Mississippi was certainly the hell-hole of the South. How glad I was to have had the opportunity to work at Chockie's and have my first experience working with Black people. I enjoyed it a great deal, and I learned so much about the South and the racism there since many of my co-workers were from the South.

Once I became pregnant in 1947, though, I stopped working for some time. I wanted to be just a mother and learn how to be a mother. Billy was born in 1947 and named after his father. His middle name, Earl, was taken from Earl Finch, the "Godfather" of the 442nd Combat Team. A year after Billy was born, we succeeded in getting into one of the low-income housing projects—Amsterdam Houses—on 63rd Street. It was a predominantly Black and Puerto Rican housing project located next to the Lincoln Center, and it was there we had the rest of our children. How lucky we were! We had our own kitchen, bathroom, bedroom, and living room. The projects were a haven, and thanks to New York City's post-war resolutions, dozens of projects sprouted all over the five boroughs. The waiting lists were long but well worth it.

Audee was born in 1949 and named after my two close friends, Audrey Chavez and DeeDee (Yuri) Taono. We gave her the middle name, Tsuma, after my mother but later found out that my mother's name was actually Tsuya.

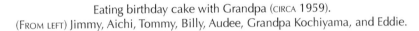

Eating birthday cake with Grandpa (CIRCA 1959).
(FROM LEFT) Jimmy, Aichi, Tommy, Billy, Audee, Grandpa Kochiyama, and Eddie.

Courtesy of the Yuri Kochiyama Collection, UCLA

Three years later, Lorrie was born in 1952. Her middle name, Aichi, which she began using when she got involved with the civil rights movement as a teenager, was a combination of the names of my two sisters-in-law, Aiko (Pete's wife) and Chiyo (Art's wife). Her English name, Lorrie, was derived from Gloria and Terry Croskrey, two dear friends from San Pedro.

Eddie was born in 1955. We gave him the middle name, Yutaka, after Bill's father. His English name came from Bill's buddy, Ed Singleton, another Sheltering Arms brother. Jimmy was born two years later and was given the name, James Wade, after our pediatrician and obstetrician. He gave himself a Japanese name, Chikara, since we had forgotten to give him one. Tommy, our last son, was born in 1959. We didn't know if he would be a boy or girl, but I wanted to name the baby after my Aunt Tami (Kondo-no-obasan). When our last baby turned out to be a boy, we just made Tami into Tommy. We gave him the middle name, Seiichi, after my father.

Since New York was Bill's hometown, Bill knew how to get around. At a meeting of newly founded American Veterans Association, Bill met a writer, Dan James, who was from Canada. We were invited by Dan and his wife Ruth to a theater party for a Broadway play, "On Whitman Avenue." It was probably the first play with an all-Black cast to make it on Broadway. Bill and I were very excited, and it seemed all the Black theater elites and well known Blacks in varied fields attended. I found out at the event that Ruth was part of the famous Duke Ellington family. She was the Duke's sister and known in her own right as a social figure. She had her own radio show and was active in the Black community. Ruth was constantly busy hosting important social events in Harlem and was very kind and generous to include Bill and me. She introduced us to famous figures like Cy Oliver and the "On Whitman Avenue" lead actor, Canada Lee.

Several years later, when Jimmy was born, we asked Ruth to become Jimmy's godmother. She was not only generous in providing clothes for Jimmy when he was young, but she would also give us ten tickets at a time to any concert that Duke Ellington was playing. We proudly passed them out to our neighbors in the Amsterdam Houses who would otherwise never be able to attend such notable events.

The friendliness of the Amsterdam Project residents, especially those in our building on 249 West 62nd Street, made this period a wonderful experience for our family. Our children joined the Boy Scouts and Girl Scouts

Jimmy, Tommy and Eddie in baseball uniforms, 1963.

troops that were organized in the project. Genevieve Duncan, who led Audee's Girl Scouts troop, was the mother of Alkamal, who years later would end up marrying our daughter, Aichi. Billy, as well as Alkamal and Butchie Robinson, the son of another close friend, were members of the Boy Scouts troop.

Our children also began attending Sunday school at a Presbyterian Church on 36th Street in the garment district area. The ministers of this Protestant Church were quite diverse: Irish, Italian, Filipino, East Indian, and one Anglo—a progressive who had done time in prison. We were introduced to this church by a Black couple, the Robinsons, whose youngest daughter, Janice, is our goddaughter.

Family life during 1950s was not only busy with two girls and four boys, but the Kochiyama home opened its doors to many hometown, New York,

The Kochiyama family opened its home to the Nisei-Sino Service Organization on Friday nights (early 1950s).

Hawaii, and West Coast friends, and GI's. Friday and Saturday nights eventually became an open house. On Fridays, we started the Nisei Service Organization to offer assistance and a place for GI's in town from Hawaii. We eventually changed the name to Nisei-Sino Service Organization when we started meeting many young Chinese. Saturday nights were set aside for anybody and everybody else: foreign students, aspiring actors and actresses, singers and dancers, professional athletes, out-of-town visitors and neighbors. From a dozen people, we often drew crowds of fifty jammed into a small apartment, to 100 people who would be out in the halls and down the stairwell.

In 1958, nine Black high school students, known as the famed "Little Rock Nine" who were credited with desegregating Central High School in Little Rock, Arkansas, came to New York to be feted by many different civil rights groups, including the NAACP, for their courageous stand against racism. The leader who won national recognition at that time was Daisy Bates, the president of the NAACP chapter in Little Rock. Through the efforts of Juanita Andrade, a neighbor from the Amsterdam Houses, I had the good fortune to meet Daisy Bates and also see Carlotta Walls (Juanita's niece) again. I first met Carlotta when she was about seven years old. She later grew up to be a civil rights activist.

It was after my meeting Daisy Bates that I began to take a serious interest in the civil rights movement. I kept my eyes on the newspapers as civil unrest and demonstrations erupted all over the South. By the close of the 1950s, the Southern civil rights movement was active in almost all of the Southern states, including Louisiana, Mississippi, Alabama, Georgia, South and North Carolina, Tennessee, Florida, and Virginia. This set the stage for what would become a significant time period for the Kochiyama family.

A rare gathering of all the Nakahara/Kochiyama families
in San Pedro, 1955, visiting Mom/Grandma for Mother's Day.

Organization of African American Unity at a rally
commemorating the life of Malcolm X, Harlem (CIRCA 1965).

Raising Six Children in the Sizzling Sixties

The 1960s was an amazing and exciting decade to be in Harlem, a community thriving with so much activity. Socially, politically, and culturally—Harlem was on fire and we got swept up in the whirlwind. All of our children began marching with my husband and me at civil rights events, in addition to doing the normal things of their age. I am proud of how much my children have in their own way come to understand the importance of justice and to stand up on behalf of others.

In December 1960, we moved to a new housing project in Harlem—the Manhattanville Houses on 126th and Broadway. It was a low-income housing project surrounded by Latino and Black families, and it was in this new neighborhood that at the age of forty, my political activism began to take shape. Moving from our five-room apartment at Amsterdam Housing Projects in central Manhattan to Harlem was indeed memorable: it was a very cold and windy December day with a blizzard storming up. Because we did not own a vehicle or have the money to rent one, we moved by subway from midtown to Harlem, going back and forth from 62nd Street to 125th.

Our children ranged from thirteen years old (Billy) to one year old (Tommy), but the older children all pitched in and helped as much as they could. They carried clothes, bedding, kitchenware, books, canned goods, pots and pans, dishes, and towels. A few of our adult friends, like the Kimizuka family, Al Karvelis, and Hal Gold, had cars so they were able to help with the furniture.

We held many memorable community gatherings in our new home. One such gathering was to hear the words of the Freedom Riders, an interracial group of activists from all over the U.S. who boarded buses headed for the South in order to protest the practice of segregated public transportation. In 1961 several busloads of Freedom Riders from New York left for the South.

Some of the buses were overturned in Alabama and set on fire. So when the Freedom Riders returned to New York, we invited some of the activists to speak at our house gatherings. One speaker was James Peck, one of the most severely beaten Riders. He was kicked, stomped on, and ended up in the hospital with fifty-seven stitches on his face. People up North were realizing what the struggle in the South was about.

In 1962 Bill and I became members of the Harlem Parents Committee, a grassroots movement to get safer streets and integrated education in the Harlem community. On weekends, our children attended the Harlem Parents Committee Freedom School. One day, all the parents were asked to take their children to a designated location (131st and Fifth Avenue). They were to put all their toddlers in the street to protest the number of children being struck down at corners lacking traffic signals. I brought Jimmy and Tommy, who were ages two and four, respectively, and it was their first experience being in a demonstration, even though they were too young to be aware of what was really happening. Because of the cooperation and participation of so many parents, the city responded quickly in installing traffic lights at every block in Harlem.

Given the intense political environment and all that was happening around us, I realize now that the growing-up years flew by much too fast for the children, especially for the youngest—Eddie, Jimmy and Tommy—who were only five, three, and one when we arrived in Harlem. While caring for and raising my children, I became very involved in the immediate needs for better education and housing. The times seemed urgent and demanding. Our family lifestyles and priorities changed. Social gatherings became political gatherings. In retrospect I realize that it was not fair to the three youngest, who missed out on many of the frivolities of childhood and traditional activities around holidays.

The major shift in our family began in 1963 when four little girls were killed in the bombing of a Baptist Church in Birmingham, Alabama. We did not celebrate Christmas that year: no presents for the kids and not even a Christmas tree. But all the children seemed to understand that a horrible racist act of violence could not be taken lightly. Instead, we donated money to the movements in the South. In the summer of 1963, we stopped in Birmingham on the way to California so that the children could visit the church where the four girls were killed. The pictures of the young girls were front-paged in the mainstream newspapers. The younger kids were as concerned and troubled as the older three. Subsequent holidays were also observed differently from the past (although not as drastically as Christmas of 1963).

Looking back, I wonder if I was much too dogmatic and strict, if the abstentions of customary practices did not hurt our children more than help them to understand the pain of others. Eddie, Jimmy, and Tommy were only eight, six, and four years old in 1963. I feel some remorse and guilt that I denied the younger three many of the fun times that the older children experienced at their age.

1963 was a pivotal year for us in terms of our involvement and education in the movement as a family. That year I took all six children to Downstate Medical Center in Brooklyn to join hundreds of demonstrators who were demanding construction jobs for Blacks and Puerto Ricans. It was also the year of the big New York City School Boycott and the year that the whole family enrolled in the Harlem Freedom School located at 514 West 126th Street. Luckily this was just across the street from where we lived (545 West 126th Street). Still very active with the Harlem Parents Committee, our family picketed schools in Harlem to close down until changes took place. It was a wonderful experience interacting with parents from the Harlem community who were fighting to bring quality education to their areas. Soon, there was a citywide effort that spread from the Manhattan Borough to the Bronx, Queens, Brooklyn, and Staten Island. 1963 was also the year that I met Malcolm X.

By the mid-1960s the older kids—Bill, Audee, and Aichi—began showing a strong interest in the Southern civil rights movement, which was becoming front-page news in all the metropolitan newspapers and also featured on the television news broadcasts. The struggle in the South was mostly for voter rights and public accommodations. Young people, mostly college-age, left their universities in the North and ventured into Georgia, Alabama, and Mississippi to register Black voters in both the urban and rural areas. They also organized picket lines at public facilities, where Blacks were not allowed to enter restaurants, hotels, theaters, libraries, swimming pools, toilets, and parks or to use drinking fountains. The year after the three civil rights workers were killed in Mississippi in 1964, Audee and Billy made their journey to Mississippi. Instead of attending his high school graduation, Billy took off for Rosedale, Audee to McComb.

Throughout our involvement in various struggles and movements during this period, Audee and Aichi studied ballet, and through the help of friends of ours who were ballet dancers (Helen Milholland and Barbara Bartlett of Canada), they were accepted into the prestigious Metropolitan Opera Ballet School. Their teachers told me that both Audee and Aichi (still Lorrie at the time) were very good dancers and would do well in ballet. They also once danced in a Wagnerian opera production. All the young dancers were blondes, so I didn't think Audee and Aichi would be able to participate. But the teachers just put blond wigs on the two, and they performed in the opera.

By the time that Audee and Aichi were in their third year of ballet, the famous Russian ballet troupe, the Bolshoi Ballet, had arrived in New York. Because they were working out at the Met, I had the opportunity to see the elegant Russian dancers practice when I would take the girls for their lessons. They were fascinating and delightful to watch—their agile bodies so supple and strong. But it was around this time that Audee and Aichi expressed their desire to quit ballet in deference to their interest in the civil rights movement. They wanted to spend more time on the picket lines and at demonstrations with their brother Billy and their organization, Students Against Social Injustice (SASI).

In 1965 Billy, then a senior at George Washington High School, and Audee, a sophomore at Music and Arts High School, were enthusiastic about going to Mississippi. They had been active for about two years in New York and were politically mature for their age. I felt they could handle any situation that might arise. The killing of the three civil rights workers took place the prior year, which brought publicity and more protection because of the tragedy. The organizers were more cautious. Audee went south for one week with High School Student Non-violent Coordinating Committee (SNCC), a well known national organization supported by parents and church groups. I felt reasonably secure that Audee would be fine, even though she went to McComb, one of the hot spots of the South. I also knew I could not have stopped her from going because she was so intent.

Billy connected with the Mississippi Student Union in Rosedale, a county not too far from the home base of the famous civil rights leader, Fannie Lou Hamer. From one of his earliest letters from Rosedale, where Billy stayed with a Black family, he wrote of his surprise at meeting Chinese in the neighborhood. He said they were as surprised meeting an Asian coming there from the North as he was in seeing that there were Chinese in many parts of Mississippi. He learned that these Chinese had migrated to Mississippi following the building of the railroad in the 1800s, which was one of the greatest contributions of the Chinese to America.

Billy was surprised to learn that young Blacks were not just into the Martin Luther King philosophy; many "dug" Malcolm as well. The following is a short letter he wrote to the family on July 16, 1965:

> I really wish Malcolm could have just made one trip to Mississippi. First of all, he would have been pleasantly shocked to see how Black Nationalist SNCC was becoming. Secondly, so much of what the Black Mississippian wants is what Malcolm has said all along. The Black people here are always preaching Black unity, self-defense, and telling the truth just like it is. Malcolm would have found thousands of followers here. Unfortunately, the more white volunteers coming down, the less militant the movement here will be.
>
> Sure wish I could have heard the guy from the Deacons.
>
> Love, Billy

After returning to New York, Billy went away to college in Springfield, Massachusetts in 1966 and 1967. He worked summers in an Upward Bound program with youth. Billy filled his days with community activities.

While she was in McComb, Mississippi, Audee stayed at the home of several Black families. She became acquainted with the well known Quinn family and the Steptoes. During Easter vacation of 1965, Audee met Terry Williams, whose family was also involved in the civil rights movement in McComb. Terry was on his way to New York City as soon as school

Letter from Billy, Rosedale, Mississippi—postmarked July 16, 1965.

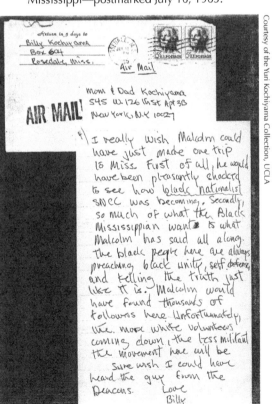

Courtesy of the Yuri Kochiyama Collection, UCLA

Asian Americans demonstrating against the Vietnam War,
Manhattan (CIRCA 1969). Rocky Chin talking to the Asian contingent.
(Some notable people pictured above: Shinya Ono, Kazu Obayashi, Audee and Aichi, Yasin
Mohamed-Ladson, Bob Miyamoto, Faye Chiang, Nobuko Miyamoto, Chris Iijima, and Steve Louie.)

ended. Because New York City is so large, Audee did not know whether they
would meet each other there. Coincidentally, it turned out that Terry's family
lived only two blocks away from us. After Terry came North to Harlem, we
saw very little of Audee. Two years later they were married and our first
grandchild, Kahlil Zulu Williams, was born in May 1968.

Aichi was like a pixie in her personality: sparkling, enthusiastic, and
sometimes ornery. Where some people thought of Audee being like "sugar,"
they thought of Aichi being like "spice." Because Aichi had been too young
to go to Mississippi or anywhere for that matter, she would sometimes brood.
She used to say she wanted most to go to Vietnam and fight as she admired
the National Liberation Front (NLF) women who worked in the rice fields
with rifles on their backs. Aichi somehow got a name of a Vietnamese activist
woman to whom she began writing. Also, when Aichi went to Music and Art
High School, she used to draw pictures and make block prints of Vietnamese
women farmers/fighters and Vietnamese mothers with their children. When
she was eighteen, Aichi met Yasin Mohammed, a Black Panther brother of

Black and East Indian descent who was from Queensbridge Housing project in Long Island City. Shortly afterward, our first granddaughter Akemi was born, and Aichi and Yasin married.

The three youngest children did not always have the most positive experiences in Harlem, especially Jimmy and Tommy. Years later I found out through Aichi, in whom they used to confide, that neighborhood kids often harassed them. They kept much to themselves, not wanting to bother me. I was sorry to learn of this and could imagine the difficulties they encountered. It showed I was not as attentive as I should have been. I had much to learn from my children. In fact, they told me straight up that I should have given more concern to them than to the movement.

Eddie, Jimmy, and Tommy belonged to their own little group—a bunch of neighborhood kids who called themselves the "Boy Commandoes." They were a nice group of kids ranging from about eight to twelve years old. Once, Bill and I planned a birthday party for Tommy and invited the Boy Commandoes. We also invited a young Black Movement brother to come do magic tricks, as we heard that he was good at them. He knew our kids, and they seemed to all get along. In fact, he seemed to get along well with everyone in the movement.

About four years later, we found out that this affable young man who was talented with magic was the main police agent who had infiltrated the Black Panther Party, Revolutionary Action Movement (RAM), and other radical organizations. He was thus more of a trickster than a magician. He even used to come out with our family to the Nisei Softball League games and played with the 442nd team.

Bill with Michi and Walter Weglyn at a reception (CIRCA 1968).

It seems he took his responsibility to keep the community and their social activities under surveillance very seriously—maybe too much. He was quite clever in making his way into the community. So many movement women later said that they saw more of him in their homes than their own husbands. He also knew how to exploit the innocence of children who readily accepted him. We still have pictures of him doing magic tricks at Tommy's party. We should have learned some lessons to be more cautious with people. At the same time, we have to teach children to have faith in people. Very few will turn out to be "lemons."

When Jimmy and Tommy were about seven and five years old, I took them to a demonstration in Central Park to commemorate the bombings of Hiroshima and Nagasaki. A news photographer snapped a picture of Jimmy and Tommy carrying candles at the march. As a proud mother, I made many photocopies to send to friends and also put it in their scrapbooks. Without these pictures, I thought, they would not remember. But as they grew older, we spoke of Hiroshima and Nagasaki and explained what transpired back then and of the thousands of people who were killed when the atom bomb was dropped on those two cities. Around the same time, our family participated in a march against American military bases in Okinawa. Again, Tommy was snapped by a photographer. When it appeared in the newspaper, the caption read, "Okinawa Youth Demonstrating." We smile today, because Tommy grew up to eventually marry a woman of Okinawan descent.

Not too long after this event, our family was involved in visits to the Mt. Sinai Hospital in New York City to see the twenty-five Hiroshima Maidens, as they were called, as they took turns receiving plastic surgery. These twenty-five atomic bomb victims came to the U.S. to receive reconstructive surgery provided by the

Tommy at a demonstration against U.S. military bases in Okinawa.

OKINAWAN YOUTH protests American military and business interests in his country.

Courtesy of the Yuri Kochiyama Collection, UCLA

Marchers make their way up Seventh Avenue (l) to a rally in Central Park yesterday in observance of Hiroshima Day. At the rally (r) a flutist plays for the crowd. Story on Page 9.

Post Photos by Vernon Shibla

Tommy (with headband) and Jimmy in a demonstration to commemorate
the bombings of Hiroshima and Nagasaki at Central Park, August 6, 1971.

hospital free of charge. When we learned that Nisei families could have the opportunity to host a Hiroshima Maiden, we volunteered. Tomoko Nakabayashi stayed with us for one weekend. Tragically, she died several months later on the operating table. She was the only one to die during their eighteen-month stay in the U.S., where over one hundred successful surgeries took place. We still have a picture of Tomoko-san with our children. We did not want them to forget her. We also wanted our children to make the connection with the atomic bombing of Hiroshima and to remember that an American Jewish Hospital gave service gratis for eighteen months of plastic surgery to the young Hibakusha women.

Not too many years later, we had our children participate at another Hiroshima/Nagasaki event, in which the focus was not only on the two atom-bombed cities, but also Nanjing, in China. The theme was "Hiroshima, Nagasaki, Nanjing—Never Again!" so that the children could learn of the

IT COULD HAVE BEEN US   *Aug 15, 1970*

Manhattan Tribune

Audee (LEFT), Aichi (RIGHT) and Bill (BEHIND
AICHI) at a demonstration against
the Vietnam war, August 15, 1970.

massacre in Nanjing at the hands of the Japanese. Not only were some 400,000 to half a million people of Nanjing killed (more than the number eliminated in Hiroshima and Nagasaki), but the brutality displayed was horrendous. The suffering due to war, feelings of hatred, and desperation of the aftermath must be taught to children so that war can be annihilated.

Jimmy, Tommy, and Eddie also participated in some Black Panther and Young Lords demonstrations, Attica events, and a few February 21st Malcolm X Commemoration marches. One of the largest marches that the three attended turned out to be a little scary. It was the big 1967 Vietnam War March to the United Nations. Two busloads of police waited in the 42nd Street underpass and unleashed an attack, liberally swinging their nightsticks and clubbing people at random. Young movement activists, seeing Tommy and Jimmy (only eight and ten) in the midst of the melee, lifted them on top of the roof of a car to safeguard them from the stampede of people being chased by the cops. Our good friend Lakaya McIntyre, who tried to rescue them from the car roof, was surrounded by about twenty police and soundly beaten. Eddie (age twelve) and his friends Martin Rutrell and Darrell Jenkins were chased by cops on horses and kicked.

By the time the children were in junior high school, the three boys seemed pretty streetwise. They were also still attending Asian American movement activities, going to the Asian Community Center to play ping pong, and interacting with the older Asians in the movement. Often at demonstrations and marches, they caught the eye of photographers because they were probably the youngest participants.

In 1971, at the age of sixteen, Eddie received the opportunity of a lifetime: the chance to visit the People's Republic of China with the second American group to be allowed into China after the Cultural Revolution—even before President Nixon! It was an all-student group, of all backgrounds but mostly college students and movement activists. There were Blacks, Latinos, whites, Asians, and an American Indian. Eddie was ecstatic about going to China, even though he knew it meant he would not be able to graduate with his class. He knew he would learn more in China in a month than he could learn in the whole semester of high school. In an essay later written the following year, he expressed just how incredible and lucky he was to have had this rare experience:

> In the fall of 1971, I had the great privilege of being invited to join a group of twenty-five American students to visit the People's Republic of China. It was a great privilege indeed because we were only the second group of Americans to visit Mainland China since the Chinese revolution in 1949.
>
> I was extremely lucky to be invited in the first place. I was only asked to go because Shinya Ono, a community organizer and leader of the Asian American movement, could not go because he was on parole. Shinya had just gotten out of jail for his participation in the "Days of Rage" demonstration outside the 1968 Democratic National Convention in Chicago.
>
> Our trip was an historic event because we went to China two months before Richard Nixon. The United States and China were just beginning discussions to normalize relations. Our delegation was a part of the People to People diplomacy the Chinese government had initiated. Prior to Nixon's visit to China, the U.S. sent their national basketball team to China, and China sent their ping pong team to the U.S. The two countries also exchanged student delegations to tour each other's cities.
>
> Our delegation was called the "Progressive Student Delegation" from the United States. We were composed of mainly college students from all over the United States. We were Black, Puerto Rican, Chicano, Asian and White. All of us were student activists, involved in issues ranging from Black

Asian Americans demonstrating in Manhattan against the Vietnam War.

liberation, anti-war, women's liberation, anti-apartheid, ethnic studies, and worker organizing.

I was the youngest in our group. I was only 16 years old, a junior in high school. I believe that I was the youngest American and the second Japanese American to visit China since the revolution. (The first JA to go to China was the late Pat Sumi.) I knew I was one lucky young brother.

Being that we were guests of the Chinese government, all of our expenses were covered, including airfare, hotels, and meals. We were even given some spending money to buy souvenirs.

Before we left the U.S., the Chinese government asked us what we wanted to do, where we wanted to go, and whom we wanted to meet. Of course we said we wanted to do everything, go everywhere and meet everyone. And we weren't joking. Nearly all our wishes were granted.

We traveled to Canton, Shanghai, Beijing, and Yenan. We visited primary schools, universities, factories, hospitals, communes, parks, restaurants, department stores, theaters, and even a People's Liberation Army base. We saw with our own eyes how socialism was being implemented.

We witnessed acupuncture being used to extract teeth and to excise large tumors. We participated in cultural exchanges with many of the national minorities. We talked to students, workers and political leaders. We were some of the first Americans to see real live panda bears. We walked in the caves where Chairman Mao wrote some of his most famous essays. We played basketball with China's national women's team. And we ate dinner with the Central Committee of the People's Republic of China at the Great Hall of the People in Tiananmen Square.

One of the many highlights of my trip was meeting Premier Chou En Lai. We had requested a meeting with the Premier and of course with Chairman Mao. Unfortunately, Chairman Mao was ill at the time. Even though we were merely a group of young student radicals, we were accorded VIP treatment.

Chou En Lai was a world-renowned revolutionary leader in the Third World, as well as a respected diplomat, even to his imperialist adversaries. He was the eloquent statesman for his nation. He was revered by the people of China for his leadership role in the Long March and for the many decades of his life dedicated to the revolution.

We met Chou En Lai along with the top echelon of China's leadership. We met Mao Tse Tung's wife, as well as the rest of the quartet later to be known as the "Gang of Four."

Needless to say, it was a very exciting experience. Here we were, this mixed group of young people from all over America, sitting in this huge hall with the leaders of the largest nation on earth.

The meeting started off real cordial and simple. Chou En Lai went around the room and asked each of us some real easy questions like, "How do you like China?" "What would you like to see?" etc. Then he asked a little tougher questions like, "What do the American people think about the Vietnam War?" and "What is the state of race relations in the U.S.?"

Then he came to me and said, "Kochiyama-san, would you like to speak in English or Japanese?" I was dumbfounded because I didn't know he could speak Japanese. But I did know that I could not speak the language. I answered, "Let's just speak in English so everyone can understand." I thought that was a clever answer and so I began to feel relaxed until he said, "Kochiyama-san, I have one more question for you." I thought, "No sweat." Then he asked, "What do you think is the principal contradiction in the world today?" I felt as though I was about to pee in my pants.

My heart just stopped and my mind went blank. I replied something like, "Do you know where the restroom is?" Not only was I profoundly embarrassed but also I was even more ashamed because this whole conversation was being filmed for the national archives! I went to the bathroom to collect my thoughts and my nerves. I relieved myself and I felt relieved because I figured that by the time I get out of the bathroom, our question-and-answer period would be over.

I coolly strolled back to my seat and then the Premier came back to me and said, "Kochiyama-san, you never answered the question."

While in the bathroom I tried to remember all the stuff I ever learned in our Marxist-Leninist study groups. I answered, "The principal contradiction in the world today is the struggle between the forces of national liberation against the forces of U.S. imperialism." Chou En Lai said, "That is the correct answer. You are a very bright young man."

There were many memorable moments in my trip to China but my conversation with Chou En Lai stands out as the most paramount.

Because of his experience in China, meeting Red Guards, and visiting the communes and schools, Eddie became more motivated about the movement here when he returned to America. The Vietnam War was escalating, so he also joined Asian Coalition against the Vietnam War, which mobilized large contingents of Asians who marched in Washington DC, as well as in New York. There was also another group, Asians in the Spirit of the IndoChinese, who also organized marches in which he demonstrated. He participated with Korean activists like Jan and Brenda Sunoo in support of the Democracy Movement in Korea. He also joined Asian Americans for Action (Triple A) in protesting the U.S.-Japan Security Treaty and Hiroshima/Nagasaki events.

He acknowledged Chris Iijima, Charlie Chin, and Nobuko Miyamoto as his role models and followed them wherever they performed. He also dug the Panthers and Young Lords

Flyer for an event featuring films on Malcolm X and Ho Chi Minh at City College of New York. Drawings are by Tommy Kochiyama.

Photograph by Yuri Kochiyama

Asian Americans demonstrating against the Vietnam War. Audee (CENTER, WITH LONG HAIR) is walking with young Zulu (CIRCA 1971).

and attended their demos. Malcolm X, Ho Chi Minh, Che Guevara, and Fidel Castro were his icons. The 1970s were an exciting time for Eddie.

Both Jimmy and Tommy liked history. I found a paper Tommy wrote in the seventh grade about Puerto Rico. I was surprised at how political he had already become and how well he understood America's colonization of Puerto Rico. He wrote:

> In my opinion, it is ridiculous to believe that the United States went into Puerto Rico with any other interest/intention than to rip off the natural resources, exploit the people, and use much of the land for strategic military bases.
>
> Today the U.S. government has exclusive authority over all questions of citizenship, foreign affairs, defense, immigration and emigration, foreign trade, postal service, radio and television, air and maritime transport. The U.S. government has judicial, legislative, and executive control over Puerto Rico. What this means is that the U.S. controls all aspects of life in Puerto Rico. Along with this is the fact that 13% of Puerto Rico's best agricultural land is occupied by U.S. military bases—not to forget about the tourist industry which brings with it drugs, prostitution and organized crime.
>
> And how has all this affected the Puerto Rican people? Well, right now, 14.3% of the labor force is unemployed. Many people have been forced to migrate to America in search of jobs. So much of their beautiful land has been ripped off and exploited. Living and working conditions are brutally oppressive and with starvation wages. And over one third of the Puerto Rican women of childbearing age have been forcibly sterilized.

Until these conditions are changed and Puerto Ricans control Puerto Rico, the Puerto Rican peoples' fight for independence, sovereignty, and freedom will continue.

When Jimmy was in the seventh grade, he also wrote an article entitled "The Chinese in America" for a junior high school newsletter:

In the 1850s when all the racism and violence was focused on the Indians and Mexicans, when a government inspector stated that the "great cause of civilization must exterminate Indians," a new dark-skinned foreigner had reached the United States coast, the Chinese. Violence found a new victim.

In 1857, a newspaper, the *Shasta Rep.*, said that "thousands of Chinamen have been slaughtered in cold blood by desperadoes that infest this state, yet we heard of but two or three instances where they were brought to justice." This was not surprising, for California had passed a law prohibiting Chinese from testifying in any case involving a white man.

In Los Angeles, in 1871, a white man was shot in a Tong war. A mob stormed the Chinese community, killed six and hanged fifteen, including women and children, from handy awnings and lamp-posts. Anti-Chinese feeling and violence spread through San Francisco in 1877. Tacoma's Chinese community was burned that year. Members of "anti-Coolie" clubs drove the Chinese out of fifteen towns. Discrimination was no longer a little thing. It was now organized.

Politicians saw advantages in this. Parties rose to power with anti-Chinese slogans. Politicians were extremely interested in the labor vote, and no party platform was complete without a strong anti-Chinese plank. The Democrats were ahead in the demand for the exclusion of Chinese. Discrimination soon became a general practice. A number of discriminatory acts were passed at all levels.

Finally California turned to Washington. In 1882, with the support of the southern Congressman and Senators, the West Coast legislators put over the Chinese Exclusion Act. This effectively halted Chinese immigration.

I felt proud that Jimmy and Tommy picked serious topics to write about and that their understanding of Asian American history seemed ahead of their time in relation to their peers.

By 1971, Eddie, Jimmy, and Tommy were already quite independent. Eddie, like Audee and Aichi before him, attended Music and Art High School, but after one semester he decided to transfer to Charles Evan Hughes, a rather tough school. Eddie liked Hughes High School because Panther and

Young Lords members used to come and speak there. Jimmy, who was attending the elite Bronx Science High School, eventually switched to Seward Park near Chinatown. Tommy wanted something altogether different. Although attending Music and Art High School and doing well, he opted to move to Los Angeles and attended an Asian American "street academy," where he was able to enjoy an Asian American cultural setting.

Years later while looking at a scrapbook, I saw pictures of Jimmy, Tommy, and Victor Shibata in the early 1970s, way out in the middle of nowhere and on their way to California. The scenery was very beautiful in some of the pictures. Later, we found the following letters that Tommy and Jimmy had written while traveling. Tommy wrote:

Hey People! What's happening?

Sorry I haven't been writing but ever since we left N.Y., we've been setting up camp, getting wood for our fire, meeting people, checking out the country, working at YB [Yellow Brotherhood], and just having a real good time.

Well, I'll just write a brief run-down on our trip out here. We finally left New York at about 5:00 on the 19th, arrived the next day (at 2:00) in Chicago. We stayed in Chicago one night and there we went to the New Youth Center in Chicago's Chinatown and met some pretty good people. From Chicago (we left on the 20th) we started for S. Dakota. It's really sick in S. Dakota because the Monument, (the one with the 4 presidents carved in the mountain) is in the Black Hills, which was a holy land for the American Indians. Near the monument, there's an information center telling about the monument and what each president stood for. For instance, Lincoln stood for freedom and the rest was bullshit like that.

Also in S. Dakota, some people are building or carving (in a mountain) a monument or statue of Crazy Horse. It'll probably be finished in about 20 or 30 years. [It is still not finished.]

Well anyway, from S. Dakota we went to Yellowstone. And stayed there for a day. Up there, we caught some trout (two 14 inches and one about 15 inches).

After Yellowstone we went to Spokane (where the World's Fair is). The fair is real small. We stayed at some relatives of one of the bros. in YB for one night.

Then we drove over to Seattle where they have a pretty big Asian community, consisting of mainly Japanese, Chinese, Filipino, and Korean people. We met some really beautiful people. The first night we stayed at some people's house named Kathy and Alan Sugiyama. They were really nice to us. One of the first places in Seattle that we went to was the Asian

Drop-In Center where we met a lot of young (about my age) street people. Some of the people are really crazy but they're all real good people. The 2nd night we stayed at Alan's brother's house and in the morning, we left for the Oregon Coast.

When we hit the coast, we had a little celebration type of thing (we opened a bottle of sake). Let me tell you, the Oregon coast is really beautiful.

Since we had to get here on the 1st, we decided to go past San Francisco and camp out. Because at this time it was the 29th. When we hit some place above Frisco, I called Aiko [his aunt]. We didn't get to talk too much but I just wanted to tell her we wouldn't be able to stop at her house. We'll probably go up sometime later this summer.

While we were looking for a campsite, everyone was getting excited. (Since we were in California), we decided to make it to L.A. as soon as possible so we just kept on going. We arrived in L.A. on the 30th at about 1:00 in the afternoon. "Ahhh, we finally made it."

Right now, it's about 2:30 and in a little while, I'm gonna go with Warren up to Gardena and meet his parents. Jimmy's at the beach right now and I'll see him there later on tonite. Tonite's the 4th of July.

Working with the people at YB is pretty nice. I really dig all the people there. Oh, could you thank Kazu Iijima for us because before we left she gave us some money. We'll drop a letter soon.

I guess Akemi must be toilet trained by now, so tell her I don't expect to be changing any diapers when I get back. Well, I guess I'll be ending this letter. So, everyone, take it easy and write back and let us know what's happening out in the Big Apple.

Love, Tommy

Jimmy wrote:

Dear Family:

How is everything with us away? Sorry we haven't written but the excitement of finally getting into something kind of prevented us from doing so. Know you must be worried. It's about 11:00 and we just finished talking to Mark and Akemi.

Well, we got in yesterday around 10 in the morning and at Holiday Bowl. Then went over to the house where we met many of the brothers and sisters from the YB. It freaks me out to see rowdy Buddhaheads. After that we all split over to Wendy's (Nick's girlfriend) house where we had a barbeque. And after that we went to a Buddhahead carnival. It was pretty small and kinda dead. But Tommy won a toaster-oven for the YB. When that ended, we went to a little party at the neighbors, John and Tomi's house. The party was for a sister named Leota. Today, some of the brothers took us over to L.A. High School where summer school is going on.

Oh, yeah, bad news. We didn't get the jobs so we'll be short on funds. It seems that all the TW [Third World] organizations were cut 80% altogether. So, it would be pretty jive for us to get jobs anyway.

So far we've seen Joanne [Nobuko], Kamau, Bob, Wendy Sahara, Chris, Karen, Nick, and a lot of other people. Kamau was pretty sick last week and had to go to the hospital. They removed his appendix. But he's all right now. He'll be laughing and acting crazy again. Oh, Chris, Wendy, Joanne, and Kamau were in an accident a couple of hours ago. Their car collided and flipped over. Luckily no one was hurt, although Wendy's car was completely wrecked. It was the other car's fault.

Might check out Vegas tomorrow night after a Chris and Joanne Concert. Wednesday, we'll get to hear Hiroshima at this dance they're having. And Thursday, 4th of July, people are going to party at the beach [Hermosa Beach]. Well, that's about all that's happening here. Oh, the trip was fantastic, but will tell you about it when I get back. P.S. Heard the Asian Center was broken into. Know you people must have been pissed. How bad was it? Please write, even if I don't.

Love, Jimmy

I believe our children who grew up in Harlem had one advantage: they were in the circumference of the civil rights movement. There were street and project activists representing a broad spectrum of backgrounds but all political: from college and middle-class participants to Black nationalists, elderly, and church people. Our children were also influenced by the different aspects of Afro-American culture: its music (jazz, blues, spirituals, freedom songs); its dance (African, Caribbean); its literature (W.E.B. DuBois, Richard Wright, James Baldwin); and its sports figures (Paul Robeson, Jesse Owens, Jackie Robinson). It was the best place to raise Billy, Audee, Aichi, Eddie, Jimmy, and Tommy. Harlem was a university without walls.

One of eleven postcards Malcolm X sent to the Kochiyamas
from his travels. This one is postmarked from Cairo.

Malcolm X and the Kochiyamas

One of the moments my family and I will never forget is when Malcolm X came to our apartment in Harlem's Manhattanville Projects on June 6, 1964. This was a year-and-a-half before he was assassinated.

The special occasion was a reception for three writers of the Hiroshima/Nagasaki World Peace Study Mission, who were on a world tour speaking against the proliferation of nuclear arms building. These three *Hibakusha* ("atomic bomb survivors") writers wanted to meet Malcolm X more than any other person in America. Because we lived in Harlem, they asked if we would make a special effort to organize a meeting with him.

We wrote months in advance to Malcolm at his 125th Street office, inviting him to meet with this Peace Mission, but we received no word. People told us he would never come. After all, he did not know us, and the time was dangerous for Malcolm. He had left the Nation of Islam only three months earlier. There were also rumors that Malcolm might be killed, but who would kill him? Who would benefit by his death? The Black movement activists felt the American power structure would benefit, not the Nation of Islam.

Meanwhile, we called on the Harlem Parents Committee to help organize a reception for Malcolm. HPC members were not Malcolm followers; they were a multinational civil rights group. But they responded with great enthusiasm because they also wanted to meet Malcolm. Despite not being sure that Malcolm would really come, we proceeded with plans for cultural performances, a few speakers, and light refreshments. A Black folk singer, Clebert Ford; a Japanese contralto; a Black school teacher, Edwardina Brown; and Isaiah Robinson, head of Harlem Parents Committee, would comprise the program. We also asked my cousin Kathy Muto and her girlfriend Emi Ikemoto to help with the refreshments. News of this reception and that Malcolm might be at our home circulated by word of mouth.

On June 6, 1964, the Kochiyama family waited excitedly. A good friend, Conway Redding, son of renowned writer Saunders Redding, stopped by early and offered to take the younger ones off our hands. He took them to see *Mary Poppins*. Lorrie (as Aichi was called then at age eleven), Eddie, Jimmy, and Tommy went with Conway. We let fourteen-year-old Audee stay and help. We can't remember where Billy was on that day, but he must have been away somewhere very important, as he would never have wanted to miss meeting Malcolm.

On that day the *Hibakusha* writers first visited a Black school and a Black church. Then they decided they wanted to walk around Harlem by themselves and not with their overly protective white hosts who helped coordinate their itinerary. They had lunch at a restaurant called "22" on 135th Street, where Malcolm used to eat. They met some Black nursing students who recognized the *Hibakusha* who were on a television program the night before. Then the group walked all the way to 114th Street. This was Jesse Gray's area, where the "World's Worst Fair" was taking place while the regular tourist-attraction fair was held at Flushing Meadows in Queens. Harlem activists thought of the unique idea of opening up a "Fair" in one of the most impoverished blocks in Harlem so that "tourists" could see how some people in Harlem had to live under the supervision of uncaring landlords and the sanitation department. The *Hibakusha* writers saw some realities of Harlem they would have otherwise missed if they did not go to 114th Street and check out the "World's Worst Fair": living quarters with broken windows, broken-down staircases, toilets that wouldn't flush and clogged-up bathtubs, and garbage piled high on the streets. The *Hibakusha* contingent finally came to our apartment. They immediately thanked us for suggesting that they first visit the "World's Worst Fair."

By the time they arrived at our home, the house began to pack up. Everyone was curious to know if Malcolm was really going to come. Shortly after the program began, there was a knock on the door—and there was Malcolm. He had three security men with him, but they blended so well with the crowd that we were not aware Malcolm brought anyone with him. When we later checked the guest book, we saw that three MMI (Muslim Mosque Inc.) men did sign. Upon entering the house, Malcolm first said that he was sorry he hadn't answered any of my letters to him; he did not have my address. He further remarked that should he travel again, he would

Malcolm X with Audee and three other teens on June 6, 1964 at the Kochiyama home.

remember to write to me. He did as he promised, writing me eleven times from nine different countries.

As he walked into the living room, people surged toward him, wanting to shake his hand. He was gracious with everyone. The living room, kitchen, and hallway were crowded. He shook hands with as many people he could reach out to. People were impressed with his warmth even before he began to talk.

Malcolm first thanked the *Hibakusha* for taking the time to go to the "World's Worst Fair." He said something to the effect, "You have been scarred by the atom bomb. You just saw that we have also been scarred. The bomb that hit us was racism." He went on to divulge that he spent some years in prison, where he educated himself. He read everything he could get his hands on, including Asian history, which wasn't too different from the history of Africa. He said that almost all of Asia, like Africa, was colonized except for Japan. But he explained that because Japan did not have the natural resources like other Asian countries, Japan was left untouched by European powers. Thus, Japan was able to develop and remain intact

Malcolm X meeting with Japanese journalists at the Kochiyama home, June 6, 1964.
(FROM LEFT) Ryuji Hamai (WRITER), Nobuya Tsuchida (INTERPRETER), and Akira Mitsui
(REPORTER)—delegates of the Hiroshima-Nagasaki World Peace Study Mission.
PHOTOGRAPH FROM FAMILY NEWSLETTER *CHRISTMAS CHEER*, VOLUME 15 (1964), P. 6.

until World War II when she was defeated. "But now," he said, "there are
American bases there."

He spoke of the People's Republic of China and Mao Tse-tung. He
admired Mao because he simultaneously took on feudalism, government
corruption, and foreign incursion. He also thought Mao was correct in
showing preferential treatment to the peasants rather than the workers
because it was the peasants who were feeding such a large country.

He spoke of one other Asian country—Vietnam: "If America sends troops
to Vietnam, you progressives should protest. America is already sending
American advisors." He also strongly commented that "the struggle of
Vietnam is the struggle of the whole Third World: the struggle against
colonialism, neo-colonialism, and imperialism." Unfortunately, Malcolm
did not live long enough to see the growth of the anti-war movement in this
country.

Malcolm was so ahead of his time. He predicted much of what was to come in the last year that he lived. No wonder he became such a revered icon. However, we must understand that Malcolm was not lionized by the press. In fact, he was demonized by both the press and those in power. Malcolm was considered a threat to those who unleashed their power to oppress the poor and marginalized. Despite how the newspapers deprecated him during the 1950s and 1960s, he was loved and admired by those "at the bottom"—the poor and powerless—especially in Black communities like Harlem. To them, Malcolm was their hero, who was not afraid to speak the truth.

Malcolm must be seen in his many dimensions: as a loving father, a devoted husband, a strong Muslim, and a man who had good rapport with the Black communities. He was also one who transformed from a Black Nationalist to a Pan-Africanist, and then to a Revolutionary Internationalist. He also transformed from being a petty criminal when racism closed options in his life to a political leader who opened doors not only for himself but also for all people.

He taught his people to be proud of their African heritage, to learn the hard road that his people had come, to seek new paths for liberation, and to fight against all the negativities in American society. He taught them to challenge racism, inequities, marginalization, and police brutality. In the social and political battles that he led, he taught all kinds of people how to fight for a more just and humane society. He also warned the youth about drugs.

Malcolm traveled widely, not only to Black communities and university campuses around U.S., but also to the Middle East, Africa, and twice to England. He was not permitted to enter France. In 1964 the Chinese Ambassador in Ghana invited him to China, but because his travel schedule was too tight, he

From the "Christmas Cheer" family newsletter, Vol. 15 (1964).

Photograph by Yuri Kochiyama

Billy showing Audee, Eddie, Jimmy and Tommy a picture of Malcolm X. From the "North Star" family newsletter, Vol. 1 (1965).

had to decline. So the Ambassador invited Vickie Garvin, a Black woman whom Malcolm had met in Ghana, to visit China. Malcolm's extensive travels made him an internationalist.

His recognition and acceptance everywhere made the U.S. government feel more threatened. Malcolm began to be followed by the CIA. He was poisoned while he was in Egypt. Other problems with his own organization brought a rift with his leader, Elijah Muhammad.

On February 21, 1965, Malcolm was assassinated while speaking to his own OAAU and Muslim Mosque followers at the Audubon Ballroom where he spoke weekly. I was in the audience when Malcolm X was assassinated and immediately ran on stage as soon as he fell to the floor. Cradling his head in my hands, I was shocked. Only one of his killers was apprehended. Two others were arrested, but there was controversy over their arrest. His sudden death was devastating for Harlem, for other Black communities, and for the Black liberation movement. However, the movement could not be extinguished. The movement continued doggedly but also in spurts. New faces, younger and more militant, filled the gap of the struggle. The movement mushroomed and become more radical.

In the wake of Malcolm's death, Black organizations flourished. The Black Panthers, the Malcolm X Society, African People's Party, Republic of New Africa, and Malcolm X Grassroots Movement emerged. Young Blacks around the country began emulating Malcolm's strong posture and articulating his ideas against the power structure. Revolutionary Action Movement (RAM), a clandestine formation, had already begun a few years prior to Malcolm's death. According to RAM's leader Muhammad Ahmad (Max Stanford), Malcolm himself was a member, but that information had to be kept quiet.

To give some sense of what Malcolm's death meant to me, I share here something I wrote two weeks after his assassination which appeared in the March 11, 1965 issue of the *New York Nichibei*:

> Though vilified by the establishment and press, Malcolm challenged and exposed the immorality of the power structure; the illusion of the constitution and duplicity of the system; the impiety of the Christian conscience; the hypocrisy of the American dream; the misconceptions of the American way of life; the deviating tactics of the mass news media; and the hatefulness of racism.
>
> For every driblet of civil rights "bestowed" upon Afro-Americans, the nation patted itself on the back. To Malcolm, this was a gross insult and an affront, as it rightfully should be.
>
> Denounced as a hater, it is enlightening to note that what Malcolm hated were: tyranny, oppression, disfranchisement, exploitation; enslavement— whether physical, mental, or psychological; race humiliation and stigmatizing; stultifying conditions and limited job opportunities, inferior education, and sub-standard housing for his people; U.S. economic and political aggression internationally; and the degrading of human lives.
>
> In his brief lifetime, he hated with fierceness the horrendous, confining, and unjust prerequisites manifested in this country, in Africa and elsewhere, which decent persons anywhere should hate and counter. Few, however, have such courage. Most people soften their protests for the sake of pseudoracial harmony, thus digressing from the struggle for freedom.
>
> What he loved was carefully omitted from the white press. He loved humanity; the quality of being a human being. He loved dignity; the attribute of being esteemed. He loved justice; the principle of dealing justly. He loved freedom, the state of being free, the absence of restraint or repression. He loved life in its wholeness and beauty, unconfined and with passionate compassion.
>
> He died young, an ebullient, energizing package of vitality, strength, knowledge and perception. He articulated eloquently, he exuded fortitude. He was a scholar, but not dogmatic nor pedantic. He spoke the language of his people in the ghetto; he understood what they were subjected to; and aligned himself to the most rejected and degraded.
>
> He could electrify a room by his presence; magnetize an audience, but he was no mystic. His source of being profound was his sincerity, humility, forbearance, selflessness, and a keen sensitiveness to the needs of others. His most generous gift to his people were the hours, days, months, and years—

the unlimited time that he spent speaking to them on the street, and in halls to liberate their indoctrinated minds and wills.

It is true that Malcolm lived and died in a state of violence, for the American climate from the beginning of its history to his people was entrenched in violence from its system of slavery and segregation. It was this same violence that won for this nation the accumulation of power, wealth, resources, and land, under the guise of adventurous spirit, building new frontiers, creating new worlds, economic assistance, and humanitarian concern.

Malcolm was surrounded by violence, as were all his people. It ensnared his every move. But no amount of intimidations, terrorizing, or pressure could still his speaking. He said what was needed to be said.

Douglas Mallock, an American poet, wrote, "Courage is to feel the daily daggers of relentless steel, and keep on living." This he did for the last two years, feeling the "daily daggers" courageously, until his last breath.

Norman Douglas, a Scotch writer once wrote, "No great man is ever born too soon or too late. When we say that the time is not right for this or that celebrity, we confess by implication that this very man and no other is required."

But Malcolm was more than a great man. He was a Curse to those who stole the rights of Black people. He was an Epic, who personified heroic action. He was an Epoch, the starting point of a new period or a striking event. He was a Phenomenon, a rare fact or an exceptional person. He was a Fountainhead, a source of a stream from which emanated strength and hope.

His legacy is his infinite love for his Black race. To all others, he leaves the fact to ponder that a man can endure the denunciations, alienation,

Courtesy of the Kochiyama Family

- ORGANIZATION OF AFRO-AMERICAN UNITY -

Mary Kochiyama

is a member of the
Organization of Afro-American Unity

Malcolm X .... Chairman

June, 1964

Yuri's membership card for the Organization of Afro-American Unity.

Yuri speaking at a "Who Killed Malcolm X" forum, 1980. Other speakers on panel: (FROM LEFT) Herman Ferguson, Karl Evanzz and Zak Kondo.

constrictions, indignities, insults; all the combined forces of inequities, without mitigating his stand.

To have lived in the same era as this remarkable man should be a personal gain of new perceptions in the affirmation of humanity.

The words of 19th century English poet Sir Henry Taylor may well epitomize the magnitude of this African giant who died for his people: "Such a soul whose sudden visitation dazes the world, vanishes like lightning, but he leaves behind a voice that in the distance far away wakens the slumbering ages."

I wrote this at a very emotional moment when Malcolm's passing was heavily felt. It was at a time when hundreds, if not thousands, of poets, writers, philosophers, and political activists were expressing their feelings about Malcolm in different ways. Generations to come will also feel the impact of Malcolm, for such an icon rarely emerges.

In the first edition of our *North Star* newsletter, which our family dedicated to Malcolm, I wrote two articles reflecting on Malcolm, both appearing on the first page. The first article, entitled "The Light Inextinguishable," began with "To live in hearts that are left behind is not to die. Thus, Malcolm lives!" I continued:

Though irreparable the anguish, and profound the grief, the fervored admiration of the unbowed Black people keep Malcolm alive in their hearts. The strength and courage that emanated from his life radiates the freedom struggle in America today.

No bullets could destroy what he was and what he meant. No sanctioned press could obliterate his image. No terror-tactic witch-hunt could crush his following. Malcolm was a mortal who became a symbol; a Black man who challenged the western world; a captive in his own land who would not be a slave nor colleague to an oppressive system; a rock that developed into a diamond through the pressures and abrasions of life—for in such ways are leaders created.

What he spawned (the ideas, purpose, and goals of black nationalism and unity) is flowering in the militancy of his people in tossing away the chains of institutionalized thinking.

A new energizing race of young Black men and women walk Harlem streets, aware and proud of their heritage, knowing from whence they came, how they were destroyed (by western culture), and where they are going (without being led by others). These are the products sown by Malcolm's unquenchable zest for liberation.

DuBois once wrote, "Throughout history, the powers of single Black men flash here and there like falling stars, and die sometimes before the world has rightly gauged their brightness. However, the many heroic Black men, and women, too (that American history books have buried), are rising out of the past. . .and their feats are being duplicated. Their deeds and their lives were not only momentary flashes like 'falling stars' but steadfast glows that lit the darkness of several centuries."

Malcolm was more than a "falling star" or an ordinary star which is sometimes visible and sometimes obscure. His life is a simile that can only be correlated with the most brilliant of all the stars in the heavens, the North Star, for the North Star is the one star that does not change position or lose its bright intensity. It is the star that set the course for mariners; and that gave direction to slaves escaping bondage; and communicated men's hope by allusion.

It is, thus, obvious and apropos that we dedicate this first issue of the *"North Star"* to Malcolm whom we feel most aptly personifies the significance of this title. Triumphantly illuminating today's stark atmosphere, giving light and direction, invincible and inextinguishable, Malcolm is that North Star shining.

In our second issue we had a shorter piece on Malcolm entitled, "Malcolm's Life: A Message."

That a man who had inhabited the "lower depth" of life could rise in triumph as a reproach to its ills, and become an uncompromising champion of his people, is in itself Herculean.

Malcolm's life is a documented fact of growth and awareness; an unceasing pilgrimage; a constant hajj in search of truth through experience and reality. Thus, he wrote: "My whole life has been a chronology of changes." That he could be flexible when it meant expanding one's mind, and be immutable in his allegiance to his people and to a cause, is revealing of his humility, judiciousness, and integrity.

He was an easy target because he towered tall. He would not cower, nor run for cover, despite threats. He dignified his trust in his people despite rumors of prophetic danger to his life. The manner in which he lived was analogous to an invitation to his death.

Like a lead warrior on a scouting trip in hazardous territory, he always unhesitatingly placed himself in jeopardy to attacks. When the bullets shattered the attentiveness of a rapt audience on his final day, Malcolm stood peerless as a leader, bearing death's brunt alone. . .as Brother Benjamin stated, ". . .to give his life for you."

Malcolm once said, "Anyone who wants to follow me and my movement has got to be ready to go to jail, to the hospital, and/or to the cemetery." What he would ask of others, Malcolm did first. . .and alone.

Perhaps the most succinct and genuine description of Malcolm was the reply that Jean Reynolds, a Harlemite and one of Malcolm's most faithful followers, made: "Malcolm was the Truth." He certainly spoke the truth to me, and he was very much like the North Star: the most brilliant of all stars, which charts the course for all who follow.

Photograph by Mary Uyematsu Kao

(FROM LEFT) Malcolm Kao, Attallah Shabazz (MALCOLM X's FIRST DAUGHTER) and Yuri at the Museum of Tolerance, Los Angeles, 1998.

The Kochiyama family, 1969.
(BACK, FROM LEFT) Bill, Audee, Zulu, Yuri, Eddie and Billy.
(FRONT, FROM LEFT) Shawn Smith (Zulu's cousin), Aichi, Tommy and Jimmy.

Tragedy and Blessing:
Billy, Aichi, and Alkamal

Billy

Two years after his Mississippi experience, our eldest son Billy was injured in a car accident. The car that he, Audee and Aichi, and his friends Lakaya McIntyre, Eddie Oguendo, Adele Jones were riding to get across the Brooklyn Bridge had stalled, so they got out and started pushing the car. Suddenly, a cab came from behind and slammed into Billy. Billy was the only one who was seriously hurt. Lakaya was tossed about twenty yards but suffered no broken bones.

Billy's leg was badly smashed at the knee. After three years of trying to save it, the doctors decided it would have to be amputated. Gangrene had set in at his heel and seemed to be affecting other areas. The amputation was thigh-high. Because we were not able to purchase a reasonable enough prosthesis that would have been comfortable for his use, Billy used his crutches. He had eight surgeries in a period of three years.

Although he married not long after the accident, the marriage was short-lived and ended in divorce. Billy also had a hard time finding a job because of his disability. Facing one problem after another, Billy always put on a strong façade. Our family was at a loss on how to help him. He was the one who was always doing for others. He was also so adaptable and resilient, and among his peers he was a leader. Billy was one of the founders of Students Against Social Injustice (SASI), a civil rights group of high school students. But we could see he was slowly changing, becoming frustrated at his inability to function physically as he used to.

BY BILLY

This year we're not celebrating Christmas. All of us K-kids agreed to this in view of what happened in Birmingham, and also for what we experienced. We want this to be a year to remember.

Even Jimmy and Tommy said they don't want any presents. If any of our relatives or close friends should send us anything not knowing of our plans, we are forwarding these on to a hospital in Birmingham.

We were terribly disappointed we couldn't join the March to Washington, but we did demonstrate in Harlem and picketed at Down State Medical Center. Mom also made the Walk from Harlem to City Hall with CORE. We're grateful for the opportunity of showing how we feel.

On our way to California, we met wonderful people like Frank Dukes and Mrs. Drews and her son, Jeff, in Birmingham; and the Rhodes family in New Orleans where we rested.

In California, it was great seeing Gramma, Uncle Art, Aunt Chiyo, and my cousins. Eric went with me to see Mike's family. I wish Eric could have met Mike too. Eric is a sophomore at San Pedro High and is going out for B football. We had a good time together at Disneyland when Gramma treated all of us. She was always doing the giving. We'll never forget her.

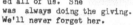

Here is a pic of some fine chicks, and a hip cat--Cindy, Becky (Mike's sister), Dave McKenna (Irene and Amy's brother) and Marcella. We had a nice time at the barbeque at the Valden's which was a get-together of People who meant a lot to Mike.

Billy's article from the "Christmas Cheer" family newsletter, Vol. 14 (1963).

On October 15, 1975, he did not return home. We called his friends and ours. No one seemed to have seen him. We called hospitals, police stations, and even the jails. No one saw anyone who resembled Billy, who was wearing his hair long, Indian-style. Six days passed before his body was finally found.

At the time we had a young couple from California staying with us, and they said they would look for him. We told them that when he felt down, he would go on a ferry boat ride, so maybe they could try the South Ferry. When they returned, they seemed reluctant to talk. Finally, they said that they were shown some crutches and told that a young Asian man left them on the ferry and jumped. They described the crutches; we knew they were Billy's. Someone also sent a Staten Island newspaper clipping, in which a young student gave an eyewitness account of someone who jumped from a Staten Island ferry.

The heartache of his passing was immense. This was the first death in the family, and it seemed too painful to take. We never knew the meaning of grief before. The loss of one's child, we have often heard, is the most painful. How true that is.

Family and friends helped ease the pain of the terrible loss. At Billy's memorial Eddie read the following family eulogy, written by Terry and Audee:

I would like to read the statement from our family. In this piece, the symbolism of the circle is important because it represents a continuum of pain and love, a struggle that is never-ending and linked together.

I want to convey the feeling that Billy's passing means more than mere sorrow. It symbolizes the beginning of hope and caring for one another, as you have shown right here. In a world where human suffering is commonplace and intensified by political and economic conditions, we have become numb to the cries of our brothers and sisters. The intensity of Billy's life and the trauma of his death has awakened our senses to recognize and feel the pain of even one person, and in doing so, to recognize the pain of all. The courage that Billy demonstrated in his final moment of anguish is the courage that inspires us to carry on the struggle for social change.

The world is a circle
A circumference of
pain and care.
His first visions eyed the
world with love and creation
with no break and no end.
He recognized a world of
colors and hope.
His nourishing years prepared him for a future to test
his gentle strength.
He became a soldier in conflict on a
Mississippi road
and his eyes gathered the sun
as a new vision of struggle
shown through and appreciated
his touch.
He saw the world for the first time
In a Mississippi reality
Splitting his theory as he became praxis.
He saw a world of pain in the midst
of plenty as a new vision emerged.
He saw Malcolm die
but his hope continued
reinforcing his commitment
to people and colors
in his circle of pain and care.
He left home, a man/child
in search of himself
to find a woman, happy times
and new worlds.
He sought an education
finding it came, not from books

but from people.
He moved with the wind
to push one of man's machines
and in the face of death, he bled.
The utter eyes of fate
Beckoned his spirit
and the world shattered his image.
The impact of the accident forced him
into a personal search
internalizing the struggle for human worth.
The introspection was not a rejection
Of a world of colors and hope
but a confrontation with his own world
of physical pain and mental anguish.
He was both so full of love and
yet so saddened and lonely.
Blood from friends and strangers
nourished his soul
while blood flowed in Vietnam
and on city streets.
He shared the agony of tortured victims.
His torment pacified by drugs
dispensed by a society
incapable of soothing the pains
yet he battled fiercely to
overcome the destruction of his mind
finally kicking drugs with
his will to win.
The day he left, he saw a
young child [Zulu] unmindful of a
Strange fruit from a twisted past.
He touched his hand and the
child was so full of vibrancy
he wept.
His painful quest for
self-fulfillment
found solace in tranquil waters.
Rain, like tears, washes away
residues of the past
nourishing the earth and
cultivating new life and hopes of

better tomorrows,
a circle never-ending.
And the circle is the world
so it is not Billy alone.
A circumference
is people, the seasons of life,
the world of
colors and hope,
pain and care,
love and struggle—
You, us, everyone.

Billy with school friends (CIRCA 1961).

Our children did not want to believe that Billy was really gone. We all wished we could wake up from a bad nightmare. But again, thanks to family and friends, we plodded back into our daily life. The Williams family (Audee's in-laws) was especially helpful. I remember they cleaned our whole house. They said it was something traditional that Black families do when a family member passes away.

Billy's passing would take years to get over. But his life was full. It was more difficult for those he left behind. There is that quote: "To live in hearts that are left behind is not to die." It is something to always remember. Despite passing at the young age of twenty-eight, Billy had lived more fully than many. Our family thanks him for the last few difficult months he shared with us, when he returned from Albuquerque, New Mexico, where he had been living with his wife Nancy.

We also thank him for those years from the time he was injured, when he took us through the hospital days of surgeries, skin grafts, pains in his knee, clumsy plastic limbs that didn't work, cast to his waist, seven-inch plate in his thigh, bed sores, etc. He took us to a world we would not have known—the world of pain, but also the world where young and old, of all backgrounds, mostly unseen, deal with their particular suffering. The hospital was a world of its own, a place where humankind fights for dignity and life.

We look back and thank so many of Billy's friends who were at his bedside, those who donated blood (over half were total strangers), and those who sent cards, letters, notes of cheer. One special friend was Lakaya McIntyre, who used to sneak into his room on special occasions like New Year's Eve and have some drinks with him. Lakaya also flew in all the way from Germany (when he heard of Billy's death) to be present at Billy's memorial service. He only heard of Billy's death two days before the service was held, but he was there.

Billy was fortunate to have had so many wonderful friends. They will be remembered with deep gratitude. Political prisoners from across the country also sent moving condolence notes. Those, too, we saved and will always cherish.

When Billy passed, our grandson Zulu was seven years old, and our granddaughter Akemi was three. Zulu was the last one to see Billy. Billy gave Zulu the last few coins in his pocket, knowing he was making a one-way subway ride to the ferryboat.

Billy's farewell letter to the family was beautiful and loving. Billy's last act was a statement. He said that he wanted to call the last shot and that he did not want to exist with his disability. He did not want to be a burden to anyone. He wanted to live, to love and be loved, to fight for what must be fought for. At one point, I think he was fighting against drug addiction. He won some battles and lost others.

The battle he lost in death was, to him, a triumph that he was in command of his final act. The leap he made into the Hudson River was his moment of liberation. We feel he did not take his life—he gave his life. He was and is

Billy with friends at Springfield College, Connecticut, 1969.

a part of the worldwide struggle for human dignity raging in many forms throughout this earth.

A beautiful letter from a Black Marxist Collective member, presumably Bill Epton, expressed it well in this way:

> He was a brother of strength concerned totally with struggling to see a people's victory. He was a comrade caught in the storms of liberation. But what lives is Billy's will to struggle for liberation—what lives is Billy's dream of victory.

Courtesy of the Kochiyama Family

Billy at a wedding, 1971.

Aichi

When our youngest daughter Aichi was eighteen years old, she met a Black Panther brother who was East Indian and Black named Yasin Mohamed-Ladson. The following year, their daughter Akemi was born, and shortly after they were married. They were married only a few years, and their marriage ended. Aichi became a single parent. But Yasin's whole family—his wonderful mother Khadijah, and his nine brothers and sisters—remained very close to the Kochiyama family. The Mohamed-Ladsons and the Kochiyamas became fast friends —truly family; even Yasin.

When Aichi was twenty-three years old and Akemi about four, Aichi became reacquainted with an old friend of Billy, Alkamal Duncan, who attended Billy's memorial. They immediately hit it off and began a relationship. Alkamal was an activist, a cadre member of the African People's Party. Many of their friends said it was like a marriage made in heaven. Both were extremely happy in spite of the fact that Alkamal had sickle cell anemia,

Tragedy and Blessing   85

Aichi with her nephew, Zulu, 1968.

a very serious blood disease. Much of his time was spent in the hospital, but both coped well with the situation. Their common-law marriage lasted fourteen years—until tragedy struck our family once again.

On November 18, 1989, in her first year at the University of Massachusetts, Amherst, Akemi came home to celebrate her eighteenth birthday with Aichi. Her Uncle Eddie said he wanted to treat them to dinner. Their good friends Peter and Emilie Wong also joined them. While waiting for a taxi after dinner, a cab came careening down the street, jumped the curb, mounted the pavement, and struck Aichi head on. It also hit Akemi and barely missed Eddie. Aichi went flying about 200 feet, Akemi twenty feet. Eddie was dazed and shocked but kept running between Aichi and Akemi to see how he could help both of them. Peter and Emilie, hearing the crash from around the corner where they were getting into their car, came back and were stunned to see Aichi and Akemi hit.

That night, I was attending a fundraiser for Mutulu Shakur at the Bronx home of Brother Shaheem and Sister Uroyoana Trinidad. When Bill called and said, "Come home right now," I could hear the urgency in his voice. When I told Uroyoana about the call, she promptly said, "I'm taking you home right now. You're not going back by subway." Though she was the host, she grabbed her coat and drove me all the way back to my apartment in Harlem. All the while in the car, I was praying that it was not a life-or-death situation. I knew something serious had happened because Bill alluded that it involved Aichi and Akemi, that Peter Wong called from a hospital, and said to rush over to the hospital. Knowing it was serious hardly prepared me for what we were soon to learn.

Bill and I could hardly believe what had happened. When we saw Aichi bleeding profusely in the Emergency Room, we knew she had scant chance to survive. Akemi, placed on the Neurology floor, was hardly conscious but kept asking why her mother wasn't there with her. As we kept vigil, practically all the "family"—the Williams, Duncans, Mohammeds, Ladsons, Holmans and close friends—somehow heard about it and came to the hospital throughout the night. We let everyone go into the Emergency Room to see Aichi. Everyone took turns rubbing Aichi's arms (the only place that wasn't bleeding) to see if they could bring some warmth to her body which was getting cold. She was bleeding from everywhere, but her face was left untouched. Blood was flooding all over the floor and was constantly being mopped up by workers. I never saw so much blood before.

One of Eddie's friends, Atsushi Odamaki, stayed all night with us and wouldn't go home to get any sleep. Eddie was making calls to the family in California. Others were also making calls for us. We will never forget the love that poured out to Aichi and also to Akemi, for whom prayers were said non-stop.

We asked the hospital to keep the life-support machine running until Jimmy, Tommy, and Audee arrived from the West Coast the following day. Eddie's girlfriend Pam also cut her vacation short and flew in to be with the family. On Sunday, after everyone arrived and it was ascertained that she was brain-dead, we had the machine turned off. A doctor then came in to announce that she had passed.

Six years before she died, Aichi prepared a document which she left with Alk, stating that she wanted all her organs to be donated. As she wished, four of her organs were utilized by four recipients.

Letters, poems, cards, and articles about Aichi poured in from all over the country. At her memorial service many eloquent eulogies were presented. Becky Hom, one of her close friends, wrote and read the following:

Each of us has our own memories of her.

I've been asked to remember her on behalf of the Asian women who came to know her through the years. Most of us met because of our political beliefs; or because of the generous "You are always welcome at our home"

TRAGEDY STRIKES: *Aichi Kochiyama (right) had celebrated daughter Akema's birthday moments before they were hit.*

MOM & DAUGHTER STRUCK BY TAXI ON SIDEWALK

NOV. 20, 1989 NY Post

By DON BRODERICK

Celebration turned to tragedy when a taxi jumped the curb on Fifth Avenue, seriously injuring a mother and her daughter on the girl's 18th birthday.

Aichi Kochiyama, 36, and her daughter Akema capped their daylong birthday party in a Japanese restaurant on 52nd Street moments before the cab ran into them about 10 p.m. Saturday.

Aichi, a secretary and fundraiser for the Japan Society was listed in critical condition at Bellevue Hospital. Her daughter was in stable condition.

"It's like a nightmare you wish you'd wake up from," said Aichi's husband, Alkamal Duncan, who was at the family's Manhattan apartment when the accident took place.

Duncan, a black-studies lecturer at Northeastern University in Boston, met his wife when they were children growing up in Washington Heights. Both were active in the civil-rights movement.

"They went out for a birthday party and now my daughter is injured and my wife is fighting for her life," said Duncan. "It makes you realize how quickly happiness can disappear."

The victims were strolling down the sidewalk when a taxi was forced off the road by a teenage driver who attempted to make a left turn from the center lane, police said.

The driver, a 17-year-old whose name was not immediately released, was issued a summons for making an improper turn in his 1986 Grand Am and forcing the cab from the road, police said.

The cabbie, Ashraf Eli, 25, of Queens, was not charged.

The women were rushed to Bellevue Hospital where they were treated for head wounds.

Akema was home from the University of Massachusetts at Amherst for a series of birthday celebrations. She had graduated in June from LaGuardia High School of Music and Art, where she was known for her oil paintings.

As they waited for medical updates at the hospital yesterday, worried friends and relatives from both sides of the family spoke glowingly of a marriage made in heaven.

"She is not my daughter-in-law, she is my daughter," said Genevieve Duncan. "This is how close a family we have been. All the children grew up together."

New York Post article reporting the car accident that took Aichi's life.

attitude of the Kochiyamas; or because of the similarity of experiences that brought so many Asian sisters together.

Aichi was raised in a family in which she was taught early on to help those less fortunate than her. The struggle to achieve basic human rights, no matter what color, what nationality, what sex, was always fundamental to her.

She was active in struggling for the rights of others throughout her life: from civil rights to liberation struggles, to the rights of political prisoners, to workers' rights, to women's rights. The list goes on.

Although her public selflessness was well observed, it took a more private turn in the last few years. Our admiration for her grew as we saw how she cared for Alkamal and how their love flourished despite immeasurable hardships. We were also inspired by how she seemed to dismantle those mother/daughter barriers, which are so often erected, through her close relationship with Yuri and Akemi.

For me, as I know for many, Aichi was a constant source of warmth, strength, and compassion. She was a positive influence because no matter what difficulties she encountered, she dealt with them directly and optimistically.

She carried a strong sense of right and wrong wherever she went. She was both revered for her character strength and respected for her moral truth. Aichi was not one to hold back on criticism when her friends needed to be set straight. Yet she had a way of telling you that made you listen without taking offense. She had the courage to stand up for what she believed—even if it meant that she stood by herself.

I've painted a portrait of Aichi of such heroic proportions that I'm sure she would say she could never live up to it. But she did. She was humble, down to earth, and always very giving of herself.

Aichi (CROUCHING, FAR LEFT) and Audee (STANDING, SECOND FROM RIGHT)
with Soh Daiko, New York City (CIRCA 1980).

It is still difficult to believe that she is no longer here. The thought that
consoles me is that while we may not be able to embrace Aichi with our
arms, we can still embrace her spirit in our hearts.

I want to end by sharing with you the image of Aichi that is etched in my
mind. It's captured in all her photographs—whether she was jogging in
Central Park, or performing with Soh Daiko, or celebrating International
Women's Day, or just greeting you with her, "Hi, how ya doin'?"—that image
is of Aichi with her radiant smile.

Eddie also read a statement—which was both personal and from the family:

Last weekend my niece Akemi had come home from U. Mass, Amherst,
to celebrate her birthday. She turned 18, so it was definitely a time to go
out and party. (Peter Wong and his fiancée, Emily, were also with us.) We
enjoyed a nice Japanese meal and then in one sudden cruel twist of fate, on
our way home to meet Alk and some of Akemi's buddies, both Aichi and
Akemi were struck by a taxi while standing on the sidewalk, waiting for the
light to change.

In an instant, our evening of joy and celebration turned into a nightmare of sorrow and grief. Fortunately Akemi survived, although she did suffer numerous injuries. Aichi passed away the following evening. Anyone who knows our family knows that we have always been a tight-knit unit. But I think that throughout the years it was always Aichi who made sure that we took care of one another. I've always admired Aichi for her ability to put things in their proper perspective. She knew what her priorities were.

First and foremost was her family. As a mother to Akemi, the two of them shared a most unique relationship. Their relationship evolved from mother/daughter, to being sisters, to being best friends.

From the time Akemi was a very young child, Aichi would constantly try to instill certain values. She wanted Akemi to always be proud of her Japanese, Indian, and Black heritage. She wanted Akemi to be sensitive to all people. She wanted Akemi to understand that in this world there exists much injustice and oppression. She wanted Akemi to know that it is not the material things that are most important in life.

At times Aichi would be frustrated, not knowing if Akemi understood what she was trying to teach. Other times Aichi felt guilty thinking she pushed too hard. I don't think there is any doubt that Aichi succeeded in what she set out to do.

Aichi has always been a proud mother but she was never more proud than when Akemi went to college. A new chapter in their lives had begun. One of Aichi's dreams had been realized.

One month ago, Aichi and Alk celebrated their 14th anniversary together. They both talked about how happy they were despite the fact that there has been so much pain and struggle in their lives. If anyone asked me to define the words, commitment and dedication, I would answer Aichi and Alk. They have stayed together through one crisis after another. I never once heard Aichi complain about having to take care of Alk. It was Alkamal's strength and courage that gave her inspiration and fortified her spirit.

One of the ironies of this tragedy is that last February, Alk was in the intensive care unit for one whole month. Things looked bleak. The whole family kept a vigil at the hospital, praying and hoping that everything would turn out alright. In that period of deep stress and fear, it was Aichi with her "gambare" never-give-up spirit, who held us all together. She never lost control and she never lost hope.

Last week the tables were turned. This time it was Alk who had to keep us all together. The fact that Aichi and Alk could endure so much pain and

NOT CROSS

Aichi at a 1971 demonstration in support of Black Panthers' NY 21, outside 100 Center courthouse where trial was being held (followed by an acquittal, May 13, 1971).

suffering is a testament of their commitment, dedication and profound love they had for one another.

During the past few years Aichi and I grew especially close. Since my brothers and sister moved out to the West Coast, Aichi and I spent a lot of time together. We talked to or saw each other almost every day. We had a lot of fun hanging out, drinking, shopping, and cooking dinner for one another. I will miss her smile and her laughter.

Most of all, I will miss the conversations. We could talk about anything. And we did. We talked about politics, music, our jobs, our family and friends, and we talked a whole lot about men/women relationships. Man, Aichi gave me advice even when I didn't ask. Sometimes, I think she was more a mother to me, Zulu, Malik, and some of our homeboys than she was to Akemi. She didn't "enryo" when she thought someone was doing the wrong thing, especially when the subject was concerning how men treat women. Aichi had no problem calling a dog a dog.

Although I may have spent more time with her these past few years, Aichi stayed in constant contact with Jimmy, Tommy, and Audee. She was always calling or sending postcards, letters and gifts. Aichi never forgot a birthday or anniversary, regardless of whether it be family or friend.

Aichi was an extremely strong and sensitive sister/woman. And I think most of her character development came from her parents who she deeply loved, respected and admired. Surely most of her political and moral beliefs and ideas came from them.

In spite of all the hardship in raising Akemi, caring for Alk, working full-time, and at times trying to find extra work to support her family, Aichi always found time to enjoy life.

Aichi loved music, particularly jazz. Whenever she had a free moment we would try to hit one of the clubs. One such time which gave Aichi much delight was checking out Miles Davis recently, in one of his very rare club gigs. At home, music was always playing. After the kids turned off the rap music, Aichi would listen to Lady Day, Sassy, Ella, Carmen, Nina, and Betty Carter. . .all strong women.

Aichi loved to read poetry. Some of her favorites were Kahlil Gibran, Alice Walker, and Langston Hughes.

And Aichi loved art. In fact, she was an artist who often combined her love of poetry and her skill at calligraphy, producing beautiful books of her favorite poems, which she gave as gifts to her special friends.

Aichi enjoyed going to museums. On the day of the accident, Aichi and Akemi went to the Metropolitan Museum, not for any special exhibit, but because it was just something the two of them appreciated. She very much admired the works of Georgia O'Keefe, Diego Rivera, Matisse, Van Gogh, Gauguin, Picasso, Monet, and of course, Alkamal.

One of Aichi's latest interests was sports, as a fan and participant. For a couple of years she had gotten into jogging. She always enjoyed challenges and she wasn't afraid to take risks. She entered many races, including a thirteen-mile half-marathon. Her dream was to run the NYC Marathon. Everyone knows that Aichi was a mellow woman but for some reason she became a huge fan of boxing because of Mike Tyson. If you were around Aichi, you couldn't dis "Iron Mike." He was the man.

By Lorrie

I couldn't make as many demonstrations as Audee and Billy did because I had to stay home some of the time to watch the three little ones.

Eddie and I did picket in the first two boycotts; and we marched with the Freedom School twice in Harlem; and went over the Brooklyn Bridge with the Puerto Rican silent march.

Audee and I went several times a week to the General Motors picket-line back in May with the 7-Arts CORE.

That was some picket-line, headed by Frances Foster and Juanita Bethea and Valerie Harper. They even had entertainment right out on the streets. Simone use to go out there almost every day. At Easter, they had girls dressed in Easter Bunnies passing flyers; and the picket-line wore Easter bonnets and hats. We sang Freedom songs to the tune of Easter Parade, automobile commercials, and Broadway hits. The reason for this demonstration was because GM was not hiring Negro performers, musicians, and models for their industrial shows.

Four other exciting things happened. Eddie and I made the "King and I" at the State Theater, featuring Rise Stevens and Daren McGavin.....Audee and I got walk-ons as pages in Lohingren at the Met. Then, right after the show ended, I got to go to camp in Bushkill, Pennsylvania through the church, and learned to swim. (Mr. Al, our head counselor, is with us in Jimmy's column). Also, thanks to Mara, I am traveling week-ends with the "Playful Dragon." During Christmas-time, we will play Richmond, Virginia where I hope to see Penny Brown.

Aichi's "Christmas Cheer" family newsletter article, Vol. 15 (1964).

Playing with the Soh Daiko group was an important part of Aichi's life. It gave us all a chance to see some of that amazing positive energy and creativity that was so much a part of her. It reaffirmed her appreciation of her Japanese culture and it literally led her to Japan, where she spent three weeks traveling, performing, learning, and finally meeting some of our relatives. That trip to Japan was one of the highlights of her life.

It is clearly evident that Aichi touched so many people in so many different ways. As I look around this room I see a rainbow of colors and a spectrum of ages. She left us all with a gift of our own special memories.

This horrible and senseless tragedy will forever leave a profound void in all our lives.

On the day of Aichi and Alk's anniversary, I asked her how she could be so happy. And she told me that we must live each day as our first, not waste time, and never take anything for granted. She left a legacy. She was a shining example of what we can all strive to be. Aichi, I love you. Aichi, we all love you. We will never forget you.

Another eulogy read at the memorial was from Muhammad Ahmad, former leader of Revolutionary Action Movement and African People's Party:

For Aichi

There have been events,
in the aeons of time
when loving, kind, sincere,
truly beautiful people
appear on the planet earth.
Aichi was one of those persons,
a rare gem of beaming honesty,
warmth,
tenderness and kindness. . .
a true loved one,
wife, mother, and
friend to all.
Aichi
is the kind of person
we wish all of us
can be.
Aichi
reflected the saying
that,
"the human family is one,"

Zulu and Aichi practicing taiko for Jimmy and Alison's wedding, 1986.

one and at peace.
We all say. . .
Peace and love to you,
Aichi,
Forever. . .

One of the people who showed special concern and did so much as soon as she heard of Aichi's accident and subsequent passing was Claire Bettag of the Japan Society. Aichi worked there at the time of her death. Claire and the Japan Society generously allowed their premises to be used for the memorial service. Even today, many people say they have never attended such a moving memorial. The most emotional moment was right after Soh Daiko, the Japanese Taiko drum group to which Aichi belonged, played their hearts out through tears. On behalf of the group, Peter Wong presented Aichi's drumsticks to Alkamal. That moment was most heart-rending and dramatic.

Unfortunately, this was not the last of the family's experience with loss. The grief that had enveloped our household would deepen even more.

Alkamal

When Alkamal was young, despite his often-debilitating illness, he wanted to see the world. Thus, right after his high school graduation, he joined the Navy. He lasted only four months before the onset of a sickle cell crisis prevented him from remaining in military service (he had lied about his medical condition to gain entrance), and he was given an honorable medical discharge. Upon his return to New York in 1966, Alkamal was drawn to the activities of the Black movement in Harlem. There, Max Stanford (a.k.a. Muhammad Ahmad), then leader of RAM and the Black Panther Party (not the Oakland branch), saw Alkamal's potential as a youth organizer and hand-picked him to head the Black Guards, a youth street group. Alkamal also became a member of SASI (Students Against Social Injustice) besides working in his neighborhood with youth drug users, teaching African American history, and engaging in cultural programs at the Double Image Theater of the Lincoln Square Neigh-borhood Center. He also took six students to Africa on an educational tour sponsored by the McGraw Hill Street Academy.

In 1970 Alk moved to Boston and became a cadre member of the African People's Party and a part of the Yoruba family. He taught Black Studies at Tufts University. In 1975 he returned to New York to speak at Billy's memorial, where he became reacquainted with Aichi and almost immediately began a unique relationship which lasted fourteen years until her death. Alk was a great father and friend to Akemi, who was just four years old when they met.

To offset the years of physical suffering caused by the painful blood disease, Alkamal turned to art, music, and cultural activities. His favorite musicians were Bob Dylan, Miles Davis, and all jazz musicians. As a painter, he emulated the techniques of Picasso, Van Gogh, and Gauguin but with a Black perspective. His spiritual strength gave him the dimension to counsel others and help assuage those in distress. Though wheelchair-bound in the last years of his life, his free spirit traveled unrestrained, absorbing, and being nourished by all that he learned.

Alkamal was one of the oldest survivors of the sickle cell disease, as most never live beyond their twenties. His brother died of sickle cell at only six years of age, and his sister at just nineteen. Only five months after the death of Aichi, Alkamal passed away after his forty-third birthday on April 8, 1990.

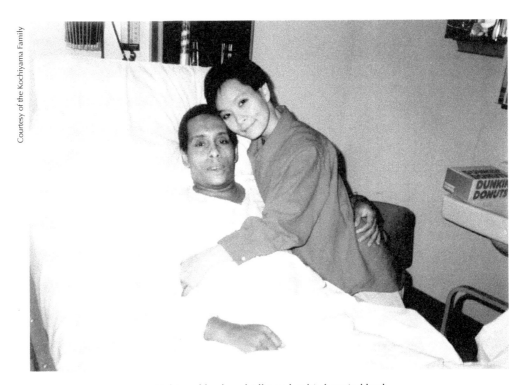

Aichi and husband Alkamal at his hospital bed.

Photograph by Yuri Kochiyama

Billy, Audee and Mike Hernandez (CIRCA 1962).

Friends Who Became Family

Not only had our family grown, but our "extended family" had also become quite large. Our extended family consisted of all the people who had stayed with us at some time—from overnight and weekends to several months or over a year. Many of our extended family members were children. They were also Korean War GIs (mostly from Hawaii) and WWII vets (like the 442nd wounded), students, civil rights workers, ex-prisoners, robbery victims, touring musicians, and visitors to New York. People from all walks of life became part of our family. It was a learning experience about people in general and the varied situations in which they could find themselves in New York.

Without exaggeration, over a thousand people stayed with us from the moment Bill and I married to the present. It would be impossible to remember half of the names, but each added more to our lives than anyone could imagine. We had a Hawaiian musical troupe under John Tsukano, a 442nd vet and musical promoter, who stayed with us until their per diem money came in. There were also a number of Korean War vets, whom we called the "Wahiawa bunch." Civil rights workers from Mississippi and Alabama found refuge with us. There were also friends of our children who stayed with us from time to time. In this chapter I would like to tell some of their stories.

One of the most poignant visitors was a teenager named Michael Hernandez. Michael was orphaned when very young but was fortunate to find wonderful parents in Esther and Jesse Valdez of Wilmington, California who adopted him. He was not only a talented artist, but was a warm, loveable youth who had good rapport with everyone who came into his life. From the time he was small, his teachers had great respect for him. When they found out that his Hodgkin's disease was advancing, they asked him if there was anything in particular he wanted to do. He said he always dreamed of going to New York and seeing some of the galleries and museums. Quietly, his teachers Helen Polin and Irene McKenna began raising money to send him to New York. They asked us if he could stay with us since we had a son the same age as Michael. We were so happy they asked us, and Billy was also excited to meet him. We also notified all the art students who hung out at our place on Saturday nights. They all wanted to get in on showing Michael around.

We had a "Welcome to New York" party when he first came and a "Farewell, We won't forget you" night just before he left. People took him to the well known galleries and museums, a movie, a ball game, Harlem Hospital, Chinatown, the Village, and even drove him to see West Point. He won everybody's heart.

The day after he left, a dozen red roses were delivered to our apartment. There was a card with his name on it and a cryptic note referring to Shakespeare's Twenty-Ninth Sonnet. We looked it up immediately. We could hardly believe that a sixteen-year-old could have thought of expressing himself in such a way, but Michael was deep and very mature for his age. We cried reading those lines:

> When in disgrace with fortune and men's eyes,
> I all alone beweep my outcast state,
> And trouble deaf heav'n with my bootless cries,
> And look upon myself and curse my fate,
> Wishing me like to one more rich in hope,
> Featured like him, like him with friends possessed
> Desiring this man's art, and that man's scope,
> Wish what I most enjoy contented least;
> Yet in these thoughts myself almost despising,
> Haply I think on thee, and then my state
> Like to the lark at break of day arising
> From sullen earth sings hymns at heaven's gate;
> For thy sweet love remembered such wealth brings
> That then I scorn to change my state with kings.

Michael passed away two weeks after he returned to California. He is buried at Green Hills, San Pedro—the same cemetery where Bill and Billy are interred and where I will also join them.

Hiroshi Ishiko, from Japan, was also sixteen years old when he stayed with us. One winter when he was studying, he fell asleep. His face fell flat against the red-hot hibachi. He must have cried out in pain. His mother rushed in and pulled his face from the stove. His skin was torn off, leaving the remnants burning on the stove. The pain must have been horrific. His lips, nose, and part of his face itself needed to be restored. The Ishikos remembered how plastic surgeons from Mt. Sinai Hospital in New York repaired the faces of the Hiroshima Maidens. They wrote to the best known of the Hiroshima Maidens, Shigeko Niimoto, who in turn contacted the doctors. Shigeko also contacted us to see if Hiroshi could stay with us since we lived near Mt. Sinai Hospital. We were happy to take in Hiroshi.

When we first saw him, he wore a white mask so we could not see how badly his face was disfigured. In fact, he rarely took his mask off for anyone to see. Through Shigeko Niimoto, the Ishiko family was able to have Dr. Arthur Barsky, one of the finest plastic surgeons in America, work on Hiroshi. There was over a year's work of repairing his face, which meant many surgeries, much pain, and a lot of patience to endure the process. It was amazing to see how well Hiroshi adjusted and how stoic he was when it came to enduring pain. He also had to deal with name-calling by project youths who dubbed him "the lone ranger." Hiroshi seemed to enjoy the three younger K's—Eddie, Jimmy, and Tommy—with whom he tagged along constantly, but Hiroshi became their leader. He listened to their English and copied their words, learning the language from them. He felt more at home with them, rather than the older K's. He enjoyed going to neighborhood stores and buying them candy and gum.

What was most remarkable was how well he adapted to the neighborhood and our lifestyle. We lived in Harlem in an all-Black area and were a large, low-income family. He came from an entirely different class, as his father owned some kind of corporation in Japan. But he never looked down on us or on our friends. Because he could not attend school, we had a tutor come to the house. We were surprised at how well the tutor connected with Hiroshi. Hiroshi, in his limited English, and the teacher, using unique combinations of spontaneous sign language, picture-drawing, and facial expressions, could understand each other. Hiroshi's English skills quickly improved, and he managed to learn some American history and world history. When Audee graduated from junior high school, we took all the children to celebrate her

Photograph by Yuri Kochiyama

Eddie, Tommy, Audee, Philippe Delacroix, Aichi, Billy and Jimmy (CIRCA 1963).

graduation by going to a neighborhood Chinese restaurant. For the first time in public, Hiroshi took off his white mask. We tried not to look at him, as we knew he was very sensitive. But we knew Hiroshi had come a long way to be able to reveal himself.

Simone Delacroix, a French woman, and her son Philippe first came to stay with us when Philippe was seven years old. Our friend Al Karvelis brought them over and asked if we might be able to put them up temporarily. They needed a place to stay after Philippe finished a stint of summer camp, so we doubled up the kids and managed. Philippe was sweet-faced and blond, and he never showed any strangeness because the Kochiyama family was Asian. Neither did his mother, Simone, who was a very attractive young mother in her mid-thirties.

Simone seemed as comfortable with Blacks and Asians as with whites. As attractive and well dressed as she was, she was never afraid of work. She was "down with us" when it came to housework. Not only did she do the dishes and prepare meals, but she also scrubbed the floors on hands and knees and tidied up a crowded apartment of nine or ten active children. She enjoyed attending whatever we attended, whether it was a Bon Odori or a picket line. She was very strict that Philippe did his share of house chores and that he learned manners.

The two stayed with us on and off until Philippe was about fourteen years old. The last time we saw Philippe was several years later, and only by sheer chance, when we ran into him at the Macy's department store. He said he had volunteered into the American military service and was awaiting orders, probably to go to Vietnam. We never saw Philippe or his mother again. We often wondered if Philippe survived the Vietnam War and whether Simone was still in the U.S. We hoped that we might encounter them again. The children got along so well, and the K kids liked Philippe very much.

Ricky Casimiro and his mother first came to stay with us shortly after he was born. His father, from the Philippines, was in the Navy, and his mother was a Japanese American. They stayed just a short while, and the Casimiros found a place elsewhere. They visited with us from time to time until Ricky was two and a half years old. Then we did not see them. Fifteen or sixteen years went by, and one day his grandfather called to ask if we remembered a "Ricky Casimiro." We said, "Of course, but we don't know what happened to him." His grandfather said, "He just graduated high school and is back in this area, and is looking for a place to stay." We told him to tell Ricky to come over, but we made no commitment about a place to

Ricky Casimiro.

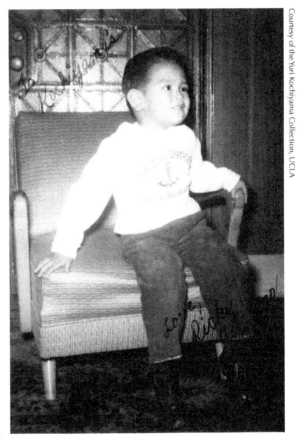

stay. When he showed up, we were surprised to find him such an amiable eighteen-year-old. We heard he had some very difficult years growing up. But Ricky was very courteous, not a teenage toughy. We liked him right away and asked if he would like to stay with us. We told him about Jimmy and Tommy who were close in age to him. He joined our family for about a year until he decided to go into the service; he chose the Navy because he wanted to go to the Philippines someday.

Wilson Makabe was one of the people who visited us from time to time when we were still living in the Amsterdam Projects in the 1950s. Wilson was an "I" Company vet with the 442nd Japanese American Combat team. While working in Pennsylvania at a chick-sexing plant, he would spend some weekends in New York with us. He became an amputee when German planes strafed an American convoy truck filled with 442nd soldiers in Anzio, Italy in 1944. Both of Wilson's legs were injured, one requiring immediate amputation.

One day while staying with us, he hung his prosthesis along with his pants on the bathroom door. Billy, who was four years old, went to the bathroom, and thinking that someone was hiding behind the bathroom door, pushed it hard. The leg and pants fell to the floor, making a loud clanking sound that woke us up. Billy came running into our bedroom frightened. Wilson was sleeping on the living room couch. Bill explained to Billy that that "leg" was Wilson's artificial limb. We still remember Billy's wide-eyed look, asking, "You mean Wilson can take his leg off?" Ironically, Billy became an amputee himself, twenty-five years later.

Another 442nd vet who stayed with us after the war ended was Sanji Kimoto of Co. K (Bill's Company). Sanji was totally blind. When the Americans were making a push to end the war in Europe, Sanji was on patrol when suddenly his eyes went out on him. He was not hit by any bullets, nor did he receive any blow to his head when this happened, but Sanji had been injured about five times before on different occasions. Some of his buddies speculate that perhaps some shrapnel near his brain moved and might have touched a nerve, which caused him to go blind.

We once visited Sanji when he was receiving rehabilitation training at the School for the Blind in Avon, Connecticut. Mr. Earl Finch, the "godfather" of the 442nd, paid for a limousine to pick us up and take us there. We will never forget the experience of seeing blinded, recently returned soldiers—some also amputees and others traumatized beyond reality—learning to walk or function as well as possible. They were mostly young, in their early twenties to thirties, from all different backgrounds. At this school one's color, class, or religion made no difference. There was so much kidding around, and the spirit of the place was so cheerful. Sanji acted as our host. He could not see, but he knew how to get from one place to another.

He visited us at our home on two occasions. When we sat down to eat, he asked us to tell him where the different food items were placed. He would ask us to place the foods according to the quarterly setting of a clock: 12, 3, 6, and 9. This would help him locate and identify the various foods according to these positions. This was a good learning experience for the children. He told us how he knocked out all his teeth one morning when he jumped into the pool before the water was put in. We marveled that he could laugh about it. When Sanji eventually returned to Hawaii, Mr. Finch bought him a seeing-eye dog, which Sanji had for many years.

Sanji went to the University of Hawaii through the G.I. Bill. Each morning he would hail a cab at the same place to go to school, and the same cab would come every day to that same spot to pick him up. The cab driver was a woman who was quite different from him, but the difference was a perfect match for Sanji. Sanji was a very shy brother from a small town in Hawaii called Kukuihaele. Rene, the cab driver, was a circus barker and a very extroverted, friendly woman of Iranian descent. The two eventually married, moved to the mainland, and adopted a lovely mixed-race baby, Diane. Sanji and Rene did everything together. They first worked at a Long Beach, California concession where they operated a shooting gallery. Then, they operated a small hotdog stand and later became Fuller Brush salespeople. Even little Diane joined them.

Sanji took on life as it came, and Rene was equally as versatile and creative, as was their daughter. When Rene passed away in the 1980s, Diane committed herself to taking care of Sanji, and both are now living in Michigan.

Paul Higa was a Hawaii islander who was in the Merchant Marines. A friend told him about our place when he was "rolled" (that's what we called getting mugged in the old days) for his whole paycheck one night at a bar. He just needed a place to stay for three months while waiting for his next ship assignment. He didn't seem too distraught even though he was down to his last few dollars. Perhaps because it happened before is why he took it well. Or maybe he was just a cheerful and optimistic guy.

While staying with us, Paul built a platform for the kitchen so I could grab anything that was stored above my reach. He also made a rack where we could hang the dishtowels. He even took Billy out during the day. When we would ask Billy, "Where did you go with Paul?" Billy would say, "Paul always gives me Coca-Cola at a nice quiet place where it's usually dark." We had to laugh, as we figured out it must have been a bar.

Another Hawaii brother who was robbed and needed a place was a young guy from Hilo named Mits. He returned home to his 42nd Street hotel room one day to find all his possessions stolen. Gone were his art and photographic equipment, golf clubs, and all his clothes and money. He had been sleeping at Central Park for a week when a Hawaii buddy directed him to our apartment, which was near the Park. The November cold was coming in, and the park was no longer the most comfortable place to be, nor the safest. When he came, we could see that he needed a bath and some new clothes. We always had ample clothes, as many Hawaii boys used to leave clothes for the next hard luck story.

We also had two teenage Black sisters, Arisika and Paula, who lived with us for days or weeks at a time. They were close to all of our children, especially Billy, Audee, and Aichi, probably because they shared similar convictions and became involved in movement activities, school integration and anti-war issues.

One time, the restaurant where I worked, Concerto West, needed someone to make the dessert for a big luncheon they were having to honor a civil rights worker from Alabama. Everyone was too busy, but Paula, only twelve years old, volunteered to make cakes. She already knew how to bake. She got up early in the morning, went to the restaurant, and baked ten large cakes for this special occasion. No one knew that Paula baked the delicious cakes. The two sisters stayed with us on and off until they became adults. They both now live in California and have remained close to our family.

People may wonder how we managed to put up all these people. For many, it was on the hard floor; we had no carpets. We often doubled up the kids. Some brought sleeping bags. There was the living room couch. Once, we put a blanket in the bathtub. A couple of times when our place got really crowded, we took our youngest child over to Roland and Barbara Shim's down the street and stayed at their place.

Looking back, I realize it wasn't fair to our own children who seldom had their own bed to themselves. But they were amazingly cooperative (though often we gave them no choice). I was also fortunate to have a husband who didn't seem to mind sharing the home. Bill was very understanding of those who needed a place to stay, perhaps because he was raised in an orphanage with 120 brothers and sisters.

We must say, however, that the generosity of Hawaii people was incredible. Once, the word got out that we couldn't pay the phone bill, and one day, an envelope with $64.00—the amount of the phone bill—was placed under our door. It came from a rather tough-seeming boxer, but a softie at heart, named Dick Sasabe, who lived in our neighborhood. At other times, Yoshinaga, a "Hawaii Buddhahead," used to leave freshly home-baked goods at our door; he was a student at the Culinary Institute of America. The Hawaii *wahines* (women) and guys used to do a lot of babysitting for us, as they loved children. We were so lucky to have so many Hawaii friends.

Our extended family taught us much about cooperation and sharing. If anything happened to any member of our family, they responded as if it happened to one of their own. One time Aichi was struck on the head by a large Coca-Cola bottle. An ex-GI Hawaiian, James Ige, who was staying with us at the time, immediately volunteered to take over the house and watch all the kids, including newborn Eddie, so that I could take Aichi to the hospital.

This extended family truly became a part of our own family. We will never forget them.

SEQUEL TO THE MIKE HERNANDEZ STORY

A promise made last year with expectations was fulfilled this August in sorrow. The promise was to 16-year old Mike Hernandez who stayed with us last November--and the promise was to visit him this summer, meet his "wonderful family," his neighborhood friends, and some of his teachers. This we did.

1302 Papeete Street in Wilmington, California became a familiar place long before we arrived there. To Mike, who was abandoned as an infant and fostered as a child, 1302 Papeete was the only house he called "his home"; and the Valdez family who lived there, "his own." For nearly 10 years, it became 'the house he grew up in'; a haven, a fortress, and in the last years--a sort-of hospital where he received from his Aunt Esther, Tender, Loving Care in unlimited portions. (Continued on Page 10)

CHRISTMAS CHEER

Volume 14   545 West 126th Street, Apt. 3B, New York, New York 10027   December, 1963

BIRMINGHAM CALIFORNIA VACATION STRIP NEW ORLEANS TOO

One of the K's King Features of the year was their Popeye-opening vacation trip to California, via the Birmingham, New Orleans and Chicago circuit. 1963 was the year--B.C.

Drawn by R.R. Lines, each episode of the three-week trek was filled with True Life Adventures and Believe-it-or-Not experiences.

Coincident to the K's departure, Carolyn Fowler (see Page 6) of Berkeley, California motored into town, and joined the K's westward caravan. Mary, being detained by court order for civil rights demonstration, followed three days later.

First stop--Birmingham. K's were met by Frank Dukes (shown with Tommy and Lorrie), P.R. Director of Miles College, and Mrs. John Drews (on Page 6 with son, Jeff), prominent Negro community leader. They were shown demonstration sites, a burned-down house, a bombed store, Gaston Motel (Martin Luther King's Hqtr.), Dynamite Hill (Attorney Shore's bombed home), Miles College campus where K's met Pres. of the college, Dr. Lucius Pitts and Dean Pearce; and the 16th Street Baptist Church where the four children were killed. (Continued on Page 8)

1963 SPARKLE PLENTIES

A moving panorama of Supermen, Reg'lar Fellows, All-Stars, and Pogo-for-Brokers, made 1963 Sparkle Plenty during the K's summer junket and at Apartment 3-B. A small fraction of Sparklers appear in the center-fold. (Because of lack of space, only a few could be shown in this issue).

During the Cal episode, K's spent an afternoon with the Louis Willises and son, Dick (below). Their other son, Jack, a former UCLAn, gave K's the contact with Frank Dukes of (Continued on Page 6)

Alfred E. Neuman "What--Me Worry?"

PONYTAIL

Little Lulu

JUGHAID

Sluggo

PEANUTS

"Christmas Cheer"—
Family Newsletter, 1949 to 1968

The year after he graduated from Long Island University with a degree in journalism, Bill came up with the idea of a family Christmas newsletter. We decided to call it "Christmas Cheer." It would be a newsy family paper relaying our season's cheers, while focusing on family and friends, weddings and births, sports and performing arts, events, mini-stories, and whatever else popped into our minds. As the children became older, they would have their own columns. One of the features was excerpts from editorials, essays, poems, and so forth that would best exemplify Christmas, its meaning, or its spirit.

Although we began publishing "Christmas Cheer" in 1950, I somehow cannot find any issue before 1952, so I'll begin there. In this issue, one of the front-page news stories was the birth of Lorrie, our third "K." The caption read: "Lorrie, Lorrie Hallelujah!" The news staff was composed of Bill, Editor; Mary (the name I used at the time), Assistant Editor; Billy and Audee, News-ances; and Lorrie, Copy-cat. Bill always used clever wording like that.

Each issue included something about Christmas: our own feelings and editorials from the writings of others. In our 1952 issue we wrote:

"Merry Christmas" may seem a flippant expression. It may also be tossed around more from habit than from feeling. Yet, it still reflects the spirit of the season with its warm, spontaneous greeting.

We are aware, however, that many of you are hardly in a place where merriment exists. Korea's battlegrounds have been a reservoir of bloodshed. We realize, too, that many of you have had losses in your home. Sorrows, tragedies, and serious illness have hit many families.

We hope, however, Christmas with its contagious warmth and joy, will touch all of you in a significant way. And may this yule-tide, shared by peoples all over the world, bring to each the wishful-thinking that "peace and goodwill to all" are not just words but a goal that can be realized.

Three issues later in 1955, the K's featured their kids as the K-Krocketeers. This was during the Davy Crockett fad. The lead story reported another birth in our family, Edmund Yutaka Kochiyama. The opening paragraph read:

As every red-blooded pioneer should know, the initials, D.C. stands for Delivery Call. (Fooled ya, huh?) Bet ya thought it was that man Davy Crockett.

Answering the call was Edmund Yutaka, a precious piece of crockery, who joined the K-set on June 16, 1955. He scaled in at 3 lbs. and 14 oz. The tiny critter was named after his daddy's old podner, Edmund Singleton, now a settler in the mild frontier of Pasadena, California, and his paternal grandfather, Yutaka Kochiyama. The K-Kids staged daily war parties, fighting among themselves to decide who'll fetch the young-un his hot vittles, haul his 4-square britches, or similar risky chores.

The "Christmas Cheer" staff now included William, King of the Wild Family; Mary, Krock full of Powder; Billy, Krockhead; Audee, Krock-ette; Lorrie, Half-Krock'd; Edmund, Krock-less. There were pictures of Edmund's godparents, Norman and Gerrie Kurlan and Hawaii friends Alice Kawato, Richard Matsu-shige, and Marsha Hayashi.

For the serious part, the K's used Peter Marshall's yule message for 1955:

Let's not permit the crowds and the rush to crowd Christmas out of our hearts . . .for that is where it belongs. Christmas is not in the stores—but in the hearts of people. Let's not give way to cynicism and mutter that "Christmas has become commercialized." It never will be—unless you let it be.

"Christmas Cheer" No. 7 (1956) featured the children's page with all of Disney's themed playlands, from Adventure Land to Fantasy Land to Tomorrow Land. Bill and I became Dizzy Landlord and Dizzy LandLady. But our Christmas message was serious, using Lillian Smith's article from the *Women's Home Companion of 1945*. It was called "The Right to Grow":

The earth we live on belongs to our children. It is theirs and they should feel at home here. They should feel free, whatever their color or creed, to move from place to place, from group to group, and know they are welcomed as human beings. Their birthright is a rich one, gathered up through thousands of years, by hands that have toiled hard and minds that have explored fearlessly and hearts that have somehow kept love alive in them. It belongs to every child, this birthright, and from none should it be withheld. Neither parent nor stranger has the right to keep it from the least of these children.

In 1957, the eighth CC was published, and Jimmy's birth was featured. The front-page caption read, "James Wade Already an M.D." The story went:

> The K's proudly hung out the shingle this year on April 28. It read, "James Wade Kochiyama, M.D."
>
> It augurs well that he has been named after Dr. James O'Rourke, the K's kindly obstetrician, and Dr. William Wade Glass, the K's dedicated pediatrician.
>
> Is there really an M.D. in the house? Yes, sir! He's Mother's Delight!

Corny as our stories were, "Christmas Cheer" was our way of communicating family news as well as news of friends under some very clever captions that Bill would concoct.

Our 1958 issue featured our international friends, calling that issue the I.G.M.Y. Year—the International Glad-to-Meet-You Year. It was also the Go-For-Broke Year, as the K's, through the help of numerous friends, made it to California for the 1958 Veterans Reunion. It was also the year that we were able to meet the courageous "Little Rock Nine"—the first nine African American students to attend Little Rock, Arkansas's Central High School—and their champion, Daisy Bates of the NAACP, who fought for school desegregation in Arkansas and won. Our Christmas message for this issue was taken from John Golden's "Unison Prayer for the United Nation," which in part reads:

> We. . .people of every faith. . .of every creed. . .join together. . .pleading for truth, justice, and charity among men. We pray for Thy omnipotent aid in this hour of imperiled civilization. . .That thou shalt cast out forever from human thought that flaming intolerance which makes for war and breeds bloody aggression. . .We pray to Thee for the restoration of concord and amity among all the peoples of the earth.

Our Christmas messages were always on the serious side, very religious at times and also very idealistic.

Our last child arrived in 1959, so the family newsletter for that year heralded his arrival: "Nikita wasn't the only K to make a stir this year. The other was young Thomas Seiichi who joined the K-Family Circle on April 1. No fooling!" Little Tommy is also shown on page 1, flanked by his godparents,

Lani Miller, George Poogi Chin, and the Rev. Akamatsu, who performed the baptism. The Christmas message for this year was taken from Harry Emerson Fosdick's condensed Riverside Sermon, "No Room in the Inn":

> No room in the inn. That was to be the Master's experience throughout His ministry—no room for his teachings in the minds of men or for His quality of spirit in their life. Consider how magical a change a little hospitality can make in our lives! A youth turns a corner of a street, and running into a new idea, makes room for it, and lo! his life is utterly transformed. Today, we lead such overcrowded lives that the loveliest things which would enrich us all are commonly excluded.

> With only one life here on earth to live, it is a pity to miss, because of an inhospitable mind, the spiritual values which mean most, reach highest, last longest and in the end make life memorable.

Six years later, the No. 14 issue (1963) printed its first editorial, which was very political. We could not believe how that first editorial and subsequent editorials brought wrath to our newsletter. Each issue preceding No. 14 was always a cheerful, pleasant newsletter with rather religious messages. Our readers (friends up until then) seemed to enjoy it. Then we became political, and all of a sudden attitudes about us changed.

Some people may have thought we were trying to clobber them with an idea. Our first editorial was just the beginning of many to come. Its only weakness was that it was too lengthy, but it was our passionate appeal to challenge the mainstream status quo, address prejudice, and send out a call for social justice:

> The gift of a life-time and many life-times, a gift in greatness to match posterity and create history—the challenge of making the American Dream of "equality and justice for all" not just a boast or wishful thinking, but reality in performance—is the Negroes Gift to America. . .

> World renown sociologist, John Hope Franklin, stated: "Almost invariably the Negro progresses only to the extent that the white man advances in understanding that a human being is a human being. The Negro cannot achieve except where the white man has advanced enough to allow him." But it is not only the white man, but the yellow man, the brown man, and men of every light pigmentation who have imbued self-elevation by lighter-coloring who are guilty of the ferment in race relationship. Each must examine himself for the varying degrees of prejudice are found in every ethnic and

religious group at every level and every area individually and en masse, not only in America, but on every continent. The cry, heard round the world, for human rights, dignity, and freedom must be answered with social justice. . .

This Yule-tide, let us not be "dreaming of a White Christmas" (does snow make Christmas any more meaningful?) or a trite Christmas, but create an essence of Christmas so viable that the dreams and hopes and aspirations that exploded with the death of the children in Birmingham, will not, likewise, be shattered in the lives of their living contemporaries.

WE INVITE YOU TO PROMOTE A FAIR WORLD

From "Christmas Cheers" family newsletter, Vol. 15 (1964).

How inconsistent, or is it "consistent," that many of the people who were "so stunned and outraged" at the bombing of a Sunday School in Birmingham never winced, spoke out against, or probably condoned by their silence, the everyday indignities and abuses in their own communities of race humiliation; social segregation; economic strangulation; disenfranchisement; housing violations and restrictions; ghettoes, inferior education, job limitations; boundered opportunities; superficial acceptance; miscarriage of and belated justice; barring public accommodations and utilities; and prohibiting miscegenation. The Negro people have endured from the subtle to the outright in ostracism, contempt, subjection, and exploitation; and have experienced all manners of treatment that are condescending, degrading, and shackling.

James Baldwin's far-seeing wisdom exhorts: "However painful it may be for people to change, not to change will be fatal." This nation must heed his wisdom and change, and accept the Gift of his people—the Opportunity to Grow.

America is not the "land of the free" but the Negroes have proven, by sheer perseverance, optimism and irrepressible desire for freedom, that this is "the land of the brave." And despite the three hundred years of yoke and chains and one hundred years of insults, Louis Lomax, one of today's most articulate Negro writers, augments the faith of his people when he summarizes: "America is still the latest outpost in Man's journey away from provincialism."

The Negroes' powerful tribute to America is the stature and caliber of their leadership, their talents, and their contributions in every field. This is their salute, which in essence, relays that the Negro people still believe and foresee their stake in America and envision their participation in the American Dream.

What more can a people give?

Our 1964 editorial was again political and incorporated more of what I was learning from Malcolm X. Here are excerpts from "Color Crisis: The Chickens Come Home to Roost":

> Borrowing the adage that last year [1963] brought railing denunciations and invectives to a most courageous and perceptive leader in the fight for freedom [Malcolm X], the maxim resounds even stronger and truer in communicating the de facto posture in color-crisis. . ."the chickens come home to roost."

> Today's color-crisis is festering and smoldering—for having inundated people's minds with a systemized indoctrination of assuming African inferiority and perverseness in miscegenation; having placed a "quarantine"; having alienated, isolated, and ostracized (while promulgating freedom, justice, and equality, and proselytizing Christianity's concept of brotherhood and love); this country that subsisted on slavery and segregation is in a face-to-face confrontation with the universal precept that all men are born free and equal.

> The enormity of the crime has untold ramifications. The African American, never having been yielded his true self-consciousness; eliminated from his participation in American history; rejected from the main-stream; excluded from the rights, protection, and immunities granted to all other citizens (who won theirs through a normal process of struggle); having had their heritage and culture torn away, and when recognized as such—having it distorted and bastardized; their people stultified; their life degraded, exploited, and made demeaning; their talents and potentials wasted or constrained; (while the "teeming masses" from Europe and Asia found entrance into the American way-of-life by adopting the same color-prejudices and segregating practices)—the Afro-American trying now to find and restore his patrimonial identification, is accused of racism; becoming more militant, he is renounced as being dangerous and ungrateful; its outspoken grass-roots leaders are called "rabble-rousers" and "anarchists"; and self-improvement projects and social actions (like rent strikes) are undermined as subversive and destructive. . .

> However, the unpremeditated riots in the Harlems of the North, spontaneously and eloquently articulated the anger, frustration, resentment,

and agony of the conditions and containments under which they are allowed to exist. Yet, most of the nation did not grasp the message. Instead, they held the ghettoized in scorn and contempt. . .

Salute to Africa and all African peoples for courageously rising against oppression and prejudice to teach the world the meaning of humanity.

In this same issue our children expressed their own opinions on human rights issues. Billy, at age seventeen, wrote in his column:

Society has criticized civil-righters in their demonstrations, saying they are not helping to "make friends," but demonstrations are not to make friends or enemies but to focus on injustices and to correct the wrongs. . .

In February, we heard the shocking news that Richard Griswold (the school-teacher who was arrested with me) was found dead in his apartment last October. The news stunned me. How sorry I am that he is gone, but I feel fortunate in having met him. He is the white Freedom Rider who was nearly beaten to death in the Monroe, North Carolina jail (a few year's back).

This brings to attention the famous frame-up case of Mae Mallory, the courageous Freedom Fighter who was sentenced from 16 to 20 years with a $15,000 bail, on a trumped-up kidnapping charge in Monroe, North Carolina involving Rob Williams.

In her column, Audee wrote about our family's memorable visit from Malcolm X:

The most exciting thing that happened to us this year was that Malcolm X came to our home. As busy as he was, he made time to attend a reception for the delegates of the Hiroshima-Nagasaki World Peace Study Mission who were interested in meeting Negro leaders. Many outstanding Harlem leaders turned out. . .

While Malcolm was away on his tour, he wrote to us from England, Egypt, Arabia, Kuwait, Ethiopia, Kenya, Tanganyika, and Nigeria. . .

I think one of the most imaginative demonstrations was the World's Fair stall-in—for it was to show that those involved felt it was more important to have "a fair world than a World's Fair"—and the few minutes that people might have to be stalled on the road was nothing in comparison to 400 years of being stalled in their right to freedom.

More criticism of "Christmas Cheer" followed, and it was clear our family newsletter was getting more political than our readers could tolerate. It never occurred to me at the time that I might lose friendships or that our friends could not understand the real issues at hand. Most said it was the editorials they really deplored. The rest of the paper "they could stomach." One person wrote: "I showed your newspaper to my brother-in-law, and he told me that Christmas Cheer was Communist influenced. Let me simply say that your paper was the deciding factor in my joining the John Birch Society." Another wrote, "I am shocked to say the least. I do not appreciate your kind of Christmas editorials." Several just said, "Don't send me any more of your Christmas Cheers. There's nothing cheerful about them." After that issue, we decided to create another newsletter to write about more political and progressive issues.

In the 1965 issue our "Pride and Prejudice" editorial criticized American foreign policy by using the titles of books as captions and themes:

Where foreign aid has been allocated, or U.S. troops have marched into, the flag, its way of life, and its racist philosophy have been implanted.

People we have known through the years write: Aren't you overcritical of America? Our answer was, Yes, that's the least we can be—critical. Can we remain silent at U.S. aggression in the Dominican Republic, coups incited in Africa, insidious operations in Thailand and Laos, vindictive transgressions against Cambodia, paranoiac image-destroying of China, the dirty undeclared war in Vietnam, and the horrendous silent slaughter of over 300,000 in Indonesia.

For all the criminal perpetrations committed by the U.S. government under the guise of saving democracy or protecting people from Communist atrocities, it is not strange that the 300,000 massacred in Indonesia were Communists and Communist sympathizers, and that the Johnson Administration "received this news with delight". . .

We salute every anti-war organization and every individual voice across this country vociferating, not for mere peace, but more so denouncing U.S. foreign policy, intervention, and assault, use of napalm, phosphorus, arsenic, and cyanide; exposing U.S.'s grotesque and inhuman path of annihilation and subjugation, and its fraudulent arguments (inciting fear and hatred of Communism) to justify this war.

More criticism and denunciation continued with each succeeding "Cheer," as our editorials opposed war, racism, and imperialism. One of our supposedly close friends even blasted us:

This should come as no shock to you. Being an atheist, I can not quote God. I can only quote myself. You, Bill and Mary Kochiyama, are hypocrites.

How can you keep the men of the 442nd in mind and also Malcolm's relationship in the same breath?

Also, I came out of my mother's womb a white baby. I grew up in a white man's society, but I fight for the Negroes too. I fight for everybody. I am not a yes-man to anybody. And you and anybody else won't tell me how, when, and where to turn to.

Another wrote:
I didn't get my Christmas Cheer this year. Are you discriminating against baggy old blonds? But I don't like what you say. This country isn't perfect because the people that make up this country aren't perfect. But has our society really forced our standards and values on other countries? Or did other countries see something in our system and adopt it for their own? Why is the kimono disappearing in Japan? Why does the younger generation dig American music, hairdos, clothes? We aren't forcing these things on them. They adopt them because they like them. This also applies to democratic procedures. Of course, our society dictates what is right and wrong. Name me a society that doesn't.

We could not argue with some of their points, for they certainly had a right to their own opinions, but we continued writing our editorials. We felt there was much to say. The 1960s were a period where politics needed an airing. Our family newsletters gave us an opportunity to voice our feelings and air our opinions—a place where we could be honest and did not have to hold back—not necessarily because it was "our" paper, but because we felt some things needed to be said. With each attack, however, we became more vociferous. The editorial in our final 1968 issue, entitled "Why C.C. Went Political," explains:

Once upon a time—for some 15 years, C.C. was a comfortable family news-sheet, a way and means of keeping in touch with the myriad friends who came into our life. It was strictly a "friendship" paper—warm, homespun, individualistic, with the kids having their own columns through the years.

Subtly it disseminated idealistic philosophy (the supposed ideals in the deeper meaning of Christmas). It was international in scope. Features promoted lives deemed inspirational. No religion was proselytized, though all inconsequential, the measurement of a human being was in the actuality of responses and reactions, attitudes and mentality, values and ideas.

About four years ago, C.C. became political. That is, we projected social problems and took positions; we vociferated our feelings on ills; we gave exposure to societal prerequisites, reiterating historical and traditional trends of this country.

We could feel that a great number of C.C. readers were upset. Through their letters and from the grapevine, we could sense their feelings ranged from disappointment at our un-Americanism to shock and anger at what seemed like insubordination and subversiveness.

Many queried why we brought up politics at Christmas-time; why not stay within the area of religion, was asked. We felt, however, if at any time politics should enter, it should be at this so-called "joyous," but solemn occasion; when peace and hope and love is promulgated and extolled, yet the world is seething in a savage confrontation initiated by those in power, and those in power persistently rationalizing their transgressions.

Battlegrounds are everywhere, wherever foreign domination places its tentacles, and indigenous people strike out in defense—as in Vietnam; or here in America, where Black people long stigmatized and incapacitated by a discriminatory way of life are now awakening to a consciousness of Blackness and self-esteem and are asserting their desire for independence...

Young people, students, and workers (hopefully) are battling archaic systems and institutions, tearing down meaningless shrines. A new world must dawn...

To each his own in the choice one makes in what area of life he wishes to give commitment and devotion. May each of you find that which you seek—fulfillment and satisfaction to enhance your life. We say "sayonara" and "aloha," "adios," and "auf wiedersehen"—remembering past kindnesses and friendship always.

This was the K's "Christmas Cheer" goodbye to all our readers and friends. As we became more politically involved, we became more active in writing letters and annual holiday greetings to our political prisoners, POW supporters, and close friends in the movement. Also, because postage was always hard for us to pay, we felt it was best we stay in touch with those who were really supportive of us and interested in our concerns.

Our family had truly come of age, but we were sad to lose longtime friendships because of our political involvement in human rights issues. All in all, this eventually prompted us with a stronger conviction to concentrate our resources and energies on the "North Star," our new family newsletter.

"North Star"–
Family Movement Newsletter, 1965 to 1969

Malcolm X

The mid-1960s was a tumultuous period, not only with the rising tempo in the Black movement, but more so with the assassination of Malcolm X. Malcolm's life was a message to the Black struggle. He was the epitome of the "light inextinguishable."

The K family felt we needed to show our love and respect for Malcolm in some tangible way. We also wanted to depict the struggle that Malcolm was leading in New York, particularly in Harlem. So we began a newsletter to honor Malcolm's name, calling it the "North Star," for that was exactly what Malcolm meant to the people in the struggle: the star that would always be shining as the guiding light.

We were only able to put out five editions, from 1965 to 1969, but in each of those issues, we tried to give some current aspect of the Black liberation struggle, with many pictures of activists in the folded middle section. In the first edition we featured Black artists as being the new compass:

> To become the mouthpiece of a new reality in action is the role that Black revolutionary artists are playing. Unity, nationalism, communication and rapport are reverberating in the works of new black writers, musicians, painters, and performers.
>
> Young Black intellectuals, the often no-degree'd, street educated, splendidly distinguished articulators are mushrooming out of the ghettoes everywhere, sparkling their awareness and literary talents with a fiery burn-baby-burn fervor. Losing themselves in the people and with the people, and expressing

the heart of the people, as Fanon would say, they are shaking ghettoes out of the lethargy; awakening, and becoming "fighting, revolutionary, national literature." These are the powerful writers of *Soul Book, Black America, Black Dialog, Liberator,* and smaller mimeo'd sheets that appeared across the country. . .

In music, artists like Andrew Hill utilize mediums that totally ignore western values, forms, and concepts, creating new exciting sounds that articulate blackness—be it beautiful black fury or beautiful black gentility, expending his creative genius in a social role.

Painters at Black Arts Repertory School depict in their work what they see and feel and understand; images of themselves—for what they see, in essence, is what they are.

In the field of drama, nowhere except at Black Arts is black reality projected as infinitely and correlatingly. . . . As writer Charles Patterson, elucidates: "On stage an actor can only live when he is acting out of his life; that which is most familiar to him is the character he can act out of."

Thus, Black artists became the new compass through the Black Arts Theater School headed by Amiri Baraka, once known as Leroi Jones. Perhaps the only school of its kind in this country, Black Arts focused on the soul power of Black artists on Black people, giving Black people the sense of themselves—who they are, what they feel, what they see, and what they have undergone.

The centerpiece for the 1965 issue was a captioned article called "Black Leadership Blazes Pathways Lighting Minds," which also included a picture of many grassroots leaders encircling Amiri Baraka. On Black leadership, this article emphasized that:

Negro spokesmen speak for many organizations, but "black leaders" hewn out of the coarse boulders and crusty crags of ghetto life speak in an understandable soul-felt idiom communicating Black nationalism and unity.

Today's militant eloquence spawned from the heart of oppressed people, vociferated (as did Malcolm) to de-brain-wash, re-educate, and re-orient Black people (and possibly radical whites) in the black and white reality of everyday life. That these Black mentors are bent in the direction of nationalism, and that its Black following find attraction, security, and hope in its content, manifests its need and its receptivity.

Black nationalism was not born to propagate racism, as was white supremacy, but in direct opposition to stem its tide. Black nationalism is an anti-racist nationalism to combat megalomaniac race tendencies historically propagated by Western mentality. Black nationalism may be chauvinistic (but which is healthily needed when a people have been robbed of identity and heritage, and their culture distorted). Black nationalism is a stage towards progressive nationalism transitory to internationalism.

Spread out across the centerfold are some of the most radical Black leaders who are blazing a new outlook despite some differences of ideology and approach, asserting that many roads lead to the same destination. . .

SNCC & Black Panther Party

The following year, our second "North Star" issue front-paged two organizations, the Student Non-Violent Coordinating Committee (SNCC) and the Black Panther Party (New York's). SNCC, founded in 1960, was a Black American student organization that fought segregation through non-violent action. The Black Panther Party was the first Harlem, New York Black Panther Party, under RAM, and is not to be confused with the Oakland, California Black Panther Party.

Our article on SNCC introduced the organization to our readers, describing meaning and importance of "Black Power" and the organization itself:

Rocking the nation with a mere two words that caught like fire in the South's Black Belt and swept across the country, North and West, SNCC and Stokely Carmichael (now Kwame Ture) burst into the '66 headlines as the newest threat to the racism of White America, becoming Black America's most promising champions.

With audacity, brilliance, succinctness, ferver, and a Malcolm-like sense of timeliness, Carmichael flung two Black Magic words from city to city,

The first issue of *North Star* (December 1965).

enlarging Black following and enraging white opposition.

The two words "Black Power" pierced the white power structure, cut through the mainstream, sank white security, darkened ivory towers, while it uplifted Black masses, brightened the ghettoes, embarrassed the Toms, and worried integrationists. Black Power, a way of advocating self-determination, came about after a lengthy in-depth search of the frailties within the civil rights movement. The weakness, Carmichael deduced, was integration. Carmichael's evaluation of integration became a bombshell that exploded a myth—a veneer.

"Integration," Carmichael explained, "is irrelevant to the freedom of Black people. Negroes have always been made to believe that everything better is always white. If integration means moving to something white is moving to something better, then integration is a subterfuge for white supremacy."

Thus, SNCC's new insight and outlook on integration is a dynamite-loaded concept based on reality, practicality, and truth. Black Power, too, is more than a slogan. It is an idea to inspire a new image; assert a Black self; create basic changes, govern one's own destiny; achieve, not for personal attainments, but for all Black people. Black Power can also build a new harmonious world for all where all can energize power.

The Black Panther Party in Harlem was one of the biggest political organizations in the 1960s. It was because of the efforts of Malcolm X that the Panthers became so influential and effective. Their ten-point program was also similar to Malcolm's. In fact, many Black organizations adopted Malcolm's thinking about being free, being Black and proud of one's African ancestry, and learning about Africa's history and its wars with colonizers.

Our article on Harlem's Black Panther Party, entitled "The Power of Positive Thinking," reinforced the importance and power of Blackness:

Suddenly revealing itself on the political horizon is a new symbol of Blackness, a black cat—known as the Black Panther, a species of wildcats not found in the Western hemisphere (says the dictionary) for panthers originate in Africa and Asia. Thus, symbolic with a hereditary base, and with the "Power of Positive Thinking," an all-Black Panther Party was born, first in Lowndes County, Alabama, and now in Harlem in 1966.

This Panther Party, an independent freedom party with no ties to the sanctioned Republican or Democrat parties, was organized to serve Black people through the political realities that dominate their lives; to press for issues and demands that will bring about constructive and meaningful changes within

Black communities; and to relay that Black people will have absolute control over their own destinies.

Young in leadership and following, this party is trying to create a Black roots political outlook based on self-determination. It needs the support, encouragement, and participation of all Black-thinking, Black-proud men, women, and youths. . .Black is the power of positive thinking, and the unity of this Blackness will be channeled in the area of better schools, jobs, housing, activities for young and old, legal counseling, protection, group support, cooperatives, tutorial aids, cultural programs. . .

That the symbol, the Black Panther, can be more than a disembodied spirit or apparition, but a moving force to serve a community, each dollar will help to build a Black political, economic, and cultural reality. Mail or bring in personal contributions to: The Black Panther Party, 2409 Seventh Avenue, Harlem, New York 10030.

Bill Epton

This "North Star" issue also featured an activist under the banner "Profile in Courage." This story was about a good friend of mine, Bill Epton, who was once Executive Secretary, Harlem branch, Progressive Labor Party:

Bill Epton stands tall and solid, a bulwark, not only for Black people but oppressed people everywhere. His stature is in his courage to speak out, challenge and denounce, publicly and unmitigatingly, governments and political concepts that exploit and degrade the powerless while the elite and bourgeois, in comfort and respectability, maintain the status quo. No clandestine figure, whatever Bill Epton does and says is done openly. Following are excerpts from his fiery oration to the courts in February 1966, just before his sentencing on a criminal anarchy charge regarding the '64 Harlem riots:

"You have judged me guilty and have labeled me a 'criminal' and also 'dangerous.' Now, let me examine what I have been found 'guilty' of doing and saying—

"I have been found guilty of agitating against the conditions that my people are forced to live under in New York and all over the country; of protesting the murder of James Powell by Thomas Gilligan, a New York policeman; of organizing Harlem against police brutality; of standing up for the right of all men to be free; of proclaiming that capitalism is an oppressive system and that socialism is the only solution for mankind to live in peace and humanity; of demanding that the U.S. government take its troops out of Vietnam; of asking the question of Black boys and men, 'What are you doing in the U.S. Army fighting your colored brothers around the world who are engaged in battle against the same government that is oppressing you?'; of being an outspoken critic of the U.S. government and its para-military police force; of publicly advocating socialism; and finally, of being a communist and a Black one at that!. . .

"But who are the real criminals? Who, completely, through planned acts of genocide, destroyed the great Indian nations that once inhabited this continent? Who raped Mother Africa to enslave and murder 60 million Africans to build this nation with their bodies, sweat and tears with almost 250 years of free labor? Who lives on greed, corruption, and the exploitation of man by man? Who murdered and destroyed the language, culture, religion, and dignity of the Black men and women who were brought over here as slaves? Who, through military power and under the slogan of 'manifest destiny,' colonized the Philippines, Cuba, Puerto Rico, and parts of other countries and reduced South America to nothing but a source of raw materials with its people among the poorest in the world? Who is attempting to reduce this nation to nothing but robots to parrot their racist and fascist policies? I will tell you—it is the criminal U.S. government that is considered the most dangerous by the people of the world.

"And now, I, Bill Epton, stand before the court—found guilty of being a communist, judged a criminal because I dared to fight back and called dangerous because I have ideas. If these are the crimes that I have been found guilty of committing, then I am guilty a thousand times over, for I have done all these things proudly."

The courtroom rose to its feet and roared its cheers and applause. The judge immediately ordered the courtroom emptied of disturbers. Bill Epton was sentenced, but the victory was his.

Vietnam

Many people today have forgotten about Vietnam or are not even knowledge-able about that period. Our December 1966 article, "Brave New World," was written during the war and it was important to tell our friends, family, comrades in struggle about Vietnam:

What is Vietnam? It is more than a tiny S-shaped country in the corner of Southeast Asia. . .Possessor of a proud and ancient civilization whose 2000-year history is filled with foreign occupation and passionate quest for independence and unity, it has aroused the world by its heroic stand as

Vietnamese guerilla forces with virtually nothing but their hands, mind, and heart matched themselves against the most powerful, sophisticated, economic and military might of the world, the United States.

Vietnam stands as a beacon in a starkly dismal world. It is a North Star to liberation movements; a gleam of hope to the so-called "backward nations" dominated by foreign powers. It is the personification of the struggle in Africa and Latin America; and also Black America.

To understand what Vietnam desires, the following is the summary of its programs:

1. Overthrow the disguised colonial regime of the U.S. imperialists and the dictatorial administration—lackey of the USA—and form a national democratic coalition government.

2. Bring into being a broad and progressive democracy.

3. Build an independent and sovereign economy; improve the people's living conditions.

4. Carry out land rent reduction and advance toward the settlement of the agrarian problem so as to ensure land to the tillers.

5. Build a national and democratic education and culture.

6. Build an army to defend the Fatherland and the people.

7. Guarantee equality among the various nationalities, and between men and women; protect the legitimate rights of foreign residents in Vietnam and Vietnamese living abroad.

8. Carry out a foreign policy of peace and neutrality.

9. Re-establish normal relations between the two zones and advance toward peaceful reunification of the Fatherland.

10. Oppose aggressive war, actively defend world peace.

Here then are the demands of the DRV [Democratic Republic of Vietnam] and the NLF [National Liberation Front]. Does the U.S. have the right to destroy their aspirations? These are the people who have opposed French domination, Japanese fascism, and now, American imperialism. They are proving to the world what a tiny, determined, united liberation front can do!

The Challenge of a Black Nation

In the 1967 and 1968 "North Star," we emphasized frame-ups, jailing of political prisoners and new bills. Continuous provocations and distortions marred and revealed reality as the police force and other right-wing groups escalated their attacks on the Black community with the hopes of flushing out and crushing Black militants. Our 1967 issue summarized it in this way: "Hysteria-seeking headlines, inflammable news articles, smears, house-raids, beatings, jailings were par for the course for Black 'un-assimilables' who deviated from the American Way, or criticized U.S. policies too loudly."

Also during that time, anti-riot bills were pushed, and emergency regulations with bans on gatherings were imposed in Philadelphia. A legitimate Negro Rifle Club, located in the Jamaican community of Long Island, New York, became implicated in a "conspiracy." Witch-hunting for RAM members became a national pasttime. Both faculty members and students considered "too black" were expelled from the "seats of higher learning."

The increasing number of political prisoners can also be seen as the measuring stick by which the establishment manifested its growing fear of Black political awareness and revolutionary fervor. Prime targets were Huey Newton, Martin Sostre, Max Stanford, Leroi Jones, Ahmed Evans, Herman Ferguson, and Arthur Harris. They were the avant-gardes of the 1968 struggle who persuasively promulgated nationalism and separation that was a crushing blow to integration efforts. The idea of a "Black Nation" on this continent to this day looms as a threat to whites and others, but is considered a hope, dream, and challenge to many Blacks.

Republic of New Africa (RNA)

In the 1968 issue of "North Star," we printed the eloquently expressed "Declaration of Independence" of the newly formed Republic of New Africa. Excerpts of the document read:

Ours is a revolution against oppression—our own oppression and that of all people in the world. And it is a revolution for a better life, a better station for mankind, a surer harmony with the forces of life in the universe. We, therefore, see these as the aims of our revolution:

—To free Black people in America from oppression;

—To support and wage the world revolution until all people everywhere are so free;

—To build a new society that is better than what we now know and as perfect as man can make it;

—To assure all people in the New Society maximum opportunity and equal access to that maximum;

—To promote industriousness, responsibility, scholarship, and service;

—To create conditions in which freedom of religion abounds and man's pursuit of God and/or the destiny, place, and purpose of man in the Universe will be without hindrance;

—To build an independent nation where no sect or religious creed subverts or impedes the building of the New Society, the New Government, or the achievement of the aims of the Revolution as set forth in this Declaration;

—To end exploitation of man by man or his environment;

—To assure equality of rights for the sexes;

—To end color and class discrimination, while not abolishing salubrious diversity, and to promote self-respect and mutual respect among all people in the society;

—To protect and promote the personal dignity and integrity of the individual, and his natural rights;

—To assure justice for all;

—To place the major means of production and trade in the trust of the State to assure the benefits of this earth and man's genius and labor to Society and all its members; and

—To encourage and reward the individual for hard work and initiative and insight and devotion to the Revolution.

In mutual trust and great expectation, we, the undersigned, do join in this solemn Declaration of Independence. And to support this Declaration and to assure the success of our Revolution we pledge without reservation, ourselves, our talents, and all worldly goods.

Asian American Movement–New York

Up to now, I had been very involved in almost every area of struggle except for the Asian American struggle—until I met Kazu Iijima. Some of the organizing activities of the Asian American movement activities going on in New York are described in our family's last "North Star" issue (1969):

Although small in number, Asians of varied backgrounds have come together in New York, forming at least three organizations—Asian Americans for Action ["Triple A"], Asian American Political Alliance at Columbia University, and Concerned Asian Students at CCNY. [I Wor Kuen had not organized yet, but shortly after became one of the most popular organizations and was based in Chinatown.]

The success of Triple A in New York was largely through the efforts of Kazu and Tak Iijima, Mary Ikeda, and Min Matsuda, activists from the World War II era of Japanese-American Committee for Democracy. This group (JACD) was probably the only contemporary radical Asian political organization of that time.

Striking hard against racism, imperialism, and colonialism, Triple A demonstrated at the U.S. Mission, demanding U.S. forces and weapons out of Okinawa and the end to the U.S.-Japan Security Treaty; marched during the Hiroshima-Nagasaki Observance Week denouncing U.S. aggression in Vietnam; picketed S.I. Hayakawa protesting his award in education by the New York Council of Churches; joined the massive march in D.C. against the Vietnam War; and picketed against Sato with the Committee of Returned Volunteers on November 19.

Chinese members who have become involved in Chinatown around the school issue (Two Bridges) are working with youth there and also are exposing the "zooism" of Chinatown tour guides.

Triple A has also sent monetary support to the Ahmed Evans Committee in Ohio; and to Tran Que Phuong, the Vietnamese professor who lost his position at the University of Montreal. Triple A supports Martin Sostre, Rob Williams, the Black Panthers, Los Siete de la Raza, San Francisco's Red Guard contingent, draft resisters of Puerto Rico, the Fort Dix 38, and the Chicago 8.
. .

The 1969 officers and Steering Committee members are: Chris Iijima, Lynn Iijima, Don Yee, Elizabeth Fong, Tak and Kazu Iijima, Don Wong, Terry Dofoo, Mary Ikeda and Taxie Wada.

Due to lack of time and finances, we could no longer afford to continue the "North Star." It was also getting increasingly difficult to pay for all the postage; it also seemed what little money there was available might be better spent to support important issues. In the years to follow, I would devote most of my time to political prisoners and learning about the struggles in Cuba and Peru.

Supporting Political Prisoners:
Mtayari Shabaka Sundiata,
Mumia Abu Jamal, and Marilyn Buck

There are over two million men and women, mostly of color, warehoused in prisons across this country, which is more than any other nation. Many are innocent, and many should not be in prison but rather, in hospitals. There are 150,000 women in prison, and over a million and a half children have parents in prison. There are also another five million people on parole. The prison industrial complex is building more prisons and more youth prisons. The majority of prisoners are Black and Latino, and American Indians make up a high percentage of the prison population. The Kanaka Maoles (indigenous Hawaiians) have the largest imprisoned population in their island country.

When we think of the statistics which impact people of color, we cannot help but surmise that racism, classism, and politics weigh heavily in the criminal justice system: in jury selection, poor defense, prosecutorial misconduct, police intimidation of witnesses, and withholding evidence. Once locked behind the walls, there are guard brutalities, withholding of medication, denial of basic needs, long stays in solitary confinement, taking personal property from prisoners during shake-downs, allowance of prison rapes, and the pitting of one racial group against another. Prison is not a place of rehabilitation; it is a place for punishment, isolation, and humiliation.

Of these two million plus prisoners, there is a small percent who are political prisoners or politicized prisoners. Because the definition of a "political prisoner" varies, it is difficult to make any definite boundary lines of who would be in the category of political prisoners. America denies that they have ever placed political prisoners within their cages, but Sacco and Vanzetti in the early 1920s were framed for a murder, imprisoned, and executed for a crime they did not commit. They were political prisoners. They were anarchists and openly disagreed with U.S. policy of World War I. They were a poor fisherman and a cobbler who won worldwide support because they maintained their principles and remained steadfast of their innocence. But that did not save them. Fifty years after their deaths, the State of Massachusetts recanted and publicly apologized. As the saying goes, "Justice delayed is justice denied."

In the 1950s, the propaganda against communism was rife. Communists were pariahs, and their doctrine was demonized. They lost jobs and homes, were unwanted, and derogated, and many were arrested and sent to prison. In the heat of the communist red scare and red baiting, leftists Julius and Ethel Rosenberg were charged with espionage for giving military secrets to the Soviet Union—which was not true. There was no real evidence that they committed such an act. Like Sacco and Vanzetti, political progressives fearlessly supported them, but in the end they were punished by death.

Who are political prisoners?

Political prisoners are African American, Puerto Rican, Cuban, Chicano, Native American, Asian American, white anti-imperialists, Kanaka maoles, Arabs, Muslims, and South Asian.

In 1990, an international group of jurists were invited by American activists and movement lawyers to a conference in New York to discuss and agree on a definition of political prisoners that would be the most acceptable. After much discussion, the conference participants came forth with the following definition: "To be considered a political prisoner, one must have been a movement activist before being imprisoned; have had some association or affiliation with a recognized political group (like the Black Panthers, Young Lords, American Indian Movement, Red Guards, Republic of New Africa, SNCC, CORE, etc.); or have engaged in some action, including clandestine acts which were political."

But there are also countless politicized prisoners who went to prison on some social violation but became heroes to movement activists. The most notable were George Jackson, Eldridge Cleaver, Hugo Pinell, Ruchell Magee, the San Quentin Six, and the Soledad Brothers. There were also internationally acclaimed political prisoners engaged in the struggle for independence, such as Puerto Rican Independentistas like Lolita Lebron, Raphael Miranda, Andres Cordero, Oscar Collazo, and Irving Flores.

Yuri talks with young people at "Free Mumia" event in San Francisco, 2001.

Political prisoners were lionized by those in social and political struggles and supported because they fought against injustices and evils in society. They raised the consciousness of those around them by their own practice and social ideas. The sacrifices made by those imprisoned in the 1950s, 1960s, and 1970s ignited the zeal and dedication of the grassroots movement activists of that time.

I would like to present the stories of three political prisoners with whom I corresponded: Mtayari Shabaka Sundiata, Mumia Abu Jamal, and Marilyn Buck. They represent the many men and women whose political involvement inspired civil rights, human rights, and liberation struggles.

Inside the New African Prisoner: Letters from Mtayari Shabaka Sundiata

Mtayari was my first teacher in the Republic of New Africa's (RNA) Nation-Building class. He was also the RNA official who on September 13, 1969 administered the RNA oath to me in the Brooklyn consulate, making me a citizen of the Provisional Government of the Republic of New Africa. This changed my political course, giving me a deeper meaning of Black liberation, or more correctly, New African liberation, with the added dimension in understanding the importance and necessity of a land base. As Mtayari used to say, "There is no national liberation struggle anywhere in the world without the struggle for land."

The following is a collection of letters from Mtayari while serving time in Green Haven Prison in the 1970s in New York. Mtayari joined the Black

Liberation Army sometime after he was released from prison. He was killed by the police on October 23, 1981, shortly after he and his comrade, Sekou Odinga, were captured near the Shea Stadium in Queens. He was down on the ground when he was shot. Sekou was beaten unmercifully, tortured, and taken to prison.

I saved all the letters Mtayari had written because they expressed the gut-level insight into prison life: its miserable conditions, its warped harshness, its lonely isolation—all of which gnaw into the human psyche but which also reveal the uplifting potency of a warrior for his nation and its people. He says it candidly in one of his letters:

> After being locked in a cement tomb for years, suffering the agony of brutal-izing experiences in a dungeon with no release in sight, it takes a very strong and dedicated man to survive this war of the mind. He must have something to stimulate his will to survive this war of the mind; otherwise, he will blow his mind by surrendering himself to the octopus. I guess you can say this is the road that we are forced to travel because we moved outside of the sunlit prison we know as the American dream.

The six years of correspondence and visits with Mtayari while he was in prison, from 1971 to 1977, were like extensions of his classes. He was an extraordinary teacher who read, studied, and researched whatever he could get his hands on—even behind the wall—and shared generously with others. He was also a good listener who showed care and sensitivity to both political arguments and personal problems. His eagerness to know what was happening outside in the "larger prison of American society" and the world at large were never seen in isolation but in relation to one another—the Vietnam War, struggles in Africa, American Indian movement, and the Puerto Rican independence struggle. Mtayari wanted to know what was happening to our President Imari Obadele and the RNA 11 in Mississippi's Parchman Prison. His breadth, depth, and scope were unbounded, and his primary commitment, devotion, and love were for his country, the Republic of New Africa. To Mtayari, the RNA, though still just a provisional government, was not a mirage, a dream, or something more than hope. He believed it was a land that would be developed, protected, and represented by Blacks.

His political philosophy was revolutionary Black nationalism, yet his concern encompassed the world. Mtayari knew explicitly what he was fighting for, whom he was fighting against, and what the ultimate options would be. Malcolm simply said: "to prison or to the grave." Mtayari was a living heir of Malcolm's ideas. In one of his letters, he writes:

> Revolution finds the seeds of its growth and the justification for its development in history. Revolutions make psychological use of the past for it plunges into the future. The role that the victims are destined to play is simply a matter of growth. Growth means to change. To change means revolution. And to resist change means death.

Mtayari and Sekou symbolize New African manhood at its highest level. Mtyari lived the New African Oath to the fullest and reiterated it on many occasions, "For the fruition of Black power, for the triumph of Black nationhood, I pledge to the Republic of New Africa and to the building of a better people and a better world, my total devotion, my total resources, and the total power of my mortal life."

As an elusive freedom fighter who had no permanent home, material wealth, or monetary gain, his letters from prison are the few remaining mementos of his revolutionary nationalist spirit and strength that spurred him in his involvement. In a 1971 letter he writes:

> I would like to quote Ndugu Kwame Nkrumah. He states, "Before the guerillas hands are armed with guns, his mind must be armed with ideas and his soul with the spirit of dedication to the people."

> I have accepted my role as a righteous African warrior. I am sanctified by the divine wisdom of my African Ancestors, whose knowledge of life is the principle upon which my life rests, and whose understanding has given substance to my being, for I am the personification of my ancestors. I'm a New African.

Mtayari's 1973 letter becomes more passionate:

> In your letter you spoke of the death of another comrade. The death of a comrade is never an easy thing to accept, even though, in war we realize that deaths are inevitable for some so that others might live in dignity and respect in a society predicated on freedom for all and not a selected few. The death of a comrade and Ndugu makes some of us realize for the first time what war of attrition really is. The burning steel that entered the black body of our revolutionary Ndugu and snuffed out his precious life, did not silence the voice of freedom, but rather confirmed our belief in revolution. Therefore, the greatest tribute we can offer our falling warrior Ndugu is to emulate him in the cause for which he gave his life—the fight for the freedom on an oppressed humanity.

Mtayari also revealed to me the human side of warriors: their need to be sustained, a need for a woman to interact with, to love and cherish. He expressed a need for a woman who could be a part of his revolutionary life, and reciprocally, his life would be part of hers, so that together they could build their New African Nation. But throughout his prison life, it was difficult for him to find even a correspondence relationship that could be sustained for any length of time.

In another letter he explained:

Letters allow one to transcend the gray walls of alienation to seek one's identity and longevity among the living. For surely this is the grave of the living dead. We are legally declared outcast[e]s of life by society, a class of men whose social orientation surely does not meet the appreciation of society at large. We are declared as a class of men defined by society as the wretched of the earth, the declass whose social philosophy, so they say, threatens society per se.

But, we, ourselves, realize that we don't belong here. We are not criminals. Rather, we are the victims of a brutal, self-perpetuating, racist, depraved, sadistic system predicated on robbery, murder and genocide.

Mtayari understood well the history of America, not only in terms of what the U.S. government did to Blacks, but to the Latinos, the indigenous, the Asians, and poor whites. He was an internationalist. Once, after a visit with him, he wrote:

You made me realize that life doesn't necessarily end in this physical grave where human degradation is the norm of human existence. You penetrated the gray walls of human misery where human beings are called outcasts of life. You were not deceived by that myth. You saw the reality of our existence and you understood the whole concept of correctional reform, which is, in reality, a facade for systematic genocidal domestic warfare. A war is being perpetrated against the African diaspora and other non-white people, who we prefer to call oppressed humanity, a humanity in the iron-grip of a society based on racism, oppression and exploitation. . .

We are oppressed as a nation; therefore we must rise as a nation, not as an individual. We must not fall victim to individualism. The nation is more important than the individual.

Often Mtayari would exhort and encourage the brothers and sisters to continue the struggle with more zeal:

Tell my ndugu na ndada to continue the struggle until freedom is won.

There are so many of us with chains on our minds. Our great struggle against colonialism, oppression, and fear must continue until these evils are destroyed from the face of the earth.

I shall never allow them to crush me. I shall continue my struggle against oppression and racism in Amerikkka. I will not succumb to Amerikkka's oppressive system. So many don't understand what is happening to them; they don't know why they are here.

He would end letters with, "Hoping to see you all soon on the battlefield of the people's war against oppression."

Mtayari eventually emerged from prison but no sooner was he released, he became involved in the most revolutionary aspect of the struggle: the armed struggle. He was prepared for whatever would ensue. On October 23, 1981, he, along with brother/comrade Sekou Odinga, was captured in a car chase by the police, and while eagle-spread on the ground, was executed on the spot. Sekou Odinga was beaten, tortured, and imprisoned. Mtayari lived by the New African oath to the fullest. He gave his total devotion, resources, and power of his mortal life. How fortunate I was to have had Brother Mtayari Shabaka Sundiata as my mentor and comrade.

Mumia Abu Jamal

The case of Mumia Abu Jamal has reached global dimensions, as his support has grown from local grassroots activists to overseas labor unions, European parliaments, the Japanese Diet, and to international prison groups. The reasons for the expanded interest in Mumia's case is not only because of the death penalty issue and the many aspects of unjust violations, but more so because of the kind of person Mumia is. More than any other political prisoner, Mumia has been able to galvanize support for not only himself but also for all U.S. political prisoners.

Mumia is an award-winning Pennsylvania journalist who exposed police violence against minority communities. On death row since 1982, he was sentenced for the shooting of a police officer. His attorneys and many community supporters stand firm of his innocence, especially in the light of new evidence involving the recanting of a key witness, ballistic and forensic evidence, and a confession from one of the killers of the police officer.

Denied privacy and contact visits with his family, Mumia has been in punitive detention for over twenty years. His case is currently on appeal before the Federal District Court in Philadelphia. Mumia's fight for a new trial has won international support. More people worldwide have become interested in political prisoners since Mumia began advocating for those behind-the-wall like himself. But he also is engaged in the struggle against war and government repression, advocating for peace and justice.

Mumia is not just a radical activist or a revolutionary. He is also a father, grandfather, an articulate speaker, an eloquent journalist, and an extraordinary political activist. He was only fourteen or fifteen years old when he started his grassroots activism and began organizing the Black Panther Party in Philadelphia. His skills were recognized early, but it was probably his radicalism, his audacious support for the Move family, and his rapport with people in general that began posing a threat to the powers-that-be in Philadelphia, to the police department, to the FBI, and to the ruling class. By the late 1970s and early 1980s, Mumia was surely being watched.

Mumia's case began in the early morning hours of December 9, 1981, when Mumia was moonlighting as a cab driver. He saw a Black man being beaten by a police officer down the street. He drove to the very spot and was surprised to find that the "brother" being beaten was, in fact, his own brother. Mumia jumped out of his cab to help his brother, who was being beaten by Daniel Faulkner. Seconds later, shots rang out. Both Faulkner and Mumia were shot and left bleeding on the street. The place was chaotic, and some people were seen running from the scene. The nightclubs and bars had just closed, and people were swarming on the street to see what happened. A police back-up team arrived and immediately began kicking around and brutalizing Mumia. Both Faulkner and Mumia were taken to the hospital. Mumia was beaten again. Seriously hurt, Mumia received surgery and survived. Faulkner died.

The case came into court in the following summer of 1982 amidst hysteria and negative publicity. The trial judge selected, Judge Albert Sabo, was considered one of the toughest and most racist. He was known as the "hanging judge" because he had sent more prisoners to execution than any other judge around the country. Mumia was not allowed to have a representation of his choice. Andrew Jackson, who later collaborated with the judge, had to be dismissed. Awarded a weak defense lawyer, he was not allowed to have an allocation of more than $150.00 for witnesses for investigation.

Asians for Mumia, New York City, 1996.

At his first trial he was ejected from the courtroom for most of the trial proceedings. The whole trial was a farce filled with lies, half-truths, witness intimidation, and hiding evidence—the Philadelphia court was hardly a place where justice could have prevailed. The entire case was so flawed by prosecutorial and judicial misconduct that charges against Mumia should have been dropped, and Mumia should have been freed. But during the years that passed, Governor Thomas Ridge of Pennsylvania signed a death warrant, which was stayed just ten days before Mumia's execution date in 1995.

In the 1990s, a new law team that included chief legal counsel Leonard Weinglass and his co-counsel Daniel Williams took Mumia's case but it ended disastrously, so Mumia fired the whole team. Another team consisting of Los Angeles attorney Eliot Grossman, Chicago attorney Marlene Kamish, British barrister Nick Brown, and Philadelphia attorney J. Michael Farrell were accepted by Mumia. They appealed for a new trial, as there was now new evidence to submit. A confession by Arnold Beverly needs to be brought forward, as well as a revealing affidavit by one of Mumia's former lawyers, Rachel Wolkenstein. But the court has denied all this crucial evidence. Another new lawyer, Robert Bryan, became Mumia's lawyer in 2003.

Mumia's life is seriously endangered. Many demonstrations have been organized, and supporters for Mumia must not let their guard down. Mumia's two most ardent support organizers are Pam Africa of Philadelphia and Julia Wright of Paris, France. A public response, including worldwide response such as occurred in 1995, must be rebuilt again. The struggle for Mumia must be taken to a new level. For more information and latest developments on Mumia's case, visit **www.mumia.org.** and **www.freemumia.org.**

Mumia is a phenomenon like Malcolm X. He is needed in this society where injustices have been the growing norm. Mumia's extraordinary leadership is needed on the streets, not behind the walls. Mumia's life must be saved.

Marilyn Buck

Political prisoners are women as well as men. Their commonality is that the similarity of their politics embraces the same motivations and goals: to condemn and obstruct injustices and evils, and to encourage justice and liberation. Among these are the Puerto Rican sister freedom fighters, like Carmen Valentin, Dylcia Pagan, Lucy and Alicia Rodriguez, Alejandrina Torres, and Haydee Beltran Torres (the only Puerto Rican sister still in prison).

In addition to these inspiring Puerto Rican revolutionaries, there is also Marilyn Buck, a white anti-imperialist who is doing the longest prison term held by any woman political prisoner. In California's Dublin Federal Prison, she was given a sentence of eighty years, of which she has completed twenty-two. Why the long sentence? All political prisoners are given long sentences because they consciously struggle against colonialism and U.S. government imperialist policies. Such acts are forbidden in the U.S. and other imperialist countries. Thus, there are several hundred political prisoners in U.S. prisons because they confronted U.S. arrogance and abuse with political affiliations, political ideology, and political acts. Militant activities were not uncommon in the 1960s and 1970s. Most activists accepted Black leadership, and leftist politics prevailed. Marilyn was involved in the Black liberation struggle, as well as unjust domestic issues with the hope of creating a better world.

I first heard about Marilyn in 1974 when someone sent me a *Los Angeles Times* clipping about the arrest of a young white woman activist who was suspected of helping a Black militant organization. I thought that this Marilyn must be quite a different kind of white activist, not one that just yells slogans. Someone gave me the address of where she was incarcerated, and we have been writing to each other since. Although I don't see her as much as I would like, I have tried to visit Marilyn each month since 2001, thanks to movement comrades who have given me rides to see Marilyn at Dublin Prison.

I faintly remember the day I first saw her, at one of the trials of the Conspiracy Case in Washington, DC. I didn't meet her face-to-face, but I waved at her in the courtroom. I have now come to know her through the monthly visits to Dublin, and it has been an immense learning experience to hear her share her political wisdom and principles, and her indomitable spirit and energy.

My most poignant memory of her was her personal compassion for me when I had contemplated suicide in 1999. Plagued and depressed by failing health problems, I wanted to end my life. Where most of the responses from others were without understanding or not taken seriously, Marilyn had genuine empathy for me. Though brief, she sent me a thoughtful note expressing her understanding of how I felt my situation was so strangely unbearable.

Courtesy of the Kochiyama Family

(FROM LEFT) Matef Harmachis, Diane Fujino and their baby, Kano, visiting with Marilyn Buck, Dublin, California, August 2001.

Like other anti-imperialist comrades, Marilyn is a dedicated, principled, people-loving activist who has been involved for many years fighting against racism, inequity, poverty, and social injustices. She has been charged with several acts of conspiracies, aiding and abetting a prison escape, and speaking out and acting against U.S. government and military violence. How did she become such a radical and bold revolutionary?

Marilyn was born in Texas in 1947 to very socially conscious parents who did not abide by the general Southern cultural norms of racism and color divisions. Her father was a pastor of a Black church, thus her consciousness matured while still a youth. By the time Marilyn was attending college, both in Texas and in Berkeley, she became an activist in the most progressive circles. She joined Students for a Democratic Society and worked with

Newsreel, a very radical filmmaker's collective in San Francisco.

She began supporting the Black liberation movement. It was then that she caught the attention of the FBI's counterintelligence program (COINTELPRO). She was twenty-six years old when she was arrested for purchasing firearms. She was given ten years and sent to Alderson Women's Prison in West Virginia. There, she met other revolutionaries like herself. She met the internationally known Lolita Lebron of the Puerto Rican Nationalist Party and Bo Rita Brown, a white anti-imperialist of the George Jackson Brigade.

Marilyn must have been a model prisoner at Alderson in the 1970s, as she was given a furlough, a temporary release. Marilyn had no idea of going back to prison. She was a revolutionary who had work to do. Eight years later in 1985, she was back in prison with Linda Evans and others. She and Linda became part of the Resistance Conspiracy Case of Washington, DC. When the group realized that a co-defendant, Dr. Alan Berkman, was seriously ill with Hodgkin's Disease, Marilyn and two other white comrade sisters pled guilty in exchange for Berkman's release. This was one of the most magnaninous acts of comradeship and sacrifice that movement activists had ever demonstrated. This spontaneous act of compassion that white anti-imperialists like Marilyn displayed made a deep impression among all comrades in the broad movement in America.

By this time, Marilyn's sentence totaled eighty years. Her twenty-two years behind the wall has neither changed her politics nor her outlook on life: to pursue justice and liberation. But it probably has changed what methods she would use to bring the best results. While in prison, she has completed a BA in psychology, worked as a literacy teacher, assisted immigrant women, taught yoga classes, has done HIV/AIDS education, and won awards and recognition as a poet.

Marilyn's health, though, has eroded. She is a thyroid cancer survivor, suffers from rheumatoid arthritis, and still has a bullet in her leg that causes a slight limp. But visiting Marilyn, one would not know of her deteriorating health. She is constantly upbeat, dazzling in her personality, laughs and jokes, and avoids talking about her health. She is an inspiration to those in struggle and is a reminder of all the white anti-imperialist women who served time in prison or are still confined: Linda Evans, Susan Rosenberg, Silvia Baraldini, Judy Clark, Kathy Boudine, Donna Willmot, and Laura Whitehorn.

Asian and Asian American Political Prisoners:
Steve Yip, Yu Kikumura, David Wong, and Eddy Zheng

It is not often that one hears about Asians in prison, especially a political prisoner. But there have been many Asian American leftists on the West Coast and in Hawaii whose progressive labor and union activities resulted in their arrest and serving time in prison. In the 1960s, there was Shinya Ono, a member of Students for a Democratic Society who was given a prison sentence in Illinois for his participation in the 1968 Days of Rage Democratic Convention demonstration in Chicago. Since that time, there have been a few more Asian Americans who have become regarded as political prisoners, such as those involved with anti-Vietnam War and civil rights demonstrations.

Steve Yip

Steve Yip was a member of the Revolutionary Communist Party, and he committed a bold act in New York at the United Nations on April 30, 1980. He and another Asian American comrade entered the chambers of the United Nations Security Council with two coffee cans filled with red, non-toxic paint and two red flags tucked in their back pockets. Two diplomats also walked in, one a U.S. dignitary and the other a Soviet Union representative. Steve and his comrade then unceremoniously splashed the two diplomats with red paint, and raising their red flags in the air, cried out at the top of their lungs, "Down with U.S.-Soviet war moves! Our flag is red—not red, white, and blue! On to revolutionary May Day!" They were immediately taken away by security men.

The timeliness of their act and the setting at the UN were a relevant and bold statement. They publicly revealed the warmongering intentions of the U.S. and USSR. The maneuverings of the two super-power nations were trying to set off a world conflagration. Steve Yip and his comrade became political prisoners after this act.

I have kept in touch with Steve Yip. He was sent to New York's Danbury Prison, and it was from Danbury that I began communicating with Steve. His first letter reveals his initial impressions of prison life:

Like many people, I never had the notion that one day I would find myself in prison. For many Asian families, being imprisoned, let alone being arrested and going to trial, had a stigma attached to it. And those offenders tended to get ostracized in the community, or at least, some talk will proliferate. . .

Already, at FCI Danbury, this "country club" prison is feeling the sharp edges of cutbacks. The whole semblance of "rehabilitation" will soon disappear in a cloud of smoke as they trim the prison budgets of the fat, which the educational and training programs come from. As one case manager in cynical bluntness declared to an inmate wishing to enter college, "There is no such thing as 'rehabilitation' here. . ."

On the evolving prison movement among social activists, he wrote:

Growing up during the late sixties and early seventies was like being in a political cauldron, whose brew was erupting with controversy and turmoil challenging young, developing minds. One of the movements that increasingly caught the attention of many social activists was the prison movement. Increasingly, large numbers of political activists and draft and military resisters were being sent to jails and prisons.

We all became familiar with George Jackson and the Soledad Brothers. We remembered Malcolm X's "rehabilitation" when he converted to Islam and entered the Nation of Islam. The prison writings of Eldridge Cleaver, George Jackson, and others were inspiring and thought-provoking "musts" for countless high school and college students. The prisoners' movement became vanguard spokesmen whose sharp polemics galvanized a growing section of people brought into political life.

He also wrote of Danbury itself:

The Federal Correction Institution at Danbury is a medium-security facility of the Federal prison archipelago. Located on a reservation on some mountain, FCI Danbury is one of over 40 federal penal facilities stretched out around the country. Danbury was the home for many political activists during the sixties. The Berrigan brothers, the radical Catholic priest-activists, spent their time here.

Reminiscing at one point in a letter, Steve expressed thoughts back to the days prior to his incarceration:

Being an internationalist by political conviction, I, too, felt beset by a strange "neurosis," a temporary bewilderment and an equilibrium displaced by an unsure anxiety. I paid closer attention to the content of people's conversations and maintained a very open and honest political approach. I did not hide my political orientation. While there developed several kinds of circumstances which I was not surprised by—mindless incidents of harassment by more backward elements for being Asian—I parried these jabs, while counterpunching diplomatically, and with sharp response if necessary. As a revolutionary communist, I was viewed by some as an oddity, almost celebrity status, while many others (of all nationalities) welcomed me as a friend and comrade: "That's my communist friend."

Steve also explained about the unequal treatment of Muslims:

The prison population at FCI Danbury is roughly 650 inmates (and climbing). At least half of the population is Black and Hispanic. A good one third of the Black prisoners are of the Islamic faith. Together with the non-American Muslims—Persians, Pakistanis, and Arabs—Muslims are a large percentage of Danbury's "residents."

Muslims adhere to strict dietary laws: the handling and consumption of pork is taboo. When the mess hall serves pork as a main dish (which is quite often), the administration shows off its consideration by providing a substitute—usually two hard-boiled eggs or peanut butter.

His final letter was very reflective on the many Asian Americans like himself who wanted to change the world:

In the passionate period of the sixties where temperamental and revolutionary nationalism had arisen, many Asians could not find the proper political fulfillment from campus activism alone (though it was itself important). We threw ourselves into the "community," whether Chinatown/Manilatown, San Francisco, or Little Tokyo in Los Angeles. Regardless, we were both affected by and in turn influenced by those exciting days of commitment to struggle and activism.

We rejected white racist American society and its institutions. We battled for Third World Colleges on the campuses and against the imperialist war in Indochina. We sought new models of social systems and human relationships.

We acted with an exhilaration, a dawning confidence and pride in our new-found ethnic awareness. We shared lofty visions of a new man and a new woman and the total elimination of all forms of racism, oppression and exploitation. We were alive and acted accordingly. We wanted to change the world and could not be content with the way things were.

Arrest, trial, and imprisonment. Steve felt the act itself would be of substantial significance and was worth his effort. His moment of limelight, his year in prison, would also prove that this system is more concerned with locking up those who take bold stands than with punishing those within its upper echelon who opt for unnecessary wars.

Yu Kikumura

The case of Yu Kikumura is a federal case. Yu Kikumura is a Japanese national, not an Asian American. Yu is an anti-imperialist peace activist, and for that reason he is categorized as a political prisoner. The International Tribunal of Jurists in 1990 selected him as one of some 150 political prisoners in the U.S. He was an activist in Japan where he supported the homeless, the jobless, and workers at the lowest level. Most of this was done at Sanya, where so many marginalized people in Japan live, such as the Burakumin and Koreans. Burakumin are Japanese pariahs, marginalized people looked down upon as a lower class because of their work with animals.

I became involved with his case when Attorney Bill Kunstler invited me to Kikumura's first hearing. I began personally corresponding with Yu and found out he was a political activist from Japan. A committee in New York subsequently formed to support and bring greater visibility to his case. The Yu Kikumura Support Committee is a small group of activists who have maintained communications between Yu, his lawyer, and other supporters around the country. Wayne Lum is one of the New York organizers. In Southern California, there is Mo Nishida and Misako Tsuchida. In Japan there is also a strong support committee called the "Yu no Kai." The Committee defined its position: "We receive no funding and rely solely on support from other concerned forces. We will not allow the media and U.S. government to taint Yu Kikumura (or any other revolutionary political activist) as a 'terrorist.'"

The stigma of "terrorist" is part of the demonizing and criminalization of political activists. "The U.S. is the most consistent and outrageous purveyor of indiscriminate, reactionary violence seen not only within its own borders—but around the world," is a quote by Dr. Martin Luther King. King continues:

> From the systematic elimination of the native peoples of America; to the enslavement of African peoples; to the forcible annexation of Mexican lands; to the war against the Iraqi peoples; and the "humanitarian" massacre of Somalian civilians fighting against foreign military occupation—U.S. imperialism continues to prove that its "new world order" still dominates and strangles with an iron fist.

The Yu Kikumura case began on April 12, 1988, when Yu was arrested by a New Jersey State Trooper at a rest stop on the New Jersey Turnpike on an illegal search and seizure charge. Allegedly three explosive devices were found in his car. The FBI also said that Yu Kikumura was linked to Libya and was a member of the Japanese Red Army. Without evidence, they claimed that Yu was plotting to avenge the U.S. raid on Libya in 1986, when the bombing killed Kadafi's two-year-old daughter.

Without any legal foundation, the presiding judge in the case declared that Yu Kikumura had intended on "murdering and maiming countless numbers of people for no other reason than they are Americans." While he has never discussed his possession of the explosive devices, he did state at his sentencing, "I'm not linked to Libya. I do not have the background claimed by the United States."

In this atmosphere of the Reagan-Bush Presidential years, the government and media were able to railroad Yu Kikumura into a thirty-year prison sentence—a sentence solely based on hearsay evidence presented (not during the trial but during sentencing). This outrageous sentence was imposed despite the efforts of his attorneys and the Federal sentencing guidelines mandating twenty-seven- to thirty-three-month sentences for illegal possession of explosives. Several years later, Attorney Ron Kuby reduced his thirty years to twenty-two years.

Despite the fact that the U.S. government states that there are no political prisoners in the U.S., the 1990 Political Prisoners Tribunal recognized Yu as a political prisoner. He is one of the few Asian political prisoners among the over 150 recognized political prisoners in the U.S. today. In a statement to the Tribunal, Yu said, "In America, democracy criticizes the people, not only the political prisoners but also the ordinary citizens."

Efforts were underway to lessen this twenty-two-year sentence to ten years, but he has already finished more than twelve years. He is currently in a twenty-three-hour lockdown facility at the notorious supermax prison at Florence, Colorado. Previously, he was held at USP Marion in Illinois. Yu was not allowed to receive literature and/or to speak with visitors in his native Japanese; a legal petition was filed to challenge this. Although the petition was later denied by the Federal Appellate Court, a political victory was attained as a result of the critical judgment brought upon the prison warden within this very same decision. The wording by the Appellate Court may influence the ability of other prisoners to receive materials other than in English.

Another Japanese national considered a political prisoner is Tsutomu Shirosaki. He is someone who stands squarely with oppressed peoples around the world against oppression and imperialism. In order to sustain the fight for Yu, Tsutomu, and other political prisoners, please become involved by joining political prisoner support committees. The Yu Kikumura Support Committee can be contacted at: P.O. Box 520021, Flushing, New York 11352. He can also be reached directly at: Yu Kikumura/09008-050, P.O. Box 8500, Florence, Colorado 81226-8500.

The David Wong Case, 2003

David Wong is a Chinese national who came to this country from the People's Republic of China in the early 1980s. He was about eighteen years old when he arrived as an immigrant and is one of three children whose mother and siblings live in Hong Kong. We learned about him through Shelley Wong, a New York Chinatown activist/leader who called a meeting to discuss David's case. A David Wong Support Committee subsequently formed in New York in 1990. David Wong's case has all the elements of racism, anti-immigrant sentiment, prosecutorial misconduct, and poor defense.

On June, 1984, David was imprisoned in Suffolk County, New York on theft charges [his first and only criminal offense], and he was later transferred to the Clinton Correctional Facility in Dannemora, New York, fourteen miles from the Canadian border.

On March 12, 1986, an inmate, Tyrone Julius, was stabbed to death in Clinton Prison. On the order of a tower guard, over 100 yards away, David was immediately apprehended, but he was not even in the immediate vicinity where the stabbing occurred.

New York Chapter of the David Wong Committee, 1994.
Picture of Bill (CENTER); Yuri and Kazu Iijima (SEATED AT RIGHT).

The medical examiner testified that the wounds on Tyrone were so deep that the attacker's clothes would have the victim's blood soaked in them. There was no blood on David or on the Chinese newspaper he was carrying. In fact, no murder weapon was ever found. The tower guard who was over 100 yards away from the incident presumably recognized David from over 700 inmates similarly dressed—many wearing hoods. The only other witness who testified against David was given parole for his testimony. Many inmates of color offered to testify that David did not commit the murder, yet they were not called to testify at the trial; they were all Black and Latino. Tse Kin Cheong, a former inmate, was with David at the time of the murder and testified that David was innocent. But the State did not provide a skilled translator who spoke the same dialect as David, raising much doubt to the authenticity of the translated statements represented as evidence in his trial. Lastly, Tyrone Julius had

Asian and Asian American Political Prisoners   145

been transferred to the prison only two weeks before he was murdered. David never met Tyrone Julius.

In August 1987 David was convicted of murdering Tyrone Julius and sentenced to prison for second-degree murder. David was an easy target for a frame-up. He spoke little English, was unfamiliar with the legal system, did not know his rights, and had no family or friends in the United States.

After David's conviction, Tse Kin Cheong, David's inmate friend, tried to help David by contacting a Chinatown community organization. In response, Asian Americans for Equality asked an associate, Shelley Wong, to act as a liaison in David's case. It was not until 1990 that Asian American students, workers, and professionals responded and formed the David Wong Support Committee to address the gross injustices suffered by David resulting from his wrongful murder conviction. Wayne Lum and over a dozen other David Wong Committee members have devotedly supported David over 10 years.

David is now serving his time at the Shawangunk Correctional Facility in upstate New York. He works daily in the prison workshop and occupies himself with reading and other activities. His main interests are philosophy, meditation, religion, Zen, physics and psychology. He has maintained his innocence to this day and actively participates not only in his own defense but also other political cases. During his incarceration, he has vastly improved his knowledge of the English language and has written letters to former President Bush, former President Clinton, and former Governor Cuomo, as well as to numerous prisoners and human rights groups. Today, he has many supporters, friends, and correspondents.

David's case is now in the hands of an experienced law professor and expert in criminal law, Professor William Hellerstein, and a Center for Constitutional Rights (CCR) lawyer, Jaykumar Menon. The case is at a crucial stage, as the two-day evidenciary hearing on April 10 and 11 was not productive. His legal defense committee is waiting for a response from the judge whether he will receive a new trial.

Because of him and the injustice he's suffered, many Asian American communities have galvanized to form committees on his behalf. There are now David Wong Support Committees in Minneapolis, Minnesota, under Liz Kaufman and Ian Shiroma, and in Oakland, California, under Joannie Chang. Until her passing in 1997, Mary Choy of Hawaii diligently sent information about David's case to the people in Hawaii. Through her efforts, contributions have been forthcoming from the islands. Maggie Ho and her husband Rick Sin are doing the same thing in Canada.

The David Wong Support Committee in New York, which, under the leadership of Wayne Lum and Patti Choy, is still sustained through the devotion and consistent work of a committed and loyal group of supporters. All the people who helped start and support our own committee have shown tremendous dedication and have been tireless in their organizing to educate people about David Wong. Those who would like to show their support for David Wong can write to: David Wong/84A5320, Shawangunk CF, P.O. Box 700, Wallkill, New York 12589. To get the latest information and update on David's case, please contact the David Wong Support Committee at P. O. Box 52536, Flushing, NY, or for email addresses and all kinds of other information you can go to their website at **www.freedavidwong.org**.

Eddy Zheng

Eddy Zheng is a thirty-three-year old native Chinese prisoner who has been in San Quentin Penitentiary since he was sixteen years old. From a rebellious young teenager who committed a thoughtless act, Eddie has been transformed into a role model prisoner and has become a bright, talented, refreshing writer.

In the years he has been in prison, he has learned English, become an avid reader and skillful poet, taught himself American law, and made countless friends through correspondence. Even though he would not be classified as a political prisoner, he has become a politicized prisoner who has organized educational activities and studied in prison to earn a college degree.

Eddie was introduced to us through an article published in the *San Francisco Weekly* about Asian prisoners fighting for Asian American Studies at San Quentin. After corresponding with him and then finally meeting him, I was deeply moved by his journey to what he is today. I asked him if I could print his poem that articulates very well his life and his painful but significant journey. It is entitled "Autobiography @ 33," and it demonstrates the human possibilities of change even in the marginalized world of prison. Two other Asian prisoners there are Mike Ngo and Rico Remedio.

I am 33 years old and breathin'
It's a good year to die

To myself

I never felt such extreme peace

Despite being mired in constant ear deafening screams.

From the caged occupants—triple CMS*, P.C.s* gang validated,

        Drop outs, parole violators, lifers,

        Drug casualties, three strikers,

        Human beings.

In San Quentin's 150-year-old solitary confinement

I don't want to start things over

@ 33

I am very proud of being who I am

I wrote a letter to a stranger who said

    "You deserve to lose at least your youth,

      not returning to society until well into middle age. . ."

After reading an article about me in the San Francisco Weekly

I told him

    "A hundred years from now when we no

    longer exist on this earth of humankind the

    seriousness of my crime will not change or be

    lessened. I can never pay my debt to the victims

    because I cannot turn back the hands of time. . .

    I will not judge you."

Whenever I think about my crime I feel ashamed

I've lost my youth and more

I've learned that the more I suffer the stronger I become

I am blessed with great friends

I talk better than I write

        Because the police can't hear my conversations

The prison officials labeled me a troublemaker

I dared to challenge the administration for its civil rights violation

I fought for Ethnic Studies in the prison college program

I've been a slave for 16 years under the 13th Amendment

I know separation and disappointment intimately

I memorized the United Front Points of Unity

I love my family and friends

A young sister named Monica

Who is very pretty wanted to come visit me

Somehow I have more female friends than male friends

I never made love with a woman

Sometimes I feel like 16
But my body disagrees

Some people called me a square
Because I don't drink, smoke or do drugs
I am a procrastinator but I get things done
I never been back to my motherland
I started to learn Spanish
Escribió una poema en español
At times I can be very selfish and vice versa
I never been to a prom, concert, opera, sporting event
Or my parents' home
I don't remember the last time I cried
I've sweat with the Native Americans, attended mass with the Catholics,
went to service with the Protestants, sat and chanted with the Buddhists
My mind is my church
I am spoiled
In 2001 a young lady I love stopped loving me
It felt worse than losing my freedom
I was denied parole for the ninth time
I assured Mom that I would be home one day
After she pleaded with me to answer her question truthfully
          "Are you ever going to get out of prison?"
The Prison Industrial Complex and its masters attempted to
Control my mind
                    It didn't work
They didn't know I've been introduced to Che, Paulo Friere, Howard Zinn,
Fredrick Douglas, Assata Shakur, bell hooks, Maurice Cornforth, Malcolm X,
Gandhi, George Jackson, Mumia Abu Jamal, Buddha, and many others. . .
I had about a hundred books in my cell
I was internalizing my politics
In 2000 I organized the first Poetry Slam in San Quentin
I earned my Associate of Art degree
Something that I never thought possible
I've self published a 'zine
I was the Poster Boy for San Quentin
Some time in the '90s my grandparents died
Without knowing that I was in prison
@ 30
I kissed Dad on the cheek and told him that I love him for the first time

I've written my first poem
I called myself a poet to motivate me to write
Because I knew poets will set us free
In 1998 I was granted parole
        Then it was taken away
The governor's political career superseded my life
Sometime in the '90s I participated in most of the self-help programs
In 1996 I really learned how to read and write
I read my first history book, "A People's History of the United States."
My social conscious mind was awakened.
In 1992 I passed my GED in Solano prison
I learned how to take care of my body from '89 to '93
In 1987 I turned 18 and went to the Pen from Youth Authority
The youngest prisoner in San Quentin's Maximum Security Prison
I was lucky—people thought I knew kung fu
@ 16
I violated an innocent family of four and scarred them for life
Money superseded human suffering
I was charged as an adult and sentenced to life with a possibility
No hablo ingles
I wished I could start things over
I was completely lost
@ 12
I left Communist China to Capitalist America
No hablo ingles
I was spoiled
In 1976 I went to demonstrations against the Gang of Four
Life was a blur from 1 to 6
On 5/29/69
I inhaled my first breath

                              —Eddy Zheng, 7/22/2002

* Correctional Clinical Case Management System's mental health condition prisoners

\+ Protective Custody prisoners

The Trip to Cuba:
The 19th Venceremos Brigade, 1988

It had always been my dream to go to Cuba with the Venceremos Brigade, but I didn't think that would be possible as I was in my sixties—sixty-seven years old to be exact—when I applied. I didn't think that anyone as old as me would be accepted, but I later found out there were others even older than I was! I filled out my application, turned it in, and was accepted. I thank my husband for being supportive and helping me with the funds needed and taking care of the family while I was away.

I was also very grateful to Vilma Ramirez, a Chilean activist who kept encouraging me to try and apply. I was surprised to learn that of the 149 North Americans comprising the 19th Venceremos Brigade, some fifteen were senior citizens. The 1988 Brigade to Cuba ranged in age from fifteen to eighty-one.

After Cuba's victory, so many activists wanted to see what a socialist country would be like. The Venceremos Brigade, a left-wing solidarity organization, developed work brigades to give grassroots organizers and activists an opportunity to go to Cuba to work together with the people there and experience first-hand their way of living. It was such a golden opportunity to work, study, and learn about global liberation struggles and socialism in Cuba. There are still Brigades going to Cuba today.

Under the slogan "No More Contras Anywhere," the Brigade represented a broad cross-section of students, workers, professionals, and retirees from all over the U.S. The gender breakdown included seventy-two women and sixty-nine men; the ethnic composition was sixty-two whites and seventy-nine people of color (thirty-eight Latinos, thirty-two Blacks, three Middle

Easterners, three Native Americans, and three Asians). The wide array of Brigadistas, however, was unified in their praise and admiration of Cuba's concerted efforts through self-determination, its continuous struggle against the vestiges of racism and colonialism, and its effort to build a solid foundation for nurturing tomorrow's new socialist men and women.

The host organization, Cuban Institute for Friendship (ICAP), was instrumental in setting up tours and meetings, handling logistics, and recruiting speakers, translators, and camp work crew who were all exemplary hosts/hostesses and emissaries of friendship.

Both eye-opening and mind-boggling for the North Americans was the spontaneous warmth and kindness of the Cuban people; the caring nature of medical practitioners (through the Family Doctor Units or hospitals); the humane policies of the penal system; the special programs for the elderly; the intensive construction work of the micro brigades; the work/study combination in the educational system; and the deeply imbued patriotism of defending their revolution which seemed ingrained in all ages in the Cuban society.

Throughout our bus travels around Cuba, Brigadistas could see the tremendous amount of construction work sprouting in the hinterlands, by the ocean, or in the towns to meet the needs of housing, education, and health care. Cuba is truly a nation whose primary concern is the basic needs of her 10 million people—beginning with the neediest. How different, we thought, from the U.S., where construction is geared toward building condominiums, luxury hotels, fashionable suburban homes, and high-rise offices for corporations, while tens of thousands of Americans are homeless, jobless, and on the streets begging.

Members of Poder Popular took us to the Alamar area where workers (both men and women) in hard hats were busy at a construction site. They explained how Micro Brigades began in 1971. Castro's plan for 32,000 houses in a ten-square kilometer area for 83,000 inhabitants was initiated. At the time of our visit, 25,000 had already been built as well as fifteen daycare centers, seven boarding schools, one polyclinic, sixty-eight family doctor units, ten supermarkets, four trade centers, a furniture store, two textile factories, a coffee factory, a centralized laundry and kitchen, and three centers.

It was also obvious that education was one of the priorities in their socialist society. The Brigadistas were taken to a number of educational facilities and schools. In a Social Science class at an intermediate school, a Brigadista threw out the question "What is Marxism?" Without hesitation, a youngster rose up and explained: "Marxism is a doctrine to be followed by workers. It is a scientific philosophy where general problems of society can be handled by understanding matter and ideas. It gives us the possibility of performing the historical role of socialism." Although some Americans may consider the answer rhetorical and simple, most Brigadistas were impressed by the answer, which revealed the seriousness with which students absorbed their lessons.

The concept of combining work and study, we learned, was proposed long ago by Jose Marti, whose prophetic ideas have given a solid base to Cuban education. At a nursing class for thirteen-year-olds, young girls were preparing to aid a birth. The realism of their demonstration was impressive. They even took the blood pressure of some of the visiting North Americans who watched in awe. At the Pioneer Center, dedicated to Che Guevara, youth from ages ten to fourteen were running the school's sugar cane factory, while high school science students were actually testing the sugar. Nine-year-olds were raising rabbits and chickens.

Another aspect of Cuban life is the importance of the elderly. Upon visiting a senior citizens complex where some 500 to 600 seniors congregated daily for exercises, excursions, and cultural activities, Brigadistas learned that 26,000 citizens in Havana belong to the Senior Citizens Club. The elderly are considered an integral part of Cuban society rather than being marginalized.

In fact, no one seemed marginal. Visiting a women's prison reinforced the socialist objectives of creating humane conditions everywhere. Inmates are allowed the right to work and earn salary. Bankbooks are issued to keep record of their earnings. A marriage pavilion allows the women to bring in husbands or boyfriends for conjugal visits. Even penal leaves are allowed to visit a sick child. A mother may go home for a year, then come back and finish her time.

In touring the prison, we noticed its dining hall had tablecloths and beds in cells had attractive covers. There was a beauty parlor, sewing room, library, pharmacy and medical facilities. Noticeable in the library collection were the autobiographies of Angela Davis and Malcolm X, and also the *Case*

Image of Che Guevara, Havana, Cuba, 1988.
(Inscription reads "Hasta la victoria siempre"— "Till victory always.")

of Dred Scott and the *History of the Black Struggle in America*. The finale of the prison visit was the presentation of the most fabulous musical imaginable, filled with vibrant talent, gorgeous costumes, and the enthusiastic backup audience of fellow inmates who roared approval along with the Brigadistas.

However, why were there a disproportionate number of Blacks in prison? At a hospital facility a Black woman doctor gave her personal experience of having been once at the "lowest rung" of hospital work as a clean-up person. "After the revolution," she explained, "Cuba made overt changes in outlawing racism." So she was able to enroll in a nursing school, became a nurse, was later admitted to a medical school, and today she is a full-fledged doctor.

On several occasions, Cuban leaders have brought up the issue of racism giving historical background from the Spanish conquest, the annihilation of the indigenous, and the colonization of a mixed-race people. They admitted that vestiges of racism exist, but they feel that institutional racism is being wiped out.

One of the most moving experiences for our North American brigade was visiting the Camp for Disabled Salvadoreans. They were young men, ranging from thirteen to thirty. These young men and youth were once guerillas engaged in battles against Salvadorean government tyranny and the U.S. mercenaries. They had seen their mothers and fathers killed, brothers taken away, villagers massacred. Many were without limbs, some on crutches, and others in wheelchairs. Yet, they expressed optimism for the future of Salvador. They were the quiet, unheralded heroes in the grim civil war for liberation, airlifted out of the war zone for medical treatment and rehabilitation, harbored in the safety of the Cuban hinterlands. Meeting such freedom fighters was a humbling experience.

Another exciting moment for us was when we attended the International Workers Day March, held annually on May 1, when President Fidel Castro led a contingent of over 500,000 participants through the Jose Marti Revolution Square. Wave after wave of an almost unceasing flow of people marched for two hours in a spectacular parade of humanity, interspersed with giant floats that represented all the various branches of work and industry.

Colorful and moving were the banners and people representing the number of nations and liberation struggles fighting in the Third World— young men and women who were attending schools in Cuba or beginning new lives in this international, socialist society. Some of the countries and organizations represented by the flying colors were Ethiopia, Angola, Mozambique, the African National Congress, Southwest Africa Peoples Organization, Nicaragua, and Palestine. The finale of the marchers was the impressive regular army of Cuba, marching in clipped cadence, and the heroic survivors of the Moncada Barracks struggle.

As the Nineteenth Venceremos Brigade, we felt proud to be part of this historical march, which is well known in the states as former Brigadistas have carried on word of this event through the years.

An unexpected highlight for many Brigadistas, especially the Blacks, was the brief encounters with the highly esteemed, recognized folk-hero, Black revolutionary Assata Shakur. Seeing Shakur and her daughter looking well and strong was heartwarming. Another delight for us was the quick meeting with Don Rojas, the former press secretary for Grenada's beloved martyred Prime Minister, Maurice Bishop, on the last night of our stay.

The Brigadistas were impressed with the meeting and hearing of the leadership of the Committee for the Defense of the Revolution (CDR), the political and revolutionary arm of the Communist Party. Working on the level of the Block Association, the CDR leaders defined and explained their intricate role, accessibility to their communities, obligations, training, selection process, and the social issues they guide constituencies through using Marxist-Lenin philosophy.

We were also elated to have the opportunity to meet and talk with some of the leadership of the Women's Federation, during which a free exchange of questions and answers took place. Women's issues involved the family code, women in the labor force, parenting, childcare, divorce, prostitution, and homosexuality.

All in all, our two weeks in Cuba was an extensive learning experience of a post-revolutionary building era of rectification and progression that would impact our own community work when we returned to the U.S.

We found the Cuban people not just work-intensive but life-intensive—buoyant and joyful. The national psyche of Cubans was best manifested when the Brigadistas were invited by Poder Popular to a rousing block party in the town of Santa Cruz, in Jibacoa. The hospitality, generosity, openness, and gaiety of the party were earthy and spirited, and the Latin/Caribbean and Afro-Cuban music and dance was plainly endemic to life and culture in Cuba.

The Julio Antonio Mella Camp (named after the Cuban martyr) was the home-away-from-home for the 149 North Americans that made up the Brigade. The contingent felt sorrowful in leaving, but grateful for an unforgettable and heartwarming experience. We expressed our sentiments in unison many times, hoping the echoes of our shouting "Cuba! Cuba! Cuba! *Venceremos te saluda!*" ["We will win!"] would reverberate until the next brigade arrived. *Recuerdo siempre.* [Always remember.]

People's War in Peru:
What is its Significance Today?

In 1992, I became aware of and very interested in a war going on in Peru. The war began in the 1980s between the Peruvian government and the indigenous and peasantry. It was in 1992, though, that Phil Farnham of the Revolutionary Communist Party (RCP) gave me all kinds of information about its history and why there was a revolution. I began to read every leftist newspaper I could get my hands on and wondered why more people were not supporting this struggle for equality and justice of the marginalized in Peru.

In 1993, Phil said that RCP and the International Emergency Committee in England were putting together an international delegation to go to Peru to visit political prisoners and check out conditions of Peru and its prison system. Some Europeans and Mexicans were preparing to go, and they were looking for Americans to join them. I was so excited to have been asked, even though my family expressed their reservations.

As soon as I arrived in Peru and was riding with Phil Farnham, I saw the poverty and the lifestyle of the poor worsening as we rode into Lima. I noticed the blatant contradiction between the wealth of plush hotels and the crowded sidewalks where the urban poor tried to make their daily living selling whatever was accessible (fruits, nuts, socks, t-shirts, toilet articles, and so forth).

To most Americans, this war is insignificant, as they are unaware of the role of American policy behind this conflict. They know nothing of the suffering of the people on the lower strata of Peruvian life. Very little is known about the war itself, for as the saying goes, "the first casualty in war is Truth." In both Peru and the U.S., the media—with its specialists on Peru—work closely with their governments, making it difficult for people to

Women and children in Peru, 1993.

know what is really happening in that country. Torn by class and racial division, the "haves" live in fear of the "have nots" and keep a stranglehold on the lives of the poor.

The Disinformation Campaign, which has been ongoing from the very beginning of the war, has reduced the liberation struggle of the underclass to guerilla warfare (poor people's warfare). But the civil war in Peru is about a People's War for a more just society. The Ashaninkas, the major tribe in Peru, under the guidance of the Peru Communist Party, organized a purposeful, disciplined, protracted struggle ultimately to bring about a new egalitarian society. Their principal goal was, and is today, to prepare a people politically, morally, spiritually, and economically to destroy and overturn the existing power structure. They hope to shape a new society, which will allow for the greater satisfaction of human needs and the further development of the human potential.

If you go to Peru today, you will see poverty, dispossession, marginalization of the poor and indigenous, and a whole different world of a different standard of life from the rich and powerful living in comfort and distanced from the poor. The brutality of the Spanish conquest of Peru—the capture and killing of the Inca Emperor, the enslavement of his people, the pillage of Peru's resources, and the destruction of the Inca civilization—is a legacy so tainted in cruelty and utter disregard for humanity that one need only anticipate the day when "the chickens will come home to roost."

In order to understand this People's War in Peru, one must trace the unraveling developments of a movement known as the "Shining Path." *Sendero Luminoso*, or the "Shining Path," has been considered an answer to poverty and oppression. Abimael Guzman, a university professor-turned-revolutionary, became their chosen leader to teach the indigenous and peasantry to move forward to the future. By 1990, Guzman was captured and was not to be seen again except for a brief moment on television, when he was moved from one prison to the next in 1993.

Grinding poverty and brutality of the oppressors have driven and continue to drive out millions of peasants from the Andes countryside. Many go to the jungle highlands looking for a better life, but once there, they find out that government policies make it impossible for them to grow anything to survive—except for cocoa leaves, the raw material for cocaine. The peasants, however, don't make anything off the cocoa trade because the profits go to the capitalist drug cartels, in addition to Peru's Army and government officials. Cocoa production amounts to half the value of Peru's legal export, so without this, its economy would collapse.

Many poor and indigenous end up in Lima and other cities. Since there are no jobs, they end up peddling cigarettes, nuts, candies—anything they can get their hands on. Millions are crammed in shantytowns. In Lima—a city of 8 million people—4 million live in shantytowns. There is no water or electricity in these areas, as the government has not allowed the building of pipelines or electrical installations. More than 200,000 children work in the streets of Lima scraping a few pennies a day to supplement their family's meager income. But people can eat in these shantytowns because there are communal kitchens where all the women work together to feed the people.

In 1990, 76,000 children in Peru died before their first birthday because of poverty. Almost three-quarters of the people live below the official poverty level. Over half the population is on the brink of starvation. The masses of people eat more poorly than those who lived in this region 500 years ago, before Columbus and the Spanish invasion. Thousands of people die each year from diseases like cholera and tuberculosis, which could be prevented by simple health and sanitary measures. In 1991, cholera spread throughout Peru and claimed 2,500 lives. This was the worst cholera epidemic in Latin America in the twentieth century. It is obvious the Peruvian government has not provided for even the most basic needs of its people.

In 1990, the government led by President Fujimori's regime carried out an economic "shock" program ordered by the International Monetary Fund to squeeze more profits so their debt could be paid. The brutal policies involved slashed wages, reduced health care and other services, and contracted growing crops for export instead of food for the people. Consequently, the cost of food tripled in a single month. The Fujimori regime is fulfilling its debt payments to IMF of as much as $90 million a month—but it is money that comes from the blood of the people.

We need not wonder why the people are fighting so hard. They are fighting for survival, for the future of their children. They are fighting the Peruvian government; its police force and army; the *rondas* (peasants like themselves who are given arms by the government to fight against the *Sendero)*; the U.S. government advisors and special forces; CIA connections; the secret police; and the National Intelligence Service—all of which come under the umbrella of U.S. imperialism. The people's enemies are also the reactionary media whose lies and disinformation have been used to portray the revolutionaries as a sinister, terrorist force who perpetrate violence on the people, including the peasantry.

On the evening of my first day in Lima, April 3, 1993, the television was saturated with repetitive scenes of Abimael Guzman being transferred to the San Lorenzo Prison, which was surrounded by land mines. His transfer was shown many times so that the wealthy class could be assured that Guzman would never be able to escape. It was also a message to the human rights groups that he was still alive, and thus, had not undergone human rights violations. Front-page newspaper headlines blared, *"Bajo Tierra Para Siempre"* ("Underground forever"). President Fujimori also appeared often on television triumphantly assuring that Lima was now safe.

Our international delegation of five people from Spain, Mexico, England, and the U.S. hoped to meet with Guzman and other political prisoners and lawyers also imprisoned for life; however, such efforts were quickly thwarted. I was also disappointed not to be able to see Marta Huatay, a woman lawyer who was beaten and tortured to a point that she is considered permanently brain-damaged. Whenever we mentioned the name Abimael Guzman to bourgeois representatives, immediate negative vibes could be felt. After all, he was the icon for the poor and indigenous. But every newspaper, even the supposed progressive ones, had the same anti-Guzman/anti-*Sendero* slant. Also, the United Left hardly seemed different from the middle or right. The same characterizations of Guzman and the *Sendero* persisted here in the U.S. The silence on this issue was disturbing.

Despite Guzman's capture and the large number of guerillas who were massacred in 1992, the revolutionary actions of the *Senderistas* did not abate. During our short stay in Peru, newspapers reported skirmishes between guerillas and the Peruvian police and soldiers, as well as the bombing of a prison where *Sendero* prisoners escaped. This revealed that the *Sendero* movement was alive and well, and the fact that there must be grassroots support from many quarters enabling the guerillas to continue the struggle despite casualties, imprisonment, and government-instilled anti-*Sendero* sentiments.

Young Peruvian boy peddles bicycle cart to transport his mother who lost her legs, 1993.

While preparing for a press conference, one of our guides warned us against it and suggested that instead we visit a shantytown. Since we were intrigued by the role it seemed to play, we gratefully accepted the opportunity. The visit to a shantytown was the most moving experience of all in my trip to Peru. It was that one visit that helped me understand the struggle in that troublesome, divided country. It also gave us some insight into the mentality of the "Shining Path" guerillas, their political ideology, their fighting spirit, and their leader Abimael Guzman.

It was there in the shantytown that despite the paucity of basic needs, the human spirit of warmth and hope could be felt, as well as the depth and breadth of commitment and zeal. One woman said, "Guzman's capture was a loss, but the struggle will continue as always. Our happiness is the revolution." Our guide, who drove us to the shantytown, used a metaphor to explain the essence of Guzman and the "Shining Path": "The Shining Path is like a river. Some water may have been scooped out, but the water will continue to flow. It will never run dry."

The shantytown had no water or electricity. The government made no provisions to make such basic needs available. But the people manage. Each family makes its own hut consisting of homemade mud bricks, sliced canes, and burlap bags. The kitchens are communal. Women take sentry duty just as the men do. There are medical clinics, sports fields, farm animals, and children in abundance. Despite the lack of basic materials, the people make do with whatever they have. Despite attacks by the government army, police, and *rondas*, the shanty dwellers protect their turf. They now have more than one-third of the country, especially the rural and mountain areas. As we were leaving the shantytown, the people there asked us to please let the world know what we had seen and heard.

We who were fortunate to go to Peru want to break the wall of silence and lies about the Shining Path people. The counter-campaign is being waged, not only by the right-wing, but also by the moderates and so-called leftists. State terror and repression is not criticized. Alternatives of revolutionary acts are considered terrorism. Smear tactics have been par for the course. Prison, torture, and assassinations are not condemned or are being accepted as necessary to crush revolts by the stigmatized "troublemakers."

The *Sendero Luminoso* is waging a courageous struggle against centuries of harsh and unjust treatment of the indigenous, their impoverishment and marginalization, and their rejection as members of its own nation. Though their political ideology is demonized, these stalwarts—young and old, men and women—will continue. Many women have participated in armed struggle. Their important roles and contribution in the struggle continue today.

Now that I have gone to Peru (although brief the stay), I witnessed and listened to both sides and feel that a necessary civil war is taking place between the poorest and most marginalized against the rich and powerful who have no concern for the destitute who are indigenous. I believe the struggle is a true People's War, involving Peru's impoverished indigenous and peasant masses and fighting to liberate a nation so that a new humane society can be created. For years, I too, after reading about "Shining Path," or *Sendero Luminoso*, in various American newspapers and magazines, questioned its political validity as a revolutionary entity, and whether they were the terrorists that some liberal writers depicted them to be.

What is the significance of the *Sendero*'s People's War? It is probably the only continuous struggle of its kind in the Western Hemisphere, taking on not only a right-wing dictatorship, but U.S. imperialism as well. Without aid from any other country, the peasantry and indigenous have combined their own forces and resources to fight for liberation. Although western media has tried to block out the reality of this struggle, this small war is being watched guardedly from distant shores. It is the modern David and Goliath battle.

Three Icons in the Movement:
Lolita Lebron, Assata Shakur,
and Leonard Peltier

Lolita, Assata, and Leonard were three political prisoners who did not see the movement as just something guided by ideology. They fervently saw the movement as a struggle to maintain their turf (their land) with arms, heart and soul, and plant seeds of the future into the coming generation. Through armed confrontation, they sent a political message to let the U.S. know that they would not be colonized. For that reason, they became singled out as targets to be punished.

Greatly admired in the movement, Lolita Lebron is a Puerto Rican nationalist. Already a legendary political activist, she was a significant part of the struggle for independence for Puerto Rico. On March 1, 1954, she, along with comrades Rafael Cancel Miranda, Irving Flores Rodriguez, and Andres Figueroa Cordero, literally took her case into the halls of Congress. They fired their guns to signify their protest at how the U.S. was planning to make Puerto Rico submit to its colonial authority. These Puerto Rican freedom fighters—men and women—were adamant about keeping Puerto Rico free.

I wanted to tell her what an inspiration she had been to the movement. When someone gave me her prison address in the late 1950s, I began writing to her. I could not believe it when I received her first letter! We continued our correspondence until she and her comrades were released in 1979. I finally met her for the first time at the most exciting packed-house welcome at St. Paul's Church on 59th Street. It seemed every Puerto Rican in New York was there. To wrap my arms around this icon was unforgettable.

Protest march in New York City. Banner reads
"Asians for an Independent Puerto Rico."

Another sister icon to the movement was Assata Shakur, known as the "soul" of the Black Liberation Army (an underground, black liberation group). She was one of the Black Panther members targeted by the U.S. government's COINTELPRO as a dangerous political dissident. A powerful leader in the Black Panther Party, she boldly demonstrated her position on political repression, racism, and violence that dominated the U.S. government's policy toward people of color. People have regarded Assata's audacious deeds as brave and have considered her an inspiration for those active in the struggle for black liberation.

One such deed took place in 1973, when Assata and her two friends Sundiata Acoli and Zaid Shakur were pulled over and ambushed by state troopers on the New Jersey Turnpike. A state trooper and Zaid were shot to death; Assata was severely wounded by three bullets. Sundiata escaped for a brief moment but was captured a short while later. Assata's almost movie-like escape through the efforts of the Black Liberation Army, her tryst with a comrade while being held in the courtroom holding pen, and her birthing a baby while imprisoned have made her into a rare legend.

I will not forget my visit with her at Riker's Island. She walked into the visiting room like an awesome Black queen in African attire and with a most regal presence. But she was still her warm, unpretentious self. She was a proven freedom fighter, a female counterpart of Malcolm. She told me that she was the only prisoner placed by herself in a building to make sure nobody would assist her with escape—no contact with anyone! A few years later, I had an opportunity to see her once more when I made my trip to Cuba in 1988. This was an incredible moment—everyone on the Brigade wanted to meet her as well.

Lastly, Leonard Peltier is Native American leader and indigenous rights activist who in similar ways was not going to allow the U.S. government to take away his people's land. He, along with members of the American Indian Movement (AIM) and other local Native Americans, also fought with arms, sending a strong message to the U.S. government. His bold act was in protest to the injustices against their tribes and the violation of the many treaties. He exposed the abuse and repression against his people. He writes about this injustice:

> We Indians are all guilty,
> Guilty of being ourselves.
> We're taught that guilt from the day we're born.
> We learn it well.
> To each of my brothers and sisters, I say,
> be proud of that guilt.
> You are guilty only of being innocent,
> of being ourselves,
> of being Indian,
> of being human.
> Your guilt makes you holy.
> —*Prison Writings,* p. 16

He is remembered for his courageous fighting at the seventy-two-day occupation of Wounded Knee in 1973, and two years later at the Pine Ridge shoot-out, where Leonard became the obvious target of the U.S. government, leading to a wrongful conviction. In each case the armed FBI responded with military-style assault against the Native Americans. In the end official hearings to bear testimony on local conditions and treaty violations of the U.S. government were never convened.

Leonard's biography, *Prison writings: my life is my sun dance* (New York: St. Martin's Press, 1999), is his personal diary that includes moving poetry and prose written while in prison. It is an inspiring work of his thoughts, values, and principles that could help every individual activist learn about humility, social consciousness, and political awareness. Leonard further reinforces my strong belief that struggle must bring out truth, reveal the enemy, and support allies who fight for human rights and justice in this complex world. He writes "a message to humanity":

> Our work will be unfinished
> until not one human being is
> hungry or battered, not a
> single person is forced to die
> in war, not one innocent
> languishes imprisoned, and
> no one is persecuted for his or
> her beliefs.
> —*Prison Writings,* p. 199

Sometimes, it seems that Third World heroines and heroes appear when needed the most—to spur on the struggle. Lolita, Assata, and Leonard played their real-life roles as revolutionary freedom fighters. Regarded by their radical comrades as courageous and bold, men and women like these three will be honored by all activists who fight for their people and native countries.

The Asian American Movement

Something phenomenal happened throughout the United States in the 1960s and extending into the 1970s. Presidents Eisenhower and Johnson led our country during this explosive time. Young people began making history by challenging the status quo and the duality, hypocrisy, and inequities in American society. They also opposed U.S. involvement in Vietnam because they felt it was an intervention and transgression in the internal affairs of another country. The anti-Vietnam War movement became huge, and hundreds of thousands of people marched in protest. We even took our granddaughter Akemi, who was just a toddler at the time, to one march. Over three million Vietnamese and 50,000 Americans had died.

The Vietnam War was a very long war, from 1965 to 1975. The Vietnamese protected their country from the French, Japanese, and the U.S. The U.S. transgressed into Vietnam because it did not want Vietnam to become a Communist country. The U.S. was afraid that if Vietnam became Communist, all of Southeast Asia, including Laos, Cambodia, and Thailand, would follow. This is America's "domino theory." The leader of North Vietnam was the great Communist leader, Ho Chi Minh. Vietnam was a poor peasant country but fought and defeated the arrogant, well militarized, and wealthy Americans, which surprised the world.

One remarkable aspect of this movement was that a sizeable percent of our own young Asian Americans became involved. From coast to coast, Asian American students and community activists jumped into this domestic fray wholeheartedly. Young Asian America's response to the social/political upheavals that rocked the country was like cracking the barriers and breaking previously accepted stereotypes: the quiet, obedient, inhibited, studious, mind-your-own-business, just-become-successful Asian—the kind of Asians that most white Americans liked, accepted, and upheld as "good Americans."

Many first-generation Asians (products of exploitation and racism) diligently nurtured the development of these stereotypes in the effort to help, protect, and guide their offspring to a "better life."

A series of extraordinary events and a new type of charismatic, anti-establishment leadership from the minority communities catapulted the movement into the lives of a nation of young Asian American sleeping tigers. There came the San Francisco State strike; a nationwide movement against the Vietnam War and the draft; Ethnic Studies; and grassroots organizing from the Asian American Political Alliance, Asian Americans for Action, the Red Guard, I Wor Kuen, and the Van Troi Brigade. Also coming into the movement and struggle scenes were the likes of Wounded Knee, George Jackson, Black Panthers, Malcolm X, Che Guevara, Young Lords, Brown Berets, Hard Core, Yellow Brotherhood, *Gidra*, International Hotel, My Lai, Palestine, Aztlan Nation and a host of other eye-opening, mind-boggling movements and events.

Already involved with many other struggles and issues in New York, I was drawn into the Asian American Movement by Kazu Iijima. It seemed to me the sensible thing, since all issues of struggle addressed human rights and social justice violations of one sort or another. Kazu, together with Min Matsuda and Mary Ikeda, formed a pan-Asian group called Asian Americans for Action (Triple A). This was about 1968, about the time that the San Francisco State strike took off. In the West Coast the Vietnam War was becoming the most important issue. Don Yee, Yu Man Chan, and Yu Han Chan also joined this organization, and as soon as Bill and I heard of this, we were very much excited and joined also.

Bill and I learned from Kazu, Min, and Mary that Asian Americans were politically active with leftist formation since the late 1930s before World War II. They told us of left-wing Asian movements that fought against the red scare of the 1950s.

Kazu was the most informative and compelling Asian American woman on the East Coast. She said she felt that social and political awareness must be brought to the attention of the Asian American communities. I remember she would often say, "We must create an Asian American perspective of the Vietnam War. An Asian nation is being bombed, and Asian Americans will be going to Vietnam and fighting against the Vietnamese too." She would also insist, "We must know what this war is really about." We knew that most of us Nisei folks were apolitical. We knew that Kazu was right. We had to organize discussion groups, read progressive viewpoints about the war, and learn about American foreign policy.

Courtesy of the Kochiyama Family

Greg (LEFT) and Steve (RIGHT) Morozumi with Yuri.

Kazu and Min suggested inviting speakers and reading books on socialism, communism, and capitalism. I knew so little about ideologies and politics, so I was happy that Kazu, Min, and Mary were leading us neophytes in the right direction.

Soon after, other groups came to the fore. While Triple A's membership comprised mainly of an older Asian constituent group, all the youth went to Chinatown to become a part of I Wor Kuen (I.W.K.), which was birthed in New York's Chinatown. The name was taken from the group in China who around the turn of the century challenged the British and other foreigners during the Boxer Rebellion. I.W.K. was the equivalent to the Black Panthers and Young Lords in militancy and politics, in grassroots organizing to the choice of apparel (black leather jackets and black beret). In California there was another group who called themselves the Red Guards, and Alex Hing was one of its leaders. Greg and Steve Morozumi were also radical activists.

Other Asian American groups were Asian Americans for Fair Media, Asians in the Spirit of the Indochinese, Asian Women's Group, Group of Khmer Residents in America, Katipunan ng nga Demokratikong Pilipino, Worker's Viewpoint, Japanese Americans Help for Aging, Vietnamese Students Association, Union of Democratic Thais, Koreans for Democracy, Asian Americans for Equality, Chinese Progressive Association, and Asian Coalition Against the War.

Back then, at the beginning of the Asian American movement, we saw that there was an identity problem, like other ethnic groups. Who were we? What should we call ourselves? Pan Asians? Asian Americans? No longer did we want to be just "Americans."

We Asian Americans also saw lined up on the international horizon such world-renowned Asian figures as Ho Chi Minh, Mao Tse-Tung, Madame Binh, Kim Il Sung, and Sukarno. In our own backyard Asian Americans found some of its time-tested role models, such as Chinese American Grace Lee Boggs, Detroit; Japanese American Karl Yoneda, San Francisco; Korean Americans Sonia and Harold Sunoo, St. Louis, and Anthony Kahng, New York; East Indian Eqbal Ahmed, Chicago; Bangladeshan Prafulla Mukherji, New York; Filipino American Carlos Bulosan; and of course, Kazu, Min, and Mary.

Greatly influenced and inspired by the civil rights movement and its many student-led protests, demonstrations, and rallies, young Asian Americans suddenly grew up, felt proud, stood tall. Unafraid to speak out, they began to take action and organize in their communities. They could detect an identity crisis and realize their lack of knowledge of their own Asian American histories, cultures, and languages. Their inability to relate and communicate sometimes with their own Asian brothers and sisters, and more so with Third World folks, was evidence that something was sorely amiss. They were disturbed by the American dream of wealth, prestige, comfort, and the feeling of superiority over others. But a new Asian America was being honed as the Asian American movement was birthed, and new goals, perspectives, values, priorities, and even lifestyles began to change for many. Their eyes and minds began to focus on the world of the oppressed, exploited, and marginalized.

Some challenged American policies; others derided the ivory towers of higher education. Some saw the elitism in media, film industry, and the arts; saw moral erosion in everyday life; were disturbed by objectives in the field of science; scoffed at the money mania in the sports world. Religion as generally practiced seemed superfluous. A more meaningful culture was sought.

Out of the chaos and criticism, a new breed of cultural artists and thinkers emerged—people-oriented, dynamic, creative, innovative, politically motivated as well as artistically inclined musicians, poets, singers, playwrights, filmmakers, actors, painters, cartoonists, comedians, writers and entertainers. Some of these include: cultural artists Nobuko Miyamoto, Chris Iijima, and Charlie Chin; filmmakers Loni Ding, Curtis Choy, Chris Choy, Renee Tajima, J.T. Takagi, Wayne Wang, Peter Wong, Robert and Karen

Nakamura, Duane Kubo, Linda Mabalot, John Esaki, and Steve Tatsukawa; film groups Visual Communications, Asian Cine Vision, National Asian American Telecommunication Association, and Third World Newsreel; playwrights David Henry Hwang, Phil Gotanda, Rick Shiomi, Velina Houston, Momoko Iko, and Wakako Yamauchi; producers/directors Roberta Uno, Lane Nishikawa, and Tisa Chang; Jazz groups Mark Izu and the Front Line, Fred Ho's Afro-Asian Ensemble, Francis Wong, Glen Horiuchi, Anthony Brown, and Kobi Narita's Universal Jazz Coalition in New York; musicians/cultural performers Robert Kikuchi-Ngojo, Nancy Wang, Brenda Wong Aoki, and Jude Narita; poets Janice Mirikitani and Nellie Wong; dance groups Chen and Dancers and Nobuko Miyamoto's Great Leap; and powerful political writers Ninotchka Rosca, the late Michi Weglyn, the late Caridad Guidote, Frank Chin, Merle Woo, Evelyn Hu-DeHart, Mari Matsuda, Gary Okihiro, Ron Takaki, and K.W. Lee.

These are only a "drop in the bucket" in the reservoir of Asian American cultural and intellectual production workers. Professionals in various fields such as law, medicine, education, journalism, and religion with prior political orientation also evolved and mushroomed. Many are intertwining their professions with community work and purposeful objectives. Banding together to become a stronger force and voice for their people, formations such as the Asian Law Caucus and Asian American Legal Defense and Education Fund had been formed. As for the field of health care, non-profit organizations such as Asian Health Services, National Asian Pacific Center on Aging, and Asian American Drug Abuse Program were envisioned by Asian American professionals committed to providing culturally sensitive and appropriate health care to their community. Asian alternative health care such as acupuncture, shiatsu (acupressure), chiropractic, homeopathy, herbology, Reiki, reflexology, and nutrition has also grown in popularity and demand.

In the 1960s and 1970s, students on college campuses protested against apartheid in South Africa. Students also saw a need to reinforce their hold on Asian American Studies programs. Japanese Americans worked for redress/reparation for Nikkei who were sent to camps during World War II. Filipino Americans have been pursuing the G.I. Bill for their WWII service and mobilizing a movement to force the American military out of the Philippines. Korean Americans have been fighting for reparation against the Japanese government for sex slavery, outrageously called "comfort women."

Community activists also began showing interest in refugees, immigrants, sweatshops, and gentrification.

Asian Americans have also confronted domestic issues such as hate crimes against Asians and Asian Americans. The brutal killing of Vincent Chin in Detroit awakened Asian Americans to the grim reality that racism against Asian Americans still persists. Although support for justice in the Vincent Chin case from coast to coast intensified, the finale of the case revealed what Blacks have known for a long time—that justice in American courts is still sorely lacking. The "not guilty" verdict passed by the Cincinnati jury was a revolting rollback for American justice and a stunning blow to all Asian Americans.

The Vincent Chin case was only one of several dozen incidences of violence visited on Asians and Asian Americans of every ethnic background. In New York City one of the most effective organizations created to speak out against such violence is the Committee against Anti-Asian Violence (CAAAV), under the leadership of Dr. Mini Liu. CAAAV has worked with Blacks and Latinos to broaden its scope, especially in its campaign against police brutality. CAAAV has also supported South Asian cab drivers, as well as working with youth in Southeast Asian communities. As CAAAV changes leadership, its chairpersons continue to be held by women. Now located in the Bronx, CAAAV is currently under the leadership of Jane Bai.

Another Asian American organization in New York that won the admiration and commendation from grassroots organizations was Chinese Staff and Workers Association (CSWA), based in the heart of Chinatown. The bulk of their work has been supporting workers—restaurant workers, garment workers, and all workers on the lowest echelon of pay or those struggling for unions. Their record of victories in winning labor disputes against sweatshop conditions is phenomenal. Their leadership is under Wing Lum. CSWA has opened an office in Brooklyn.

Two of the most successful (in terms of servicing their community) groups in New York is JASSI (Japanese American Social Service, Inc.), under the directorship of Midori Lederor, and NAKASEC (National Korean American Service and Education Consortium), located in Flushing's Koreatown. NAKASEC was founded in 1994 to address the needs and concerns of Korean Americans through programs in education, social service, culture and advocacy. Some of its work has been in providing an annual Summer Youth Program, Naturalization Clinics, scholarships for Korean American students, and multicultural projects. South Asian and Southeast Asian formations have also begun organizing, some publishing their own newsletters. At this moment the protection of and support for South Asians, Muslims, and Arabs are urgent issues.

Yuri speaking at Vincent Chin demonsration, April 1992.

As to the future of Asian America, which is changing even in complexion to a more diversified, lovely hue of colors, the road ahead is full of possibilities and opportunities. With the array of enthusiastic young activists of diverse Asian American and Pacific Islander backgrounds today, the future of the Asian American movement is promising. The pan-Asian aspect of the movement will help to maintain both diversity and unity. Already there have been exciting, progressive left-wing events both on the West and East Coasts. New cultural performers and writers are emerging even in Middle America—like in Minnesota, Rick Shiomi; Iowa, James Sato; Wisconsin, Peggy Choy; and Illinois, where Asian American theatre, hip-hop, and break-dance are sprouting. The Asian American and Pacific Islander lesbian and gay communities are becoming increasingly strong voices across the nation, and many are activists in community struggles. Korean adoptees have also become a prominent force in America, as they have developed networks to facilitate dialogue and promote awareness of issues and concerns.

Although the 1960s and 1970s were the spawning years of the Asian American movement, when seeds of political substance were sown, we will begin to see the new harvesting of the movement that is coming of age. I hope that the movement becomes more intertwined in working with other people of color and progressive whites. I also hope that the Asian American movement, with its many mutual objectives, becomes more international and supports liberation struggles around the world. We must be clear what we are struggling for and what we are struggling against. We must see that the struggle consists of both race and class, and work in concert with all those who are fighting for a more humane and just world. Long live the Asian American movement! Long live Third World unity! Long live internationalism!

Yuri with the "K Bears," 1997.

New Additions to the Family:
The "K-Bears"

Anyone walking into our apartment in Harlem would immediately wonder why there were so many teddy bears hibernating in our living room. They were sitting on the couch, along the sides of the couch, on a large French antique table, on an antique Chinese chair, and one on the floor in its own little house.

These living room bears are known as the "K Bears." Another group called "The Family Bears" was huddled comfortably on my bed in the master bedroom and, in fact, they occupied half the bed. In the beginning these bears were given to us mainly by family members.

Is the K Family really a collector of teddy bears? Not exactly. That's not the way the bears accumulated. The mid-1970s represented the "empty nest" stage for the K Family, when our children were growing up and beginning to fly the coop one by one. They were all leaving to begin their own lives, with the exception of Billy, who passed in 1975. The house was really getting empty, and Bill and I were feeling the void.

One day when I came home from the pilgrimage to Malcolm X's gravesite, Bill greeted me with, "There's someone waiting for you in the bedroom." I was immediately upset. Why would he bring someone to the bedroom? I went there and sitting pertly on our bed was the cutest yellow-brown Care Bear with a red heart on his cuddly belly waiting to be hugged. I melted immediately. Bill was so pleased to see my response. The Care Bear became very special in our lives.

A few months later, when I came home, I went into the bedroom and found another bear—the exact replica except smaller. It was a baby Care

Bear. I fell in love with it too. Our granddaughter Akemi was about five years old at the time, and we gave her the honor of naming our two bears. She wasn't very original. She just called the larger one "Bear" and the smaller one "Care." So we called the larger one "Daddy Bear" and the little one "Little Care."

Shortly after, my sister-in-law Aiko called from California and asked if I would like a teddy bear as she was making clothes for bears. I just said, "Yeah, send one." She sent us two. We named one "Aiko Bear," and the other "Jose" since it came from San Jose. This was just the beginning: four bears.

Soon after, for reasons we are not sure, close friends began gifting us with bears, and our bear family began growing. Our friends and visitors began to notice the growth and uniqueness in our new furry family. The one person who gave us more bears than anyone else—something like ten bears—is Lindy Liem, from the Bay Area in Northern California.

Little bears, big bears, medium sized bears—bears of all shapes and colors began joining the K-Bear family. There was a red Indian Bear from Pat Saunders; a homemade (also red) bear from Miyoko Tsubamoto Deschamp; a bear with a Japanese hapi coat from Renee Tajima and Armando Peña; and one from Diane Fujino and Matef Harmachis who was also wearing a hapi coat made by Diane's mother. Another bear with a Japanese kimono came from Miyoko Deschamp's daughter, Kiyomi. There was an Apollo Bear from Marsha Tajima. Famed musician Pharoah Saunders and his wife (at the time) Shukuru Saunders presented us with a black mink bear; we named it "Pha-Shu Bear" in their honor. Asian Sisters in Action, an organization in Minnesota, presented me with a bear at the Jericho '98 demonstration in Washington, DC. It was wearing a black T-shirt with the words "Asian Sisters in Action" on it, along with a picture of a revolutionary Asian sister carrying a rifle in front. On the back of the shirt were the words "Free All Political Prisoners." I later found out that the drawing of the revolutionary sister was the rendering of artist Steve Wong.

We have two unusual bears that make sounds. One of them, called "Aju-Sani Bear" (named after Ajuba and Hisani Bartley), snores if a certain sound is made. The snore is so human in sound that one time Eddie came home not knowing that we now had a snoring bear. When the door closed behind him, Aju-Sani Bear began snoring! Eddie was taken back because he didn't know where the snoring was coming from. He thought someone

K Bears at the Kochiyama Harlem apartment.

was sleeping under the living room couch. He was really scared, but once he finally figured out which bear was snoring, he was relieved and turned off the snoring gadget.

We have a "Winnie the Pooh" bear that, when you push in his stomach area, will either say, "Hello, Friend!" or laugh and say, "Hi, Honey!" This came from Susan Burnett, the spirited movement sister who was a secretary to Mumia Abu Jamal. She was also an avid teddy bear lover. She also gave me permission to see Mumia and the Move sisters in Pennsylvania, an opportunity for which I will always be grateful. Sadly, she passed away in 1999 after a lifetime of service to others.

Our two Valentine bears sit on top of the computer. The white bear holding a pink Valentine is from Julia Wright, the daughter of the famed writer Richard Wright and the leading Mumia supporter in Europe. The fluffy Gund bear is from Terry Kosakura, a former Sunday School student of mine in New York during the 1950s. There is also a cute Halloween Bear, given by Ricky Casimiro, who is wearing a black hat and an orange scarf. Sharon Maeda and Nobu and Bob Murakawa gave us a couple Christmas bears. The Murakawas also gave us one of the most realistic-looking black bears, which we once hid in a strategic place in Little Tokyo in Los Angeles just to watch the reactions of tourists.

Some of our furry additions were "cousins" to the bears: pandas, koalas, and raccoons. Our panda bears came from Aliyah Ladson, Ching Ching Ni, Peter and Emilie Wong, and Eddie and Pam. Then came dogs, rabbits, elephants, pigs, monkeys, an orangutan, a reindeer, a cow, and one unusual yellow earthworm from Asian American writer Karen Tei Yamashita.

The dogs came from Peter and Emilie Wong: one would do a perfect flip and land right on his feet again. Then there was a black-and-white-spotted Dalmatian from Rea Tajiri and her mother, and also a little yellow puppy from six-year-old Yuji Miyagi. A very huggy, once-white-now-gray rabbit with big floppy ears with white sideburns and wearing a t-shirt came from Roberta Uno and Njeri Thelwell (it looked a lot like Harlem dramaturg Garland Thompson). The stuffed rabbit coos, "Cuddle up with someone from UMass." The rabbit was named after the two, "Rojeri Rabbit." One year, a little yellow Easter bunny in a mailbox was brought over by Barbara Tsao. Now that Barbara has left us, this little "Barbara Bunny" has become very precious.

One of my favorite bears is a once-white Gund Bear, now gray, given to me by Barbara Hernandes, a Chicano activist from East L.A. We called this our albino bear, since she was wearing a Panther button. She is named "Barbara Bear," and I have carried her with me on trips along with the Care Bears.

Others who gave me bears are Man Chui Leung, Liz Kaufman, Asha Samad Matias, Mayumi Nakazawa, Amy Chen, Rex Chen, Herman and Iyaluua Ferguson, Roxana Farrell, Margie Fujiki and children, Aliyah Ladson, Maggie Ho and Ricky Sin, Eriko Ikehara, Koishi Hikaru, Nicolet Lum, Mai Nguyen, Tomie Arai, Legan and Akira Wong, Doualy Xaykaothao, Edmund Fong and Willy, Van Troi Pang, Marji Lee, Peggy Saika, Ruiko Yoshida, and J.T. Takagi.

Only two bears were ever bought: Harlem Bear and Ennis Bear. A total stranger purchased Harlem Bear for me at a knick-knack table on 125th Street, hence the naming; it really had that Harlem street appearance. Shortly after Ennis Cosby (son of Bill Cosby) was tragically killed in 1998, I bought a brown bear that reminded me of Ennis because of its smiling face. It was as if he were saying with out-stretched paws his famous "Hello, Friend," just the way Ennis did.

The most unusual bear came from Japan. It came with a note explaining to "please put the bear in a microwave on cold nights then take it to bed with you to keep warm." I wish I could remember the giver's name.

There was one bear whose giver I cannot remember, but I named it Baba Bear. I named it after George Baba Eng, an inmate in a New York prison whose warm letters nourished me through some difficult times. Baba Bear represents all the political prisoners who are the essence of those political activists behind-the-wall—the front-line soldiers who battle against guard brutality, indignities, injustices, and denial of humane treatment. I received Baba Bear about the same time I got the Salvation Army bear, which was given to all the residents at the Berkeley Home for the Elderly.

Every member of my family has given me a bear, panda, monkey, or puppy. All of these were in my bedroom in Harlem. They were gifts from my younger grandchildren Ryan, Traci, Christopher, Maya, Aliya, Kahlil; my children Eddie and Pam; Jimmy and Alison, Tommy and Julie, Herb and Audee; and my older grands, Zulu and Akemi.

After coming to the Bay Area, I received bears from Scott Kurashige (UCLA); Gary Mars (Stony Brook); a bear bank from Barbara Lubinski; and a tiny Care Bear bell from Tomie Arai. I'm not sure of all the other bears, as Audee and Herb have put them in safe storage in Oakland.

Numerous others gave me "animal huggies," but at this moment I cannot remember all their givers. It would also be impossible to write about all the bears, but they hold a loving place in my heart. They are representative of the many people who came into my life. They are not simply toys; they are an integral part of the love and caring of many friends. More than that, the bears with their different looks, colors, and sizes remind me of the world's people— of every race and background, and the preciousness of their being.

Yuri speaking at the African/Asian Round Table,
held at San Francisco State University, 1997.

Epilogue
Five Years Later

Five years have passed since I completed the first draft of this manuscript, and it all seems like such a blur to me now. After returning to the East Coast from UCLA in summer 1998, my health suddenly took a turn for the worse without warning or explanation. I began having inexplicable "head" problems, including difficulties with my balance. I was not having headaches or pains, just some strange agonizing feelings as if my head was in a trap. Perhaps I was starting to go into a depression but didn't understand what was happening to me. While my manuscript was not forgotten, I now had more pressing issues at this point in my life.

By spring 1999, Audee, who lived in Oakland, suggested that I come to California for an unlimited time until my health improved. She asked my youngest son Tommy, who lived in the Los Angeles area, to go to New York and bring me back to the Bay Area. At first, I was resistant about leaving New York, even for a short while. I had felt bad enough that I had missed the big Mumia march in Philadelphia on Mumia's birthday, and did not want to miss Malcolm X's Pilgrimage to his gravesite in Hartsdale, New York; it was coming up on May 19. Up until that time, I had never missed a Pilgrimage since 1966, which was the first Pilgrimage after Malcolm's assassination. Thus, I waited until after May 19 to leave the East Coast.

The plane ride to California was a soothing experience with Tommy. He just seemed to understand what I was going through at the time. He suggested that we do a crossword puzzle together, which I thought was the perfect vehicle to become one in mind with Tommy and distract me from leaving New York. It was the first time I had completed a crossword, and it provided a kind of bonding experience for us. Soon I was to experience getting closer to the family again after so many years of living apart.

When Audee and my son-in-law Herb met me at the San Francisco airport, a new chapter in my life began (even though, at the time, I didn't expect to stay permanently in the Bay Area). I stayed in their home for the first few months, and they did everything possible to ease my situation as they became my primary caregivers. They did all the cooking, housecleaning, shopping and coordinating my medical care, in addition to going to work and continuing their active involvement in the community.

My other son Eddie and his wife Pam, who also lived in Oakland, helped in whatever they could do—cooking, handling my finances, and taking me places. It felt good to be with the family again. Every member of the family was so sensitive and kind during a very difficult time of my life. Since I had not spent a lot of time with the rest of the family in recent years, it was nice to be living close enough to see Tommy, his wife Julie, and their children Ryan, Traci, and Christopher; my other son Jimmy, his wife Alison, and their children Maya, Aliya, and Kahlil; and my grandson Herbie.

During this time, I started to withdraw from people and didn't want to talk to or see anyone. One of the people who showed interest in my mysterious health problem was an old movement friend from New York, Floyd Huen, who was now a doctor in Oakland. As busy as he was with his own practice and other professional commitments, he would make time to see me, often making house visits. He was able to evaluate and change my medications so that I could function better. Meanwhile, I was feeling more frustrated and despondent about how sickly and unproductive I had become. I felt like I was of no use to any political struggle, much less to my family.

By summer 1999, I slipped into a depression that made me question the value of living. One day, I wrote a farewell letter to my family and took an overdose of sleeping pills. Since my daughter would call me everyday from work, she was worried when I didn't answer the phone. She asked a neighbor to check on me. The neighbor found me in bed in a dazed state. Audee also asked Herb to come home and check on me. Upon coming home and finding a suicide note, he called 911. An ambulance came and took me to the hospital.

After several weeks of treatment at Herrick Psychiatric Hospital (which is part of Alta Bates Hospital in Berkeley), I was released back to Audee and Herb's home. With the help of my family and friends as well as the hospital, I received a network of medical and psychological support. I was fortunate to have the assistance of Dr. Ann Yabusaki (a Sansei psychologist), Dr. Floyd

Huen, Dr. Marc Sapir from the Center for Elders Independence, the out-patient clinic of Herrick Hospital, the Japanese American Services of the East Bay, and home care attendants from Caring Hearts Home Care (sponsored by the Oakland Chinese Community Council, now called Family Bridges).

At the end of the summer, I awoke in the middle of the night and accidentally fell down while going to the bathroom. As it turned out, I fractured my pelvis and was hospitalized in Alta Bates Hospital for a week or two (again under the care of Dr. Floyd Huen). After my hospitalization there, I was transferred to the Elmwood Nursing Home in Berkeley where they could provide constant care and therapy. One of the occupational therapists, Jeff Saunders, used to write quotes in calligraphy to encourage and motivate patients to move forward and get well. Two of them were: "Doing your best at this moment puts you in the best place for the next moment," and "You may have a fresh start any moment you choose. Falling down doesn't mean staying down." I have kept these quotes. In fact, I ran into Jeff this year, and he was carrying a bundle of quotes on him. He gave me some, and I was surprised to know that they were all quotes from Malcolm X.

During my stay at the Elmwood Nursing Home, I realized that I needed the help of my family if I were to recover. It was the first time I decided that I could not return to New York City, since I would not be able to care for myself or find the kind of support I had in the Bay Area. While I wanted to return to Audee and Herb's home, my family decided that I needed more round-the-clock care than they could give. Thus, I spent several months at The Berkshire, a senior assisted living residence in Berkeley.

In that year and the several years following, I learned more about life than the eighty years prior. I learned new lessons about pain, agony, unpredictability, values, family concern, medical care, health, kindness, friendship, and becoming more conscious of what others go through. As someone wrote to me, "Illness and pain can be a great teacher. May it raise you to another level." I know it has. Illness and pain not only make one a more humane person, but more humble and sympathetic as well. I also learned a great deal about depression and emotional pain, which can be just as debilitating as a physical ailment. I had to accept and adjust to the changes going on within me.

In addition to my devoted immediate family, there were friends and family who visited me in the hospitals and the nursing home and offered ongoing help: my niece Liz Nakahara, Stephanie Tang, Alex Nguyen, Greg Morozumi, Atsushi Odamaki, and Floyd Huen. Later, others who helped me were Monica Ly, Michael Tran, Asha Davis, Mike Chang, Ben Wong, Anmol Chadda, Wayne and Gloria Lum, Marji Lee, Diane Fujino and Matef Haramachis, Mayumi Nakazawa, Ruiko Yoshida, Dina Shek, Jan and Brenda Sunoo, Dr. Sam Rose, Patti Choy, Olivia Wang, Chinosole, and many others.

By mid-2000, my health had greatly improved. I was able to move from The Berkshire to the San Pablo, a senior residence operated by the East Bay Asian Local Development Corporation in Oakland. This would be my last stop and for me, it was the perfect place to continue my limited work in human rights. At the San Pablo I rent a small room with a kitchenette, small microwave, refrigerator, and private bathroom. Located in the same building on the first floor, I can also conveniently get my medical care and physical therapy at the Center for Elders Independence (CEI). The entire CEI staff have been so helpful, especially Vicky Welsh (nurse), Sherri Lowery (social worker), and Esther Akiba (physical therapist). I guess I have reached that age of an octogenarian and am surrounded by a colorful mix of elderly and disabled survivors of strokes, degenerative diseases, heart and lung problems, diabetes, and other ailments. Hard-working citizens and immigrants from Eriteria, Ethiopia, Sudan, Kenya, Nigeria, Korea, France, Mexico, and Cuba brighten the informal, friendly atmosphere. The senior residents are equally diverse from Iran, China, El Salvador, the Philippines, and Puerto Rico. The majority, however, are from the U.S. southern states who have plodded rough and tough roads blighted by racism but aged with a strong positive attitude.

Surprisingly, there are some "celebrities" among the residents such as Taft Jackson, who played for the L.A. Lakers in the 1960s; a singer who sang with an opera company in China; Peggy Snow, who is the great-granddaughter of Geronimo, the American Indian leader; and an Iranian pediatrician who was wounded in the Iran-Iraq War. More surprisingly, there is a Brooklynite, Husayn Sayffudin, who belonged to Malcolm X's Muslim Mosque, Inc., and a brother from Ohio named Ramadan, who was a member of RAM.

In the past two years I have been fortunate to regain good health and spirits. I have been able to resume my movement activities and live independently. I am deeply grateful to countless friends from the Bay Area, as well as visitors and old friends from New York, Los Angeles, and elsewhere, who have enriched my life in so many ways. They have extended their help and support by picking me up to go to demonstrations, rallies, conferences, dinners, movies, and other events, or by coming to my place to help with mailings and other activities. I have also become involved with an elderly Asian women's group comprised of Mary Tomita, Ying Lee, Kiku Funabiki, Rose Buck, and Stella Wu. It has also been rewarding for me to be involved with so many local organizations concerned with social justice, political prisoners, and anti-war movements, and to be involved with such a diverse Asian American community.

I want to mention those people who even once provided me rides to rallies, marches, prisons, meetings and other events as I cannot use public transportation. My thanks to: Atsushi Odamaki, Alex Nguyen, Greg Morozumi, Elena Serrano, Christina Lee, Dina Shek, Paula Boaz, Shukuru Copeland, Raoul Estremera, Penny Schoener, Amy Little, Vicky Legion, Marilyn Kalman, Jim Cosner, Meg Yarnell, Eriko Ikehara, Mary Tomita, Ying Lee, Kiku Funabiki, Audrey Shoji, Scott Braley, Diana Block, Claude Mark, Dory Mazzone, Suzanne Ross, Monica Ly, Marilyn Fowler, Max Blanchet, Mariaposa Burciaga, Alice Arikawa, Hana Kawaguchi, Sun Hung Lee, Richard Aoki, Gerald Smith, Mamie Chow, Veronica Ang Vong, Bill Crossman, Ruth Morgan, Don Paul, Mike Cheng, Ben Wong, David Johnson, Aileen Hernandez, Raye Richardson, Anmol Chaddha, Kathy Liu, and family members Herb, Pam, Jimmy, Alison, Tommy, and Julie.

Photograph by Audee Kochiyama-Holman

San Pedro High School 64th Reunion, October 2003.
(FROM LEFT) Norma Benedetti Brutti/reunion coordinator, Yuri,
Norma's daughter-in-law, Amy Momonoi Wada, and Hildred Abny.

Photograph by Audee Kochiyama-Holman

San Pedro High School 64th Reunion, October 2003.
(FROM LEFT) Mary Rodriguez, Yuri, Rose Lauro,
Nadine Holt Truex, and Nan Carlson Grimm.

I also want to thank a special group of family and friends who helped me with mailings, shopping, research, and other chores: Liz Nakahara, Stephanie Tang, Monica Ly, Barbara Lubinski, Herb and Audee, and Eddie and Pam.

As I draw to a close to this memoir to "pass on" to my children, grandchildren, and great-grandchildren, I would like to mention some people of my past I will never forget. In the Sunday School class I taught before the war, I fondly recall Dorothy Hurley who was a very special junior high student. Close friends from San Pedro days who have kept in touch with me still are Norma Benedetti Brutti, Gloria Croskrey, Nan Carlson Grimm, Marion Peterson Lee, Mitch Mardesich, and Dorothy Mayo. I am sorry I have lost touch with Vivian Martinez (my closest friend up until the war), Zola Beardmore Crook, and Ann McKay. From San Pedro High School there were four athletes with whom I became good friends and who met unfortunate deaths either during or after World War II: Doug Adams, Merle Armstrong, Terry Croskrey, and Charles Schwartz. Some of my Nisei classmates from San Pedro High School were Monica Oana Miya, Fumi Okahana, Emi Momonoi Wada, and Yuri Endo Yoshihara. Two white comrades from the civil rights movement who have kept in touch with me are Suzanne Ross and Toby Emmer. Finally, I will always remember my Third World comrades, Bolanile Akinwole, Bibi Angola, Ajuba and Hisani Bartley, Haziine Eytina, Herman and Iyaluua Ferguson, Espe Martell, Muntu Matsimela, and especially Pat

Saunders and Nyisha Shakur. They were role model activists and leaders, all working in the Black and Puerto Rican movements.

Here are also some of the most significant moments in my movement life:

—meeting Malcolm X on October 16, 1963, and witnessing his assassination on February 21, 1965

—attending the Monroe, North Carolina hearing of Robert F. Williams after his return from China in 1968

—riding in a U-haul with ten citizens of the Republic of New Africa to a place they named El Malik in Mississippi in 1971

—attending the first Manzanar Pilgrimage in 1971

—participating in the 1977 take-over of the Statue of Liberty by Puerto Rican independentistas to demand the release of Andre Cordero, who was dying of cancer

—traveling to Cuba with the Venceremos Brigade in 1987

—traveling to Peru in 1993 on a human rights mission with Phil Farnham (RCP)

—traveling to the Philippines and Japan in 1994 to speak about the imprison-ment of Abimael Guzman and the revolution in Peru

—having the opportunity to meet Mumia Abu Jamal in prison in Waynes-burg, Pennsylvania (thanks to Susan Burnett, Mumia's visiting arranger)

—attending the well organized Tule Lake Pilgrimage in fall 2002

I want to thank those who supplied me with what I needed the most—stamps! They are Chiyo Itanaga, Suzy Ishikawa, Tuyen Tran, Sharon Maeda, Ruth Ishizaki, Shukuru Copeland, Richard Aoki, Helen Zia, Barbara Easley, Myrna Stephens, Nan Jun Kim, and family members Akemi, Tommy and Julie, Jimmy and Alison, Eddie and Pam, and Herb and Audee.

My gratitude goes to all political prisoners in the U.S., past and present, who taught me the meaning of struggle and sacrifice by fighting against racism, inequalities, evils and restrictions—that freedom, justice, truth, human dignity, and basic needs can one day be experienced by all. So, to you, political prisoners—Blacks, Latinos, American Indians, indigenous Hawaiians, white anti-imperialists and Asians—my thanks and admiration wherever you are, especially those who died behind the wall. You are the heartbeat of the struggle.

I am deeply indebted to my family for their patient, unconditional, and unselfish love for me. Up until my husband's passing in 1993, Bill was my primary source of support in so many ways—always taking care of things on the home front so that I could continue my movement activities. After Bill's death, Akemi and Zulu provided a great deal of help since they were the only two immediate family members in New York at that time. After moving to California, I was supported by the rest of the family who were living in Oakland and the Los Angeles area. It's been wonderful seeing our family grow, with Zulu and his wife Masai now having two kids, six-year-old Kai and one-year-old Kenji; and Akemi and her husband Marc with two-year-old Leilani and baby Malia. Our family will always carry the loving memories of Bill, Billy, Aichi, Alkamal, and Yasin.

I am grateful for all the people who came into my life and blessed me with their gift of friendship. To those of you from my hometown of San Pedro, California; from Santa Anita Assembly Center in California, Jerome concentration camp in Arkansas, and the Aloha USO in Hattiesburg, Mississippi; from Harlem, New York City; and now, in the Bay Area—I thank all of you who touched my life, energized my convictions, and left footprints in my heart.

Sgt. William M. Kochiyama

R E S T R I C T E D

HEADQUARTERS SEVENTH ARMY
APO 758   US Army

GENERAL ORDERS)
              :   16 July 1945
NUMBER   317)

Award of the Silver Star. I
Battle Honors - Citation of Unit. II

II - BATTLE HONORS - CITATION OF UNIT. By direction of the President, under
the provisions of Section IV, Circular No. 333, War Department, 1943, the
following named organization is cited for outstanding performance of duty in
action:

THE 3D BATTALION, 442D REGIMENTAL COMBAT TEAM is cited for outstanding
accomplishment in combat during the period 27 October to 30 October 1944, near
Biffontaine, France. On 27 October the 3d Battalion, 442d Regimental Combat
Team was committed to battle after one-and-a-half days in a divisional reserve. One of the battalions of another unit which had been advancing deep
into enemy territory beyond the town of Biffontaine was suddenly surrounded
by the enemy, and separated from all friendly units by an enemy force estimated
at seven hundred men. The mission of the 3d Battalion was to attack abreast
with the 100th Battalion and four other battalions and relieve the entrapped
unit. The mission was more difficult than it first appeared for the enemy had
reoccupied the thickly wooded hills situated within the two and one-half miles
separating the "lost battalion" from our front lines. For four days the Battalion fought the stubborn enemy who was determined to stop all attempts to
rescue the besieged battalion. Several roadblocks skillfully reinforced by
machine guns had to be destroyed while under heavy artillery fire. On 29
October the Battalion encountered a well defended hill where the enemy, one
hundred strong, held well dug-in positions on the hill and would not be dis-
lodged. After repeated frontal assaults had failed to drive the enemy from
the hill, Companies "I" and "K", then leading the attack, fixed bayonets and
charged up the slope, shouting at the enemy and firing from their hips, while
the enemy fired pointblank into their ranks. In spite of the effective enemy
fire the determined men pressed the assault and closed in with the enemy.
Nearing the enemy machine gun and machine pistol positions, some of the men
charged the gun emplacements with their Thompson sub-machine guns or BARs
killing or seriously wounding the enemy gun crew, but themselves sprawling
dead over the enemy positions they had just neutralized. Completely unnerved
by the vicious bayonet charge, the enemy fled in confusion after making a
desperate stand. Though seriously depleted in man-power, the Battalion hurled
back two determined enemy counterattacks, and after reducing a heavily mined

(over)
R E S T R I C T E D

From Yuri's "My Bill" scrapbook: the actual Citation of Battle Honors that
Bill Kochiyama's unit received. He was part of the famous battle to rescue
the "Lost Batallion" in the Vosges Mountains of Northern France.

The Role of the Nisei Soldier

By Bill Kochiyama

[The following is a speech Bill made at Hunter College on April 28, 1993. Because I was so impressed with how personal and informative his presentation was in describing the experiences and important roles of the Nisei in World War II, I wanted to include it here so that our children and grandchildren will know and never forget.]

I hope I will be able to provide you with a passing glimpse at the deep-reaching military experiences of Japanese Americans during World War II. Before I begin, I would like to preface my talk with my personal background so that you may better understand how I fit into this setting.

I was born in 1921 in Washington, DC and raised in New York City in West Harlem, where we presently reside. During the depression years (1929-1939) I was reared at Sheltering Arms, an institution that cared for children of low-income single parents and was affiliated with the Protestant Episcopal Church. Out of the 120 youngsters—sixty boys and sixty girls, ages five to eighteen—I was the only one of color. Not surprisingly, I grew up aspiring to become a Caucasian, while rejecting everything to do with my Asian, that is, my Japanese heritage. Subconsciously I hated who I was.

While growing up I seldom came in contact with other Japanese, or for that matter, with other Asian Americans—Chinese, Koreans, or Filipinos. According to pre-1940 census, there were only about 3,000 ethnic Japanese in the entire tri-state region of New York, New Jersey, and Connecticut.

In spring 1940, at age twenty, I took off to the West Coast hoping to enroll at the University of California at Berkeley. Because I was unable to afford tuition fees for non-residents, I had to find employment. In my quest for a job, I experienced the painful reality of racism. Unions, which were very powerful in California in those days, would not accept Asian Americans as members, and the white-collar world was exactly that—for whites only. For the first time in my life, I felt like a second-class citizen. Everywhere I went, I was advised to find work with "my own people," a grim prospect because I did not know anything about "my own people." In desperation I sought help from a Japanese employment agency in San Francisco's Little Tokyo that directed me to a large dry cleaning and laundry establishment in Oakland. The business serviced whites, while all of its employees were of Japanese ancestry.

About a week after Japan's attack on Pearl Harbor, the firm was forced to suspend operations. Subsequently I tried to enlist in the Armed Forces: first with the Army, then the Navy, and finally the Marine Corps. At each recruiting station I was flatly rejected. "Japs" were persona non grata. Little did I know that officially Japanese Americans were not admissible in the Navy, Marine Corps, Army Air Force, Coast Guard or Merchant Marine. On January 5, 1942, the War Department classified Japanese American men of draft age as 4C—enemy alien unfit for military service.

In swift succession an 8 pm-to-6 am curfew and a five-mile travel ban were imposed only on persons of Japanese descent. This was followed by Executive Order 9066 issued on February 19, 1942, which set in motion the mass incarceration of 120,000 people of Japanese ancestry, two-thirds of whom were American citizens.

On May 6, 1942, four days before my twenty-first birthday, I was among some 8,000 Japanese Americans from the San Francisco Bay Area who were herded into the Tanforan Assembly Center, a race track converted into a temporary detention camp, where we lived in manure-smelling horse stalls.

Six months later, on September 16, 1942, we were railroaded to Topaz, Utah, situated in the middle of an alkali desert. This permanent mass internment camp was euphemistically called a relocation center. Of ghastly significance, the Nazis used the same term "relocation" to move Jews to concentration/death camps. Ours were not death camps, thank God, but they were certainly concentration camps, which Webster's New World Dictionary defines as: "A prison camp in which political dissidents, and members of minority ethnic groups, etc., are confined."

Topaz, as well as each of the other nine mass internment camps, was a mile-square enclave, where some 8,000 to 10,000 men, women, young children (including orphans and newborn babies) as well as the seriously handicapped, the blind or paralyzed, and the very elderly were imprisoned. Barbed wire fences surrounded the camp, with searchlights and guard towers at each corner of the compound. Armed sentries of the United States Army patrolled the outer perimeters.

On January 28, 1943, the War Department announced plans to form an all-Japanese American combat unit. On April 7, I answered the call for volunteers, and on the following day I was released from Topaz and on my way home to New York, where I was reunited with my father after two-and-a-half years of separation. In May I was inducted into the Army, and on June 16, I joined K Company, 442nd Infantry Regiment at Camp Shelby, Mississippi, which was known as the hellhole of the South.

Although the fighting record of the 442nd is well known and documented, it bears repeating. Composed of men almost equally from Hawaii and the mainland U.S., this unique outfit became and remains the most decorated unit in U.S. military history for its size and length of service. In seven major campaigns in Italy and France, the regiment won over 18,000 individual decorations for valor, including the Congressional Medal of Honor; an unprecedented eight Presidential Distinguished Unit Citations, and 9,500 Purple Hearts, which translates into a 308 percent casualty rate. The total U.S. casualties per Americans in uniform in World War II were 5.8 percent. Casualties per number of Japanese Americans in uniform was 28.5 percent—almost five times greater than that of the overall American forces.

Two U.S. Senators from Hawaii served with the "Go For Broke" unit: Daniel K. Inouye, who lost his right arm in combat and who was awarded the Distinguished Service Cross for heroism under fire; and the late Spark M. Matsunaga, who won the Silver Star for bravery and who was wounded twice in action. Both rose to the rank of Captain.

The bloodiest single battle fought by the 442nd was in the rescue of the "Lost Battalion," which was surrounded by enemy troops in the Vosges Mountains of north-eastern France. In its effort to rescue the 211 men of the 1st Battalion, 141st Infantry Regiment of the 36th (Texas) Division, the 442nd lost more than 1,000 men in casualties.

Bill and friend. Handwriting reads: town of Aix, France Sept, 44
Vosges "Lost Battalion" Tragedy. From Yuri's "My Bill" scrapbook.

This is only half the story of the Japanese American soldier in World War II. Classified as "secret—restricted information" by the War Department for almost three decades is the little known account of the exploits of the 6,000 Japanese Americans who served with the United States Military Intelligence Service in the Pacific Theatre of Operations. They translated captured Japanese documents, interpreted enemy communications, interrogated prisoners of war, deciphered enemy codes, and gathered intelligence behind enemy lines. In addition, they participated in every major invasion, including going in with the first wave of assault troops at such places as: Attu in Alaska, Guadalcanal, New Guinea, Leyte, Solomon Islands, Saipan, Iwo Jima, New Caledonia, Bougainville, the Philippines, and Okinawa.

They serviced individually or in small groups and were attached to every branch of the U.S. armed forces—the Army, Navy, and Marines. In addition, they served on foreign assignment with Allied forces from Australia, Canada, China, Great Britain, India, and New Zealand.

The Japanese American soldiers in the Pacific distinguished themselves on and off the battlefields. Many were killed and wounded while performing extraordinary acts of bravery, while others did outstanding intelligence work. The decorations they won were far out of proportion to their numbers. After V-J Day, from 1945 to 1952, more than 5,000 Japanese American linguists played an important role in the Occupation of Japan, where they took part in all of the major assignments covering military government, disarmament, civil affairs, counter intelligence, civil censorship, the War Crimes Trial, and repatriation program. Top commanding officers have made the following statements about the Americans of Japanese ancestry in the Military Intelligence Service:

Colonel Sidney Forrester Mashbir, Commandant, Allied Translator and Interpreter Section—"The United States of America owes a debt to these men (Nisei linguists) and to their families which it can never fully repay."

Major General Frank D. Merrill, Commander of the Merrill's Marauders in Burma —"As for the value of the Nisei, I couldn't have gotten along without them."

Major General Charles Willoughby, G-2 Intelligence Chief of General MacArthur's Command—"The Nisei saved countless Allied lives and shortened the war by two years."

General Joseph (Vinegar Joe) Stillwell, Commander of U.S. Troops in China/Burma/ India Theatre—"The Nisei bought an awful big hunk of America with their blood."

A concluding note: the Japanese American soldiers paid their dues the hard way. Over 33,000 of them served in the United States military during World War II and its immediate aftermath, including some 300 in the Women's Army Corps and Army Nurse Corps. Their wartime record and sacrifices proved once and for all that they were loyal Americans. They earned the right to walk tall. This is the proud legacy they have bequeathed to their children and grandchildren.

A Song for Redress/Reparation

[Sung to the tune "Battle Hymn of the Republic"]

By Yuri Kochiyama

Oh, forty years have passed, and yet a people can't forget
A Presidential Order that a nation should regret
An Order that uprooted and made incarcerees
Of a single ancestry.

Chorus
It's time for Redress/Reparation
Restitution from our nation
Justice calls for compensation
for 120,000 wronged!
To deserts, swamps, and mountains we were sent across the land
To concentration camps for war's duration it was planned
We victims of hysteria and greed and bigotry
of Japanese ancestry.

(Chorus)
And yes, our brothers, fathers, sons went on to volunteer
And gave their lives in sacrifice, our futures to secure
A Regiment has carved a name in U.S. history
Of Japanese ancestry!

(Chorus)
(*Sing slowly*) And many were those left behind in camp-deserted graves
(*Sing slowly*) And those whose lives were shattered or whose minds could not be saved
But facts will be recorded of this great catastrophe
Of Japanese ancestry!

(Chorus)
[Repeat last chorus three times; last time, last line—end on high note]

Scrapbook Memories, 1942

This album is a conglomeration of snapshots and pictures, haphazardly and hurriedly scrambled together in the last week before evacuation in April 1942. The pictures, however, were not placed in this scrapbook until after the war. They were carried loosely with me from one move to another; through all of camp-life, USO-work, back to camp, and home again to San Pedro.

The pictures are but a small segment of school and hometown friends. Lack of time and space prevented me from carrying more. I took along whatever pictures I could carry on my person. The rest, left behind, were probably misplaced or lost in the hustle-bustle and shuffle.

I am only sorry I had no snapshots of many of my closest friends, neighbors, and family friends. However, the fellows and girls in these shots represent the town that meant so much to me when I lived there, and even more so when I left. They gave me the one gift that might be taken anywhere. . .to keep, to add on to, to give, and share with others. . .always. That gift was friendship.

They are assembled here. . .for "auld lang syne" and happy memories. In my scrapbook was a poem I wrote just after we were evacuated, something for my hometown of San Pedro:

You asked if ever loneliness would steal across my heart,
When thinking of the hometown with which we had to part.
Oh, yes, I often ponder o'er the town I loved so dear,
But somehow, wishful thinking brings the old friends very near.
I do not miss the seashore, I do not miss the hill;
I do not miss the old haunts where all the people mill.
Tis' not the hometown places that tears away the heart.
Tis' all the hometown faces that make the teardrops start.
I miss the little children I used to see each day.
I miss the happy school-folks who passed along my way.
I miss my fellow-classmates, I'd hope by chance to meet.
I miss the kindly neighbors and people on our street.
I miss the "skirted soldiers," the troopers of our corp.
I miss the ones I worked with in a five-and-ten-cent store.
I miss the many girls I used to have in class.
I miss the local athletes and those we'd cheer en masse.
I miss the hometown fellows who left the harbor town.
In service of their country; no thoughts to seek renown.
I miss the many others I only knew by sight,
For they, too, are the portion who make my burdens light.
Oh yes, I miss the hometown, and oft' my heart does ache,
But mem'ries close the distance, a gap it cannot make.
For sometime in the future, I do not know just when,
Our paths will knit together, I'll see them all again.

—May 1942

Yuri's Rock
By Zayid Muhammad, Front-line Artist

[A love song for Bill and Yuri Kochiyama upon the occasion of Bill's passing in October 1993]

when i last saw the two of u together
we were at the Caribbean cultural center
celebrating one of our favorite heroic common denominators
Malcolm X
thru a rich tamarind-tongued Garvey-based analysis
of Caribbean scholar Tony Martin. . .
we were mutually in between
ducking the desperately bitter bite
of a late winter wind. . .
and although we had no way of knowing it
it wd be the last time
that i wd see the both of u together. . .
but i must say
the way i saw u that nite
the way u were with each other
crystallized clearly for me
what u two have clearly meant for each other
for all these decades that u've shared and endured
together. . .
and it was the little things that did it
the little subtle things
in how u two were communicating with each other
almost without saying a word
that just made it so clear. . .
and isnt it often the little things
that do it for two people
who truly find what u two truly found
in each other?
Bill's cool and calm/anchoring
Yuri's demonstrative petite-defying passion
i mean u know Yuri
if somebody is saying something important
saying something with an analysis
and saying about Malcolm too
the way Tony Martin was
i mean u know Yuri
she even listens with a lot of energy
i mean if she had leaned anymore forward
she wd've wound up in Tony Martin's breast pocket. . .
yet with every syllable
her hand was either in yrs, Bill

or on yr lap
clinging ever so slightly
to u/her rock
and u so proud and so content
to be just that
Yuri's rock. . .
so what then did it take for u to become the rock
of somebody so precious for so long?
well, from what she tells us
it was some of yr 'smart-alecky' comic cynicism
some of yr sun-sized loyal beaming
about yr 120 brothers and sisters
some of yr embarrassing honesty about forgetting
the day u two met
and it was definitely some of yr chilled-out urban-eyed
manhattan groove. . .
it was definitely some of yr skin-saving graceful way
of using her 90some-odd love letters
to sidestep Nazi artillery and shells
definitely some of yr scars from u and 442* comrades
just as facist-skinning graceful
laying scores of those same Nazis
into the waste-can of history
it was in some of the even way u carried the outrage
of yr people being caged and bayoneted
into the hypocrisy of u.s. democracy
at home/and then their being scorched into it
under a senseless nuclear sun/back home
it was definitely some of how u handled all of that. . .
it was yr willingness to make the space u two shared
a place of refuge for those of yr comrades
who needed a place of refuge
it was yr balance about things
like dishes, cooking and cleaning
about keeping kids and a home together
and plants alive. . .
it was yr dark sparkle
whenever we praised yr precious spouse
for her precious place in our hearts and lives
and from reading her eyes, Bill
it was definitely some of yr
chilled-out urban-eyed manhattan groove. . .
u really had to have 'what it takes'
to earn and keep the honor and the trust
of someone so precious for so long. . .
and our world knows so few
so gracious so giving
so proud so tender

so modest so sincere
so tireless so principled
so determined so available
so clear so correct
so intense so nurturing
so selfless
so selfless
and so precious. . .
yeah, Bill, really had to have 'what it takes'
to earn and keep the honor and trust
of such a precious spouse
such a focused partner
such an enduring lover
such an empowering comrade. . .
and it was clear to me that nite
crystal clear
just in the little ways
u two touched each other
just what it meant for u to be the anchoring rock
for yr special spouse that u were
for so many years. . .
the personal is political
and the political is personal. . .
and just think
u two had that
for 47 years. . .
and the way brothers start dying around 35
hell, i hope to live to be 47
and to get a chance
somewhere along the way
even if just for a little while
to be
a special somebody's anchor
the way u were
Yuri's rock. . .
*not only was the late Bill Kochiyama a fine human rts
activist-husband-father; he was also a proud veteran of the
widely-heralded japanese-amerikkkan 442nd battalion that
kicked ass in ww2s european theater

bro. Zayid
30 October 1993

Third World

M. Kochiyama

Whether in the Black, Brown, Red, or Yellow movement, the term THIRD WORLD makes its appearance on flyers; is hurled about in speeches, pops up in raps; is unfurled on banners and carried on posters. What does it mean? How and where did it originate?

The words were first used at the United Nations to split the socialist ranks at the time of the Bandung conference led by Sukarno in Indonesia in 1955.

The Third World presupposes a First and Second World. United States and the Western World had been considered the First World—the "have" world of power and influence, the world of capitalism. The Soviet Union and Eastern Europe comprised the Second World – the world in progress towards communism, opposing capitalism.

The Third World is that world that the first two worlds are dominating and controlling under the channels of 'development.' This world, Africa, Asia, and Latin America, is the world of the Black, Brown, and Yellow peoples seeking independence of the first two worlds. Its ultimate goal is survival and salvation; the right to national self-determination.

Sukarno called the Third World the Bandung World, meaning the world of dark-raced peoples. In 1955, this was the uncommitted world in limbo. Today, it is the world of transition towards liberation.

Globally, the Third World is becoming united by common oppression, but also divided by the lures of "economic and military aid" enticed by the powers of the first two worlds.

The upheavals in the Third World is widespread. The realization of self-determination is electrifying. Thus, the cause of Palestine is that of Vietnam's; the liberation struggles of Mozambique and Angola are related to the guerrillas' involvement in Uruguay and Bolivia. The Philippines' sentiment against military colonialism is mutual with that of Puerto Rico's.

The Black man's degrading experience in Amerika corresponds

with the treatment of the Indians, Eskimos, and Chicanos in both Amerikas, and the Aborigines in Australia. The uprisings in the Caribbeans, the denunciations of the Micronesians, and the demands of the Okinawans are all the voices of the Third World, the world's oppressed. They are reverberating a powerful message that "paternalism is 'out' and total liberation is 'in.'."

The Third World and its descendents in the western hemisphere are in motion. It is a life-and-death struggle to cast off the shackles of imperialism and colonialism, and obliterate racism. Death is not just physical. Psychological and emotional damage has taken its toll in loss of identity even here in Amerika as revealed in the Asian movement.

The Third World must oppose, challenge, confront and halt transgression of imperialistically-inclined powers, including those in their own world, for imperialism knows no color or geographic lines. The Third World must offer an alternative—a more humane way of life, where diversity of peoples, cultures, religions, and ideologies will enhance civilization, rather than proscribe life. Economic systems must truly meet peoples' needs of commodities and services without exploitation of man by man, and without racial denigration violating the humanity and dignity of man. . .all men.

"In the Third World," states Ibrahim Makhous, Prime Minister of Syria, "national liberation and social transformation must go together, taking place at the same time. The world must be a beautiful garden, each people being a rose of their own coloring, its own perfume. Each people should enrich civilization with its own genius, its own creations, its own achievements."

From: *Asian Americans for Action Newsletter*, II:2 (Oct 1970), p. 5

A History of Linkage: African and Asian, African-American and Asian-American

By Yuri Kochiyama, Institute of Multiracial Justice newsletter,
"Shades of Power," 1:1 (Spring 1998), 3-5.

Much of the history of African/Asian and Black American/Asian American interactions is not as well-known as it should be. All peoples of whatever race or color have criss-crossed into each other's lives more than we think. But such history, like all true history, has often been hidden, lied about, or distorted. Malcolm X used to admonish: "Study history. Learn about yourselves and others. There's more commonality in all our lives than we think. It will help us understand one another." We also need to remember that history, depending on how it is told, can be used as a weapon to divide us further, or as a vehicle to seek truths that might bring us to greater mutual understanding.

Unfortunately, thanks to the mass media, we are more likely to hear about ways that we are divided. We hear about attacks on African students at Nanjing University in China, the killing of 15-year old African American Latasha Harlins by a Korean shopkeeper in Los Angeles, and anti-Korean actions following the verdict on the beating of Rodney King. These events also reveal the social and economic gaps between peoples of color.

But there is so much that unites us, which we do not learn. As Gary Okihiro observed in a paper he wrote: "Africans and Asians share a history of migration, interaction, and cultural sharing. They share a history of European colonization, decolonizatin, and independence under new colonization and dependency. Africans and Asians share a history of oppression in the U.S., successively serving as slave and cheap labor. . ."

Filipino Slaves Come

The first Asians who came to the United states were Filipino slaves, who were originally taken to Mexico by Spanish and Portuguese merchants in the 18th and 19th centuries. They escaped to New Orleans, Louisiana, where their descendants live today, in their own communities. Also in that period, people from China and India were sold to European and American ship captains as "coolies" in the same way that pigs were sold: they were put in pigpens, nearly naked and filthy, with their destinations pained on their chests. Many Chinese workers were sent to Latin America.

Between 1870 and 1890, when Congress was debating the infamous Chinese Exclusion Act barring Chinese immigrants, African American leaders like Frederick Douglass and Augustus Straker spoke out against the bill. They considered the objections to the Chinese "in kind and principle" identical to attacks on blacks, and said that their opponents were the same as those of the Chinese. Senator Blanche K. Bruce of Mississippi, the only African American in the U.S. Senate, voted courageously against limiting the rights of the Chinese people by the Exclusion Act.

During the Spanish-American War of 1898, some 6,000 Black soldiers sent to the Philippines with Theodore Roosevelt's "Rough Riders" were repelled by the American atrocities (600,000 Filipino civilians massacred). Feeling kinship with their "brown brothers, " as they said, the Black soldiers risked their lives by joining the Filipino guerillas.

At the turn of the Century, a Japanese man named Sen Katayama became the first Asian to attend a Black college in the southern United States. He went on to be an outstanding labor leader and friend of the acclaimed Black writer of the Harlem Renaissance period, Claude McKay. Together they organized the Communist Party in New York. U.S. labor history has ignored Katayama, probably because racism marginalized workers of color.

In the early 1920s another Asian came to the U.S. while in exile for his work to free Vietnam from French colonialism. Ho Chi Minh lived in the ghettoes of Chicago and Harlem, became an admirer of Black leader Marcus Garvey, and wrote one of the earliest books on racism in the United States (it was published in the Soviet Union). During the U.S. war on Vietnam he was seen as a hero by Blacks and other Americans opposed to the war, who often considered it a racist war and identified with its victims.

In the 1930s the Black historian and leader W.E.B. DuBois, visited China, Manchuria and Japan. DuBois met Mao Tse-tung and other Chinese leaders. Famed Black Americans who have visited the People's Republic of China also include Langston Hughes, Vicki Garvin, Robert Williams, and several members of the Black Panther Party.

Interaction was common between African-Americans and the Japanese as well. In the midwesten United States, immigrant Japanese related to the newly emerging Nation of Islam (NOI), and some made ties for the purpose of friendship and trade. In early 1940 Elijah Muhammed and others of the NOI went to jail because they would not support World War II against Japan and spoke out against it; they also opposed the concentration camps where Japanese Americans were sent at the time. First generation Issei Japanese worked with militant Black nationalists in those years.

The historic 1955 conference of non-aligned nations held in Bandung, Indonesia brought together African and Asian leaders in a historic gathering. The U.S. was irked at not being invited but many prominent Blacks attended, including Adam Clayton Powell and Margaret Cartwright, the first Black reporter assigned to the United Nations. The Bandung conference was organized by Indonesian president Ahmad Sukarno, whom Malcolm X held in high esteem because he would not bow down to the white man.

The 1950s also saw the United States getting embroiled in the Korean War. At a huge rally in New York, the distinguished and charismatic Black leader Paul Robeson declared that "it would be foolish for African Americans to fight against their Asian brother." He urged Blacks to resist being drafted and said that "the place for the Negro people to fight for their freedom is at home." Despite world wide recognition for Robeson's many talents—as a football hero, lawyer, actor, singer, and speaker —he came to be seen as a threat by the United States. In reality he was an anti-imperialist internationalist and lover of humanity.

The 1960s brought many acts of solidarity involving Asians and Blacks alongside Latinos and Native Americans. We find these in protests against the Vietnam War; support for the "I" Hotel in San Francisco; student struggles for ethnic studies. There was much interaction between Black Panthers, the Student Nonviolent Coordinating Committee (SNCC), Young Lords, I Wor Kuen, Brown Berets and other Chicano groups, the Red Guards, and Manila Town Filipino activists. Together Asian activists supported Wounded Knee in the West and the Attica Brothers on the East Coast; the fight to bring the People's Republic of China into the United Nations; and support for Third World political prisoners throughout the country including Puerto Rican independistas.

Beyond our borders, Mao Tse-tung, leader of the emerging People's Republic of China, said during the 1968 urban riots by African Americans: "I hereby express resolute support for the just struggle of the Black people in the United States." In that same period Mao sent thousands of workers to help build the railroads between Zambia and Tanzania in East Africa. Chinese workers also helped to construct the national sports stadium in Zimbabwe and a library in Harare. In addition, Zimbabwe received teams from North Korea. An outstanding Korean woman writer, Pak Sunam, always referred to Franz Fanon—the Martinique-born psychiatrist who became a powerful voice of anti-colonial, antiracist struggle—as "her brother."

There are many stories of solidarity featuring Malcolm X; he probably impressed Asian Americans, in particular youth, more than any other Black leader. In June, 1964 Malcolm met with Japanese atom-bomb victims who came to New York for plastic surgery and toured the U.S. speaking out against nuclear proliferation. They were deeply impressed by Malcolm's graciousness and openness. Malcolm also spoke of his admiration for Mao Tse-tung and his support for Vietnam's struggle, which he saw as the struggle of the whole Third World.

Another important area of Black/Asian interruption has been music, primarily jazz. Coltrane, Max roach, Milford Graves, Herbie Hancock and other jazz greats made periodic tours to Japan, as did reggae artists such as Jimmy Cliff. At the same time, Asian American musicians like Fred Ho, Mark Izu and Francis Wong have created jazz combos. Dancer/singer Nobuko Miyamoto and poet Janice Mirikitani are heralded by Black audiences.

There are still more examples of Black/Asian interaction. But much remains to be done to build bridges and create a united force that can challenge the system in which those with wealth and power live high off the toil and desperation of the marginalized. We must all work to break down the barriers and phobias and build working relations, while understanding that each group has its own primary issues and needs its own privacy and leadership. If we want to change society, we must begin by transforming ourselves: learning from one another about one another's history, culture, dreams, hopes, personal experiences. We must become one, for the future of humanity.

Note: This article is a condensed version of a speech made by Ms. Kochiyama at the African/Asian round Table, San Francisco State University, on Oct. 1, 1997. The author, a Japanese American born in California, is a longtime community activist living in Harlem who has worked on many issues, in particular supporting political prisoners. She worked closely with militant Puerto Rican groups like the Young Lords Party and was a member of the Organization of Afro-American Unity as well as a close friend of Malcolm X.

Note: As a result of Yuri Kochiyama's internship at UCLA Asian American Studies Center, she formed warm and inspiring relationships with many of UCLA's student activists. She had a weekly brown bag lunch with students where they would ask her whatever questions they had on their minds. This invaluable time Yuri spent with students motivated Russell Muranaka, along with Tram Nguyen, Vy Nguyen, Raymond Real Ribaya, and Kit Tarroza, to publish a pamphlet entitled "Discover your Mission: Selected Speeches and Writings of Yuri Kochiyama." Because of the popularity of this publication, we have reproduced sections of the pamphlet. Appendix 8 and 9 are from "Discover your Mission."

Appendix 8

Mothers and Daughters

By Yuri Kochiyama, from "Discover your Mission: Selected Speeches
& Writings of Yuri Kochiyama," UCLA Asian American Studies Center, June 1998

Just three words—"Mothers and Daughters." Yet how much content and substance emerges from those three words. They encompass history, bridge generations, conjure nostalgia, ramify into women's struggle. From a personal story to the larger perspective, the three words give life to "her" story—women, the world over.

The first word, "mother," as defined in the dictionary, besides "giving birth to," states—"give rise to, to care for, to protect like a mother." Thus, a woman need not give birth to, or produce a child—to be considered in the "mother category." And how many women we all know who have cared for, brought up or gave protection to—some child or countless children in their lifetime. That does not include just nurses, teachers, therapists, scout mothers, and camp counselors. Women in all fields of work have been "mothers" or surrogate mothers. All women are potential mothers, if not actual mothers.

The second word, "and," which indicates connection, the link; gives continuity, is the bridge.

As for the word "daughter,"—the offspring, the reality is that every woman is someone's daughter in a real sense—biologically.

As Asian mothers and daughters, what would be the particularities that we should express or pass on? Would there be differences in our role as Asian or ethnic mothers in this Euro-American society? What would be the similarities? Or does motherhood transcend color and race and geographical lines?

Nearly 50 years ago, as a junior high school student in San Pedro, California, I read for the first time the moving words of the Lebanese poet, Kahlil Gibran. I liked his book, "The Prophet," in which he writes about the universal facets of life—Love, Joy, Work, Pain, Death, etc. I enjoyed with relish the contents of his poem "On Children" as I was going into the rebellious teenage years. It seemed the words were meant for my Issei parents, or immigrants parents in general, who could not seem to understand their Americanizing children, never thinking about what the Isseis had to undergo in this country, or what their thoughts would be on any given matter. It never occurred to me, wither, that I would one day be a parent, and Gibran's words would be applying to me.

Excerpts of the poem read:

Your children are not your children

They are the sons and daughters of
Life's longing for itself.
They come through you but not from you.
And though they are with you, yet
they belong not to you.
You may give them your love, but
not your thoughts.
You may house their bodies, but not
their souls.
For their souls dwell in the house of
tomorrow, which you cannot
visit; not even in your dream.
You may strive to be like them,
but seek not to make them like you.
For life goes not backward nor
tarries with yesterday. . .

His words hold true in many ways that we cannot "hang on" to our children, nor shape their lives, as their lives are theirs to develop, but as I reflect in the poem today, I disagree with Gibran that we can only "house their bodies, but not their souls;" that we can only "give them our love, but not our thoughts." I believe a mother has a right and a responsibility to give her children, not necessarily "her" thoughts, but the best thoughts from whatever source that could help to bring greater depth, breadth, and understanding of life to her children.

Some assessment on this society must be made for them. Ethnic mothers must teach their children the desire to challenge and struggle against the frailties and evils of chauvinism and greed that create the rich and powerful and its counterpart, the poor and oppressed. The contradictions may seem "distant" to Asian Americans who are no longer marginal, but new refugee Asians are facing not only serious financial problems, but physical hostilities. The tragic killing of Vincent Chin in Detroit is a prime example of the dangerous possibilities—to any Asian. Neither can we disregard or obscure the demeaning, disparaging existence for many Blacks, Hispanics, and Indigenous on the periphery of this society.

Going back to the subject of motherhood, I must delve back into my own past. The reality is that when I become a first-time mother, my primary interest was hardly on any lofty plane of what to imbue in my child, but rather, in frantically trying to learn the ABC's of diapering, feeding and cleaning the baby; doing the everyday chores and watching the infant grow with awe and delight as it literally physically changes.

As a neophyte mother and a recent transplant to this hustling/bustling New York City, an apolitical provincial, motherhood and New York were both a new world and a challenge. And like most mothers, one's own mother is the most likely resource for advice, help, and direction. For the first time, I felt a real mother-daughter relationship. How often she used to say when she was young, "you won't understand until you become a mother yourself." How true those words were.

Reflecting on my mother, I feel she was the best role model of an Asian woman I could ever wished for, or have ever known. Sadly I never told her nor expressed the kind of appreciation I wish I had while she was alive. It seems there were some difficulties in communicating deep feelings. I often wondered if this was a common Japanese or Asian mother/daughter relationship.

My mother was quite like any other Issei mother —hard-working, caring, living the life of the traditional devoted wife and mother. She lived, however, an easier life than most Japanese of that time—as our whole family also did, because we lived in a "white" neighborhood. My father owned a fish market in San Pedro. The neighborhood was mostly Slavonian and Italian, and their fathers were also in the fishing business.

However, most Japanese in our area lived either in the San Pedro Hills as vegetable farmers or on Terminal Island—a Japanese fishing village, across the bay from San Pedro—as fisherman or cannery workers. We, Japanese who lived in the heart of San Pedro proper, lived like any "white" person as part of the mainstream. The lives of both the Terminal Islanders and the San Pedro Hill farmers were much harsher and isolated.

From a comfortable, secure life—abruptly came the bombing of Pearl Harbor, the FBI round-up on December 7th in which my father was taken to prison, and his untimely death a month and a half later. My mother's life changed drastically.

My admiration for my mother grew as we started our new life in the camps. Despite the shock and grief and upheaval of those few months after Pearl Harbor, my mother's adjustment to camp-life in Santa Anita's race-track Assembly Center and Jerome and Rohwer, Arkansas camps in the forest, was remarkable. She did things I never imagined her doing. She regenerated into a new person—or I never knew her outside of a stereo-typed Japanese mother/wife—although I was aware that she was a schoolteacher in Japan. Perhaps she also had to maintain a certain image of respectability of a Japanese middle-class woman.

But suddenly she was working as a waitress in the mess hall; volunteering as a chaperone at the camp's USO program; helping in the distribution of the firewood for the block; assisting in youth work; and writing to countless Hawaii, 442 Nisei soldiers as a surrogate mother. She overcame her grief. She was amply occupied.

My older brother and I left for outside jobs, leaving her alone in camp. (My twin brother was already overseas in the South Pacific.) She never tried to hold us back. She encouraged us. Ironically, I left on Mother's Day, although I didn't realize it until I was on the bus. I invited her to visit where I worked before I had found living quarters. (My work was at the Aloha USO in Hattiesburg, a USO specifically founded for the Japanese American Combat Team by a concerned Chinese American YMCA Director, Hung Wai Ching, in Honolulu.) I wrote that we would have to sleep on the USO floor—next to a young Latin army wife/mother and her baby. In fact, "Mom" thought it would be fun.

My mother's credence for independence had surfaced earlier when she allowed my brothers and I, from our teenage years, total freedom to choose our own friends (bringing them home any time), make our own decisions and mistakes, and pursue our own interests. Comparing with other Issei parents, who were stricter, I thought my mother was quite unusual. Of course, I felt very unfortunate. This freedom and trust she gave to us, I think was an important legacy to utilize when I became a parent.

Just prior to World War II, at age 20, I was attending a special class at the Los Angeles Presbytery, taking a course on "how to work with children." The teacher, a vibrant women in her 60's, brought home one point incisively, injecting it in our minds: "It is more important what you teach a child to love than what you teach a child to know." That one thought could ramify in many ways. Again, it was something to remember. Through the years her words sifted back. "It's more important what you teach a child to love than what you teach a child to know."

If ever it was more clearly amplified, it came about 30 years later in Harlem listening to the teachings of the phenomenal Black leader, Malcolm X, who has been immortalized since his assassination in 1965. Although at that time he was vilified by the power structure and the press as a "hater," the clarity of his many pronouncements transcend all the defamatory remarks made against him.

Malcolm used to admonish repetitively to be clear on what one should love—to love justice, freedom, dignity, pride, equity, and truth. He also pointed out what should be hated with equal magnitude—injustice, inequity, brutality, denial, derogation, stigmatizing, hypocrisy, duality, lies—the whole spectrum of racism. The objectives of what to strive for or against were unquestionable. The essence of love and hate were sharply defined, not ambiguous.

For a mother with six children ranging in age from 4 to 16, listening to Malcolm weekly was like attending class on ethics and struggle.

But as to any insight on the particularities of an Asian American mother's role, I was still ignorant—other than what my Issei mother left me. It was not until after the Civil Rights period was over and the fight for Ethnic Studies and the protest of the Vietnam War was underway that the movement for Asian American consciousness came into being.

It was at the point that the identity crisis surfaced and the reality of its impact had Asian American activists and students scurrying to seek their roots, learn about their history, study their heritage and culture. Again, Malcolm's wisdom was heedful. He had been saying to his people to "find your roots. Where are you from? How did you get here and why? What has happened to you?" Asians began a serious search into themselves, their foreparents, the history of their experience in America.

The role of the Asian Woman became a pertinent issue. Study and research brought out that foreign domination, Asian traditions and Confucianism had unequivocally restricted full growth, psychologically, mentally, politically; dwarfed her potentials; curtailed her activities; and limited her interests; depreciating the status of women generally. However, the Vietnam War catapulted a new Asian Woman—the courageous women of Vietnam—working and fighting side by side with their fighting men, driving vehicles, working in the factories, on the wharves; caring for the children in the village hamlets, bombed out hospitals and makeshift schools; representing their government in international conferences in Geneva and Paris; or trying to survive in the brutal tiger cages of Con Son. Yes, we had our heroines—Asian women heroines—and even my two young daughters proudly posted pictures of Madame Binh, a representative of Vietnam's Provisional Revolutionary Government, on their bedroom wall along with other women and children of Vietnam.

My daughters are Sanseis, third generation Japanese Americans, post-World War II babies; products of the environment and the times. The environment was two New York City Housing Projects, heavily Black and Puerto Rican. Their growing up years were in the midst of the historic Civil Rights period of the 60's, followed by the Anti-Vietnam era of the 70's. American social mores were being challenged. The Christian churches were being criticized. Upheavals were political and cultural. Ethnicity was being recognized. Racism was being exposed. Polarization was expanding. Radicalism was in. The streets was "where it was happening." The ghettos of major cities were burning during the summers of '66, '67, '68.

Audee and Aichi, like their older brother Billy, were breathing in the fervor and excitement of their time and their peers. (Their two younger brothers, Eddie and Jimmy, were in grammar school; Tommy was still a pre-schooler.) It was not only a period of "their" growth, but all of our growth. America was being forced to look at herself; also to change. . .at least for a while. Her dirty linens were being dragged outside the world to see. And it was youths, especially Black youths who were in the forefront of this struggle.

It was the early 60's and it was the eye-opening, mind- boggling introduction to Muslims, Yorubas, Five Percenters, Garveyism, and Black nationalism. Harlem, for the K-family, was like an open university for Black Studies.

Up to that point in their lives, Audee and Aichi, three years apart, were finding themselves in the ballet dance world and considered highly by their teachers at the Met. . .but suddenly the heat of the civil rights movement impacted their lives and they tossed their ballet slippers for sneakers. By the time they were finishing junior high school, they were into thick demonstrations, marches, picket-lines; fundraising for SNCC, petitioning the release of arrested activists, and joining an active teenage group called Students Against Social Injustice.

At the age of 15, Audee—as a member of High School SNCC, went down South in 1965, as did her older brother Billy, to get a "taste" of the more serious struggle in the rural areas of Mississippi. The three Civil Rights workers, Goodman, Schwerner, and Chaney were killed the year before.

By 18, Audee was a young mother. She had met a personable young activist with the Mississippi Student Union. Her activities had to be curtailed for domestic chores. Zulu, our first grandchild, became the family's pride and joy. Three years later, it was Aichi following suit, giving birth to a beautiful part-Indian, part-Japanese child named Akemi Kawazan. The father was one of the younger members of the Black Panther Party.

The hectic growing-up years sped by much too fast. The times seemed urgent and demanding. Our family life-styles and priorities changed. Social gatherings became political gatherings. It was not fair to the three youngest who missed out on the usual traditional activities around the holidays. It all began in 1963 with the bombing of the Baptist Church in Birmingham, Alabama where the four girls were killed. We did not celebrate Christmas that year; there were no gifts for the children. Money was donated to movements in the South. Subsequent holidays were also observed differently from the past, although not as austerely as the Christmas of '63. Looking back, I feel I was much too dogmatic and wonder if the abstentions of customary practices did not hurt more than help to bring awareness of other's pains. Tommy, Jimmy, and Eddie were four, six, and eight. They were denied the fun-times that the older children experienced before them. However, this change did not come with no rationale. The whole family visited Birmingham, Alabama that summer of '63 enroute to California. They were shown the Baptist Church where the children were killed; they met with the woman who typed the famous letter by Martin Luther King from prison; they were taken to Miles College where they met young activists.

Back in the Santa Anita Assembly Center in 1942, the famed evangelist E. Stanley Jones came to speak. I cannot help but remember what he said: "It doesn't matter so much what happens 'to' you as what happens 'inside' of you—and what you do 'after' it happens." Thus, life's blow, whether the evacuation experience that struck the Japanese Americans collectively or a break-up that jolts people individually, need not be a "knock-out" punch, but just another experience to grow on.

Thus, how do we answer the early questions posed inquiring what should be the particularities that Asian mothers and daughters should express or pass on? If it is in behalf of or promoting heritage, there must be a distinction between pride and arrogance. National pride may enhance one's demeanor; but arrogance and narrowed nationalism is no different from racism. A mother should teach her children respect for all peoples, acknowledging the history and contribution of all peoples. Our future generations need not be confined to marriages that continue a purity of race; but a search for a parity in life. Neither should marriage be a ladder, stepping stone or bridge to anything as has been used or abused in history by both nations and individuals. Marriage should not be based on race, but love and sharing and mutual interests and goals. Free choice is a must in a free society.

On the question of difference in our role as Asian or ethnic mothers, we must always keep in mind the universality of the role of mothers. I think mothers in general do try to imbue the Golden Rule to their children; also a sort of "live and let live;" and instilling the precepts of some religion or philosophy.

All mothers wish the best for their children, but even that (wishing the best) must be in weighing out priorities of needs and contradictions. While other children starve and suffer, should a mother be only preoccupied that her child "have the best" of anything? Or should her concerns entertain also thoughts of those who are in dire need? Masses of women coming together can give special attention to specific problems as women the world over are doing about the proliferating arms race. The same could be done on the severity of world hunger engulfing large portions of the earth—or the need for free education and medical care globally.

Does motherhood then transcend color and race and geographic lines? If it does not, the world is in trouble. Tomorrow's holocausts (if there is one) will be different from yesteryears'. Disasters will not be confined to one country or area. Radiation will penetrate geographic demarcations. The waters, skies, and lands everywhere must be protected. It is sad that Americans have not seen photos of the mutations brought on Vietnamese children by America's agent orange defoliated throughout Vietnam. The love, anxieties, and anguish of Vietnamese mothers are no less than stunned American Vietnam veteran's wives who have borne deformed babies. Also, the huge cost of producing "The Day After" could have been used to duplicate countless reels of the "real thing"—the burning of Hiroshima and Nagasaki.

Mothers must be observant as she watches the television or reads the newspaper—that she catch, not only the features—but learns that 20 million people are refugees living in squalid, unsanitary conditions; that 45 nations are involved in conflicts; that 4 million soldiers are in actual combat; that the U.S. has military alliances with 48 nations; that the U.S. sends military equipment to 43 countries; that 1,517,000 American soldiers and sailors are stationed in 119 countries; that U.S. has the offensive capability of destroying the world many times over.

Asian mothers, like all mothers everywhere, must be concerned about the above statistics for it will affect their children and their children's children. Economics, politics, science, media, the arts, education are all intertwined in our daily lives. Asian mothers must speak out; must join with other mothers; interact with other mothers in the major issues of the day. As women we can be part of the most potentially powerful moral force in the world. Our weapons must be our passion and compassion for all human life and living things, but not with the limited, phobic mentality of the Moral Majority.

As Asian women we have history we can be proud of. Our mothers and grandmothers were pioneers. They crossed an ocean, learned a foreign language, adjusted to a new culture. They worked side by side with their husbands on plantations and farms; restaurants and laundries; sweat shops and vegetable stands; in fish canneries and domestic work. They helped create Chinatowns, Japantowns, Manilatowns, and now Koreatowns and Southeast Asian communities. Their children's education and children's future were their priority. They gave birth to a generation of Asian Americans.

The ball is now in the hands of the third, fourth, and fifth generation Asian Americans. Some may not have the physical characteristics of their foreparents, but some knowledge of their heritage is important. And as someone quoted as an advice to parents and teachers: "There are two things you can give to your children—roots and wings." . . .a wise advice for mothers and daughters—Asian or otherwise. But the most important, I feel, is sowing the seeds of love and justice in fertile minds that its regeneration can extinguish the continuous fires of greed and imperialist wars. Mothers and daughters united—may make a qualitative difference in this world of mushrooming uncertainties.

MALCOLM X: FOR THE SECOND AND THIRD GRADERS OF
SHELLY MILLER'S CLASS /CHILDREN'S STORE FRONT

    Yuri Kochiyama met Malcolm X in Harlem on October 16, 1963—a memorable day she says she has never forgotten. She became a life-long associate until his assasination, and she takes every occasion given to speak about Malcolm X.

    Her speeches throughout the years have addressed many aspects of his life and thoughts. The handwritten notes that follow illustrate one of many class presentations she has given on Malcolm X and other topics of concern to her.

    In this particular set of note cards she prepared for a second- and third-grade class in Harlem, Yuri seems to capture the essence of Malcolm X with powerful simplicity and wisdom.

- the Editors

MALCOLM X

(for 2nd + 3rd Grade)

I I Thank Ms. Shelley Miller. Special
-treat for me to meet.
children... because mine
have grown up.

II Children — Malcolm loved
children. He had 4; I more
came after he died. (6 girls)

III Pass out the pictures
of Malcolm

IV Malcolm as a father
(Called Attallah/his daughter)
   a. Fun father, Warm,
      Not stern
   b. Buddy, a pal.
   c. Someone who listened
   d. Could tell stories
      learned about Black heros
      + African & Afric. Amer. hist

KOCHIYAMA: *Discover Your Mission*/UCLA AASC •18

2/
a. Benjamin Banneto
b. Frederick Douglass
c. Harriet Tubman
d. Mary McLeod Bethune
d. Never heard him say the whites were devils.
e. Daughter/Andrea / autograph "Please help to make this + better world for all people."

Vd at end

I Malcolm + Education:
Felt education was most important. It was denied to his own people from slave days. Slaves were punished if found trying to read a book. Denial of educ — historical Malc. Lib. School.

3/
a. School – not 4-walls and a roof
School - 2 component.
those who want to learn
those who want to teach.
All of us should be both a sometime teacher and student
"

II Malcolm + Family
Slavery was a means of destroying family life, not allowing marriage — because slaves could be sold at the whim of the slave-master. Thus, family + marriage meant everything to Malcolm.

5/ IX Malcom + Nationhood
for self-determination
" - reliance
" - defense

For Black Nation in the
Black Belt So.
GA, AL, SO.C, MS, LA

IX Malcom + Harlem
The Place he lived; called
home. Must keep it
Black/ independent, strong
Afro-centrd. unique.
People must respect this
community. Must rule.
this a positive place for
children, elderly, family.
Respect must come from
everyone. Black, Asian, Latina,
white. All negat. act. must
halt. —like drugs, liquor,
crime.

VIII Malcom & Africa
Image of Africa distorted;
caric. model for et; looked down
upon. Infuriated him.
Thus, he studied out,
researched about Africa,
and shared all he learned.

VII Malcom + International
Perspective
1983— Saw the struggle
of Vietnam as the struggle
of the Third World —
against foreign domina.
" " " intervent.
" " " take-ov
Like what is happening
in the Persian Gulf.

XII Daughter, Audee — and the autograph.

"Audee, Please help to make this a better world for all people."

This is probably the message he wanted to give to you — if he were here today.

And he is here in spirit.

"To live in hearts that are left behind is not to die."

Remember that — should you ever lose someone dear to you. If you remember, and keep love within you, that person half not die. You will keep them alive.

We, who loved Malcolm, keep him/her alive in our hearts.

XI Malcolm: Life + Death
What he stood for:
① Championed his ppl's cause
② Spoke up against the evils in society
(racism, hypocrisy, inequity, poverty, bad schools, lack of health care, poor housing, unemployment among Black)
Hated

3. Loved humanity — People; freedom - quality of being free; loved dignity (dignity for the elderly, for the poor); loved justice, loved life — mobility, respect, no boundaries; no intimidation; be able to believe in your own religion; relig. of choice

4. Why was he killed?
Spoke out agn the Power structure, the U.S. Govern, U.S. Policy.

Appendix 10

from Asian Americans for Action newsletter,
Volume 5, Number 3 (April-June 1973)

AFTER THE CEASE-FIRE — WHAT ?

By Yuri Kochiyama

Since the Vietnam Ceasefire of Jan. 27, 1973, what is the situation in Southeast Asia today?

The last of the American POWs have been returned home. American soldiers, airmen, and sailors have been withdrawn. But, has this meant the termination of U.S. involvement in Indochina?

As U.S. servicemen were returned, some 20,000 "civilians" (called 'technicians') have quietly replaced them. Some will be working for U.S. corporations on contract with the Pentagon, while others will be working out of the U.S. Embassy. The Defense Department has awarded $150 million to 23 U.S. corporations to keep the Saigon Air Force in the air (Washington Post, 12/9 & 12/11/72).

As for violations of the Peace Agreement as pointed out by North Vietnam, here are four major ones:

1) Continued and escalated bombing of Cambodia.

2) New B-52 strikes being carried out in Laos.

3) Stopping of mine-clearing operations in North Vietnam.

4) Resumption of reconnaissance flights over North Vietnam.

The breakdown of events, country by country is as follows:

CAMBODIA: -

Since February, some of the heaviest raids in the history of the Indochina War, took place with U.S. using as many as 120 B-52's per day,

for 37 consecutive days. Some 3 million people (which is half of the Cambodian population) have been made refugees since American bombing excursions began 3 years ago.

Yet today, the Cambodian revolutionary forces have liberated 90% of Cambodian land. And altho' Sihanouk was overthrown in 1970 by a U.S.-CIA coup and Lon Nol given the power, Sihanouk's government never ceased to exist. Sihanouk's Royal Government linked up with their former antagonists, Khmer Rouge, and together formed the National United Front of Cambodia and the Cambodian Peoples' Liberation Armed Forces.

/more next page

LAOS: -

A peace agreement was signed on February 21 in Vientiane by the Laos Patriotic Forces and the Vientiane government, but U.S. has made B-52 raids into Laos since the signing date, most prominently on April 16 and 17.

The Vientiane administration (as Associated Press put it, 6/20/65) was an American "adoptive child." But "child abuse" of Laos was systematic; totally controlled by the U.S. Embassy.

Fierce U.S. Air Force involvement had been raging since May, 1964, not 1971 as the American newspapers first projected. Besides the trained, equipped, and commanded "Special Forces" from the Vientiane Army, Thai mercenaries and Saigon troops were used in South Laos in Feb., 1971, without consulting the Phouma administration.

Laos, a small, peasant nation, braced by U.S. finance, has been made into a U.S. base of operation for rangers, spies, and radar stations to guide air raids against North Vietnam.

SOUTH VIETNAM: -

There are two governments in South Vietnam -- one, the government of Vietnam (GVN) in the heart of Saigon, led by Nguyen Van Thieu; and the other, the Provisional Revolutionary Government (PRG) quartered west of Saigon, led by Huynh Tan Phat.

The Paris Peace Agreement does not specify which of these two governments or other political forces should ultimately guide the future of South Vietnam. The agreement calls for a National Council of Reconciliation and Concord, where the two parties can organize free and democratic elections in order to form a new government.

Thieu, however, wants the elections to be carried out under the

↖ Vietnamese prisoner one of thousands who have never known peace. (UAR...)

control of his hand-appointed province chiefs, district chiefs, and police forces at every level of the administration.

The PRG maintains that the true political sentiments of the people can only be expressed if the PRG and the GVN are on an equal footing.

The strategy being used by the U.S.-Saigon governments is, first, tightening controls in the cities through propoganda, police, and army forces; and secondly, bombing the countryside, forcing the peasants to move into the cities under Saigon government control.

Recalcitrants and neutrals are apprehended, for Thieu considers all such as threats; and they are imprisoned as criminals. Thus, the growing number of political prisoners and the escalation of brutality within the prisons.

NORTH VIETNAM: -

The Democratic Republic of Vietnam (also known as North Vietnam) and the United States signed the historic January 27th document for peace. The specifics of implementing the agreements were

6

AFTER THE CEASE-FIRE—WHAT?
con'd

stated. Responsibilities were to be carried out by the signatories.

Despite the stipulations that U.S. must clear North Vietnam's harbor, U.S. stopped mine-clearing operations on April 19. U.S. had exploded only 3 of the 10,000 mines dropped or planted in North Vietnam waters. Also, from April 20, U.S. resumed flying reconnaissance missions in what it called a policy decision to violate the agreement to put pressure on North Vietnam.

The U.S.'s countercharge of North Vietnam's violations is aimed at the fighting in Cambodia, accusing the DRV as the infiltrator-aggressor. But the overwhelming evidence that the fighting against Lon Nol is done by the Cambodians themselves, was reinforced by the American Ambassador himself, when he told reporters in Phnom Penh, that "since the cease-fire 3 months ago, there is no documented evidence that Vietnamese Communist troops are serving combat roles in Cambodia."

Not hundreds, but thousands, of countercharges, obstructions imposed on the international Commission of Control & Supervision, indiscriminate round-up of neutral, forced urbanization, nibbling military operations, unreasonable provocations, and the premeditated, systematic neo-colonialst schemes of U.S. and Thieu's dictatorial manner of unleashing repressive acts against the people, have sabotaged the realization of peace.

The future of Vietnam will depend on many factors, political and economic, internal and external. The wounds of war can hardly be healed while U.S. will, might, and maneuverings are foisted upon the Vietnamese people.

To faciliate reconcilation and national accord, United States and all other countries must respect the independence, sovereignty, unity and integrity of the two Vietnams, not interfere in their internal affairs, and allow North and South Vietnam to begin negotiation among themselves.

THE ENEMY By Thich Nhat Hanh

The enemy is not a person
If you kill people with whom will you live?

The enemy's name is cruelty
The enemy's name is lack of conscience
Its name is hatred, its name is bitterness
It is the name of a group of phantoms

The enemy wears a coat of doctrine
The enemy wears the pretense of freedom
It wears hypocrisy, it wears twisted words
It wears the disease that keeps us apart

Think of the pity of the weak
Think of the pity of innocence
Pity the sellouts, pity the cheater
Pity those who pity us

The enemy is not in the stranger
It lies inside of each of us

The enemy's name is false accusation
The enemy's name is ignorance
Its name is ambition, its name is envy
Its name is jealous hatred

The enemy's name is covetous eyes
The enemy's name is arrogant head
Its name is a lonely heart,
its name is a narrow mind

Its name is the dream of conquest
The enemy is not a person
If you kill people with whom
will you live?
The enemy is not in the stranger
It lies inside of each of us.

Translated by Doug Hostetter

7

ON THE LINE

442nd Association

VOL. 1, No. 1   December, 1951   New York, N. Y.

442ND ASSOCIATION FORMED IN NEW YORK

They Lead New Vets Group

-- Photo by Tito O'Kamoto

Pictured are the first cabinet members of the 442nd Association. They are, left to right: Yosh Ito, Kei Yamato, Art Munch, Bill Kochiyama, Kelly Kuwayama, Norman Kurlan and Dick Hata.

Bill Kochiyama Elected First Prexy

Bill Kochiyama was elected the first president of the 442nd Association.

Serving with him will be: Art Munch, vice president; Norman Kurlan, secretary; Yosh Ito, treasurer; Kelly Kuwayama, Kei Yamato, Dick Hata, board of governors.

Nominations were received from the floor and through write-ins. Votes were cast on ballots mailed to members.

Chic Aoyama was in charge of tabulating returns.

The new president chaired the temporary 442nd Committee which was instrumental in organizing the Association. He was a member of Company K.

His wife, nee Mary Nakahara, was a leader of the Aloha USO in Hattiesburg, Miss., and the teen-age Crusaders club of Jerome, Ark.

"Go For Broke" Reunion Lunch Is Scene of Birth

At a mass luncheon-business meeting in the Miyako Restaurant during the "Go For Broke" Reunion in May, the local 442nd Association was born.

Temporary officers were elected to carry out the formation of the club and given carte blanche powers to organize.

In September the first officers and board of governors were installed.

IDEA WAS THERE

Prior to the MGM "era" of "Go For Broke," the idea of a 442nd organization in New York City was seriously discussed by local veterans.

Nothing definite happened until the 442nd Committee was formed to handle details of the reunion. At the business meeting, committee members spoke out for a permanent organization.

Their plan got unanimous approval.

DELUXE HEADQUARTERS

The problem of a meeting place was solved when arrangements were made with the 77th Division veterans to use their headquarters at 28 East 39th St., in Manhattan. This central location is complete with cocktail lounge, dining room, library, recreation room and other facilities.

THE NSO's FE-MAIL

3rd Edition   Nisei Service Organization   May, 1952

G.I.S SUPPORT HELPS FE-MAIL GROW

Servicemen, vets, and sisters of G.I.'s have gone 'all out' as Fe-Mail backers, generously contributing to the support of this paper. This past month's donations have helped this sheet grow into a four-pager for this issue.

Treasurer Flo Kozuma reports a new list of donors. The servicemen's contribution's include: Pfc. Kaz Nakagawa of Fort Dix, NJ; Sgt. Roy Namba of Fort Bliss, Tex.; Pfc. Hank Yoshikawa of Amarillo Air Base, Tex.; Pfc. Osamu Asato of the 1st Marine Division in Korea; Maxie Sakamoto, somewhere in the South Pacific; Pfc. Mike Murakami of Fort Wadsworth, NY; and Fort Monmouth's SCEL Det. boys, Pfc's. George Kasai, Ray Watanabe, Harry Kajihara, Suyeo Tomooka, George Hasabe, Sam Kakauye, and Nog Komatsu.

442 Association members who donated were: Mr. and Mrs. Frank Ochs, Mr. and Mrs. Kei Yamato, Mr. and Mrs. Tito O'Kamoto, Mr. and Mrs. Arthur Munch, Haruo Yanagi, Irving Akahoshi, Gene Herbert, and Yosh Ito.

Two sisters of G.I's also sent in money, Kay Kitada of Los Angeles, and Riyoko Tabata of Clarksburg, California.

Photographers Gene Herbert and Tito O'Kamoto, 442 veterans, donated free service covering NSO activities.

Photo by Gene Herbert

PRESENT NSO OFFICERS (l-r): Seated - Michi Teramoto, Hist.; Conrad Kuwahara, Dir.; Pat Iwamoto, Sec.; Georgie Sawahata, Soc. Ch. Standing - Sadie Kuratomi, Pres.; Sumi Young, Sec.; Flo Kozuma, Treas.; Fran Kadowaki, VP.

HOSTESS CLUB PLANS ELECTION AND INSTALLATION

SADIE KURATOMI, PAT IWAMOTO, FLO KOZUMA NOMINEES FOR PREXY

Plans for a May election and a June installation of officers, were the main topics of discussion at the general Hostess Club meeting on April 11. Candidates were nominated from the floor, with further nominations to take place by mail. All NSO girls are urged to vote.

It was also unanimously approved that the presidency would be filled by an officer in the present cabinet.

Candidates names must be submitted by May 15 to the Fe-Mail Staff. Ballots will be mailed out the week following, with election dead-line stipulated.

Those nominated at the meeting were: Sadie Kuratomi, Pat Iwamoto, and Flo Kozuma for president; Fumi Takaki, Georgianna Sawahata, Pat Iwamoto and Frances Nakamura for vice-president; Ginger Nakamura, Lucy Chin, Alice May, Yuri Nakamura, Josie Jarm, Alice Lee, and Sumi Young for secretary; Florence Kozuma and Lucy Chin for treasurer; Margaret Kuniyoshi, Georgianna Sawahata, and Lucy Chin for social chairman; Michi Teramoto for historian.

The girls also made plans for a dance at the Chinese Community Club, which was given on April 26, headed by Lucy Chin.

New hostesses present were: Roseanne Iwanaga, Yuri Nakamura, Yuri Inouye, Edna Ho, Kris Kawaguchi, and Ruth Eto.

ANNIVERSARY DANCE SLATED FOR MAY 10

Marking one year's mile-stone in NSO activities, the "anniversary ball" has been slated for Saturday nite, May 10 at McBurney YMCA located on 23rd St. and 7th Avenue.

Sadie Kuratomi, her hard-working cabinet, and hostesses, extend their invitation to all G.I.'s in East Coast camps and those on furlough.

2   ANNIVERSARY ISSUE

NSO OFFICERS
  Board Director: Conrad Kurahara
  Hostess Club Officers: Sadie Kuratomi,
  Frances Kadowaki, Sumi Young, Pat Iwamo-
  to, Georgie Sawahata, Florence Kozuma,
  Mich Teramoto
  Fe-Mail Staff: Michi Teramoto, June No-
  buto, Pat Iwamoto, Bill & Mary Kochiyama.
                           249 W. 62nd St., N.Y.C.

EDITORIAL:
LEST WE FORGET . . .

That May should happen to be the one year anniversary of the Nisei Service Organization seems fitting and timely in that May is the month that many dates are set aside in remembering those in uniform.

I-Am-An-American Day, Armed Forces Day, and Memorial Day are observed in May. "Go For Broke", the movie picture that focused much attention on Nisei G.I.'s of World War II, was also released in May of last year when the world premier was held in Honolulu.

But even with all these "special days", today's servicemen, as noted by Asst. Sec. of Defense Anna Rosenberg, are treated with lack of respect and ofttimes with contempt. Civilians engrossed in their personal problems seem oblivious what is happening in Korea.

"Casualties" so often pushed aside as 'statistics' or forgotten until national rites call them to our attention, have been in actuality the biggest factor in bringing about encouraging legislation to many of America's ethnic groups. A classic example would be the now-legendary story of the 442-nd Combat Team. Their sacrifices were great, but thanks to those sacrifices, an entire minority group has reaped the rewards: recognition of the Japanese-American, removal of a stigma, and an upward trend in the fight for civil rights.

Chinese-Americans have also in World War II, gained naturalization for their parents.

In the present conflict, the War Dept. is well aware of the high casualties from Hawaii. Some day, it will be those "casualties" that will open the door to statehood and other benefits.

To those who are serving and have served, we owe more than a verbal thanks...and we cannot sit upon the laurels of past service records. Each of us, in and out of uniform, must in our own respective capacity, live up to those men that Gen. Joseph Stillwell said, "bought an awfully big hunk of America with their blood."

GAY NITE ENJOYED AT BAMBOO GARDEN

All those who joined the NSO'ers at the Bamboo Garden in Union City, New Jersey, returned home on the night of March 15, (or should we say, the morn of March 16), with a gay evening behind to add to their memory-books.

A crowd of 70 jammed the dance floors en masse and enjoyed the delicious free chicken dinner. Photographers Gene Herbert and Tito O'Kamoto flashed away industriously as everyone tried their darndest to look unself-conscious as possible. Proprietor Tom Lee and wife June, donated to the NSO, the $1.00 charge they had previously set for the G.I's.

The "boys" came in from New York, New Jersey, Pennsylvania, Maryland, and even as far South as Virginia. (The fella from Virginia was Masaji Hatae from Fort Belvoir).

New servicemen spotted by the gals were Harry Eng, Edward Hor, Warren Moy, Ken Murata, Masa Rikimaru, and John Uyeda.

The NSO was also happy to welcome new feminine faces as Kris Kawaguchi, Edna Ho, Yuri Inouye, Terry Oikawa, Marie Kurihara, Helen Moy, Kathy Asano, and Midori Tanaka.

HIGH SCHOOL GIRLS BIG HELP TO NSO

One of the most hep bunch of gals who have been helping the NSO, are the high school cuties who are not quite 'official hostesses' because of age. These are the gals who are doing the heavy bulk of correspondence with GI's, entertaining at home, dating when asked, sending cookies to the hospitalized, and keeping the NSO posted on GI news.

One of the most active is petite "Tebbo". Phyllis Kusumi who attends Music and Arts High School. As a letter-writer and foster of GI-gal correspondents, Tebbo has burned the candles at both ends. Some of her chums she's started in this writing-fad are Sue Chapman, Jo Miras, Lillian Kazim, and Eleanor Pacis.

From Hunter High, Etsu Itokawa and Emma Duchane have certainly done their share.

Julie Richmond's Jean Imazu and Madeline Sugimoto have been sending addresses and names of GI's from "back home".

Inseparable Liz Yee and Marjorie Chin have also stimulated classmates in writing.

And, three of the most "dated" teen-agers are: Shirley Mock, Josie Jarm, and Alice Moy. (All sharp stuff)...

What would we do without you!!!

JAMES IGE
Vice-President

SUSANNA NISHIMURA
and LILLY JARM
Secretaries

ELEANOR WAKA
Executive
Secretary

AYAKO KOZUMA
President

JULIE LUM
and TOMMY NAKAMURA
Social Chairmen

NSSO FE-MAIL

22nd Edition	Nisei-Sino Service Organization	December, 1957

YURI KIMIZUKA
Publicity Chairman

MASA + JEAN NAKAMURA
Treasurers

MAY DEGUCHI
Historian

CO-DIRECTORS
GEORGE CHIN, WALTER BJORK
and JIMMY KONNO

We are happy to send greetings to all our friends, supporters, and interested parties, old and new.

Because we are no longer in position to send out monthly news-sheets, Christmas has become the only time to convey good wishes and gratitude to the many individuals and organizations that we have had contacts with through social and service mediums.

We appreciate the warm associations with members of the YBA, YF, YPF, Nisei Tennis Club, CCYC, all the Chinese College Clubs, and the Filipino Social Club, which is our latest acquaintance. Your presence at our dances and outings have added much to our group, and we hope to see more of you.

We wish to again acknowledge the continuous support from the 442 Veterans Association, the Four Seas of China Town, the editors and columnists of the Chinese-American Times, and Mr. Tooru Kanazawa, English editor of the Hokubei Shimpo. Our thanks, too, to Keoni and Iwalani and their Hula Troupe, and to Chief Two Eagle and the Indian League of America for their performances at the dances.

To the countless young folks who have helped as hostesses and hosts at social affairs, given leads to housing and jobs, or befriended or oriented newcomers to the city, NSSO feels justly proud. NSSO is grateful, too, that there are people like Rev. Alfred Akamatsu, Mr. Ernest Kozuma, Mr. Tad Yamada, Mrs. Frank Narita, Mr. Minoru Harada, and Mr. Frank Sogi, and others who have given time and effort to cope with personal problems of GI's, students, warbrides, and young people in general.

May this "desire to help others" be contagious through this new year, that more and more new faces will participate in NSSO's underlying program of-- 'fellowship through service '.

Merry Christmas!
Nisei Sino Service Organization

CHRISTMAS CHEER
STAFF
249 West 62nd Street
New York 23, New York

WILLIAM KOCHIYAMA
Editor
MARY KOCHIYAMA
Assistant Editor
BILLY KOCHIYAMA
Big News-ance
AUDEE KOCHIYAMA
Lil' News-ance

TO "CC" READERS

To our new reader-friends, this news-sheet is our way of dropping in during the Yule Season to express our Christmas Cheer. (To meet our publication deadline, the articles were written in September and October.

Some of you are new-found friends. Others of you are old friends. Some of you are GI's fighting in Korea, or pen-friends from other countries. What many of you are undergoing, we cannot imagine. We do wish, however, a Christmas that can warm your hearts wherever you are.

This sheet is a mixture of homey news, events, and people close to us. We feel bad that much of the news items sent in could not be used because of the limited space. This issue featured Go For Broke and our trip to California.

We wish to also convey our sincere thanks for gifts and kindnesses shown to us thruout the year. Such tokens of friendship cannot be measured in material goods and gains alone. Each of you have added something to our life, though some of you we have seen but once.

"In every person there is a teacher, and in every experience, some lesson in life."

Thank you for that gift of knowing you.

EDITORIAL:
CHRISTMAS... 10 YEARS AGO

As we look back to Christmas of 10 years ago, we of Japanese ancestry can recall with almost vivid painfulness, the uneasy, frustrating, insecure experiences we were forced to undergo.

Many of our Issei parents were interned. Niseis were "released" from their jobs. Schools were reluctant to accept Niseis. A curfew and 5-mile traveling limit was beginning to go into effect for us. Some trains and bus companies would not sell tickets for transportation. College students were stranded in many college towns. Some restaurants and stores refused service to Japanese and Niseis. Japanese-run stores were boycotted. Japanese farmers were molested; all fishermen were placed under suspicion. Evacuation was being endorsed by people in high political and military circles.

Newspapers blared inflammable, untrue stories of espionage and sabotage. Hollywood Class B studios began their production-line of cheap hysteria-filled quickies. A change of feeling towards those of Japanese ancestry was immediately felt in many communities. (A deep feeling of gratitude to those of non-Japanese backgrounds who stayed by their Nisei and Issei friends.)

Draft boards refused Niseis in service, and classified Niseis as enemy aliens. Those already in service were discharged, placed under guards, or sent to land training camps.

In this almost c[...] hour of emptiness, [...] seis determined t o [...] their loyalty a n d [...] their stuff", plead[...] the War Dept. and th[...]

dent to permit them to participate as any other citizen in serving their country.

Thus was born the "go for broke" story of some 10,000 Niseis from the Island and mainland who eagerly volunteered for the military intelligence and the all-Nisei Combat Team. The rest is history.

A grateful nation's thanks, her recognition and acceptance of an equally grateful minority completes the wartime saga, and opens the way whereby Niseis may continue their campaign for rights still denied.

CHARLES DICKENS SAYS IT IN CHRISTMAS CAROLS

"There are many things from which I might have derived good, by which I have not profited, I dare say, Christmas among the rest. But I am sure I have always thought of Christmas time, when it has come round, as a good time; a kind, forgiving, charitable, p leasant time; the only time I know of, in the long calendar of the year, when men and women seem by one consent to open their shut-up hearts freely, and to think of people below them as if they really were fellow-passengers to the grave, and not another race of creatures [...] other journeys.

Appendix 15

from the
"Christmas Cheer"
family newsletter,
Volume 2, 1951

Christmas Cheer workcrew: (from left) "Jocko," Billy, Audee and Aichi.

FOLK HITS OF '65

"What's that we hear now ringing in our ears?" could well be answered with, lots of "Good News."

Saturday Nite friends who have 'made it' in the theater world are too numerous to mention, but Bobby Dean Hooks tops the "hit" list with his success as director of The Group Theater Workshop (with Barbara Teer), his "Henry V" performance with the Mobile Theater, his Frederick Douglas portrayal in TV's "Profiles of Courage," and his current St. Marks production, "Happy Ending" and "Day of Absence" written by Douglas Turner Ward. Bobby is shown here.

Other K folk-hits became "willing conscripts" for change, like Al Karvelis and Karen Sidney, Saturday Nite favorites, shown above.

Other duos who saw similar "new days", were: Manny Gilyard and Yvonne Wheeler, Ferdinand Masata and Lorna Hodges, Victor Miraga and Joyce Fujiwara, Charles Johnson and Ann Kramer, Al Uhrie and Barbara Goodman, George Matsumoto and Elaine Takano, Levi Laub and Mary Maher, Leroy Nix and Deloris Hinson, John Utley and Martha Buchwalter, Mike David and Doris Zintmeyer, Reggie Allen and Alicia Corpus, Nat White and Carol Helling, Margie Kimizuka and
(Continued on Page 4)

FRIENDS HELP C.C. TRAVEL MANY A MILE

Christmas Cheer has traveled some financially "rocky roads," and its staff have oft' repeated, "Can't help but wonder where we're bound" --but thanks to the generosity of donors, the 16th issue is here.

The names of such friends and relatives who made this '65 sheet possible, are listed below.

Dad Kochiyama, Mom and Dad Nakahara (though deceased), Pete and Aiko Nakahara, Art and Chiyo Nakahara, Mrs. Kondo, Mrs. Toyama, Eddie and Aiko Imazu, Joyce Imaze, Mrs. Ogata, Mr. and Mrs. Muto, Kathy Muto, Emi Ikemoto, Sei and Chie Kondo, Ruth and Leo Toyama.

Dr. and Mrs. Charles Turck, James Ige, George and Lily Nakamura, Kay Curry, Virginia
(Continued on Page 2)

CHRISTMAS CHEER

Appendix 17

Note: Asian Americans for Action (known as Triple A)
newsletter cover for Volume II, Number 1, 1970.

Asian Americans for Action

NEWSLETTER

225 Lafayette Street, Room 713 - New York, New York 10012

Volume II, Number 1   February 1970

```
* * * * * * * * * * * * * * * * * * * * * * * * * * * * * * * *
*                                                              *
*  "The annihilation of our race is at hand, unless we unite in one com-  *
*  mon cause against a common foe...Think not that you can remain pas-  *
*  sive and indifferent to the common danger and thus escape a common  *
*  fate. Your people, too, will soon be as the falling leaves and  *
*  scattering clouds before the blighting wind. You too will be driven  *
*  away from your native land and ancient domains as leaves are driven  *
*  in the wintry storms....  *
*                                                              *
*  "By being united and all of one mind we may prevent what is left of  *
*  our country from passing into the hands of the white man, and in  *
*  time other nations may join us. Rouse up your drooping spirits, my  *
*  friends, and let us strike in defense of our homes."  *
*                                                              *
*                           -- Tecumseh (1768-1813)  *
*                              Shawnee Indian Chief  *
*  (In 1811)  *
*                                                              *
* * * * * * * * * * * * * * * * * * * * * * * * * * * * * * * *
```

- EDITORIAL -

This country is entering a critical stage.

This is an editorial on political repression and political prisoners. Why, in the "land of the free" do we need to talk about political repression? Isn't political repression the first indication of a fascist state? Yes.

Free Huey P. Newton
Free Bobby Seale
Free the Panther 21 in New York
Free the Wilmington 8
Free the Los Angeles 18
Free the New Haven 14
Free the Chicago Conspiracy 7
Free W. Kunstler and L. Weinglass
Free the Washington, D.C. 9
Free other Black Panthers in
    jails all over the country
Free the ARM students
Free Fort Dix GI Bill Brakefield
Free the soldiers in stockades
Free Ahmed Evans
Free Martin Sostre
Free the Catonsville 9
Free the Oakland 7

Free the Milwaukee 14
Free all draft resisters
Free Lee Otis Johnson
Stop the harrassment of the
    Young Lords
Stop repression of the S.F.
    Red Guards
Dismiss the up-coming cases of:
    Herman Ferguson, Raphael Viera,
    Rap Brown, all the many others
Free the Harlem Five
Free Los Sietes de la Raza
Free Tijerina
Free the Presidio 27
Free the Fort Dix 38
Free John Sinclair
Free the Newark 20

And remember: MALCOLM, MARK CLARK, FRED HAMPTON, BUNCH CARTER, JOHN HUGGINS, BOBBY HUTTON, 23 OTHER DEAD PANTHERS, BIRMINGHAM BOMBINGS, MEDGAR EVERS, MARTIN L. KING, CHANEY, GOODMAN, SCHWERNER, LIUZZO....the list is endless since the beginning of this country's history.

FREE ALL POLITICAL PRISONERS - END POLITICAL REPRESSION
+ +

THE BLACK STRUGGLE AND POLITICAL PRISONERS

By Mary Kochiyama
(a sister who has long been close
to the struggles of Black people)

"Free all political prisoners" has become more than a moving slogan in the past several years' period of the Black struggle. These words carry a message of where the movement "is at." They say, in essence, that 'brothers (and sisters too) are being incarcerated but must not rot in jail.'

Who Are Political Prisoners? In order to comprehend the seriousness of this stage of struggle wherein a racist establishment is giving vent to fear and rage, unleashing the forces of 'law and order' to crush a legitimate and inherent struggle, the term "political prisoners" must evoke some appropriate

Yuri Kochiyama: Community and Political Resume
[compiled from several sources by Audee Kochiyama-Holman and Marji Lee]

Political Education
Harlem Freedom School/Isaiah Robinson	1963-1964
Malcolm X Liberation School/Jim Campbell	1964-1965
Organization of Afro-American Unity/Malcolm X	1965
Amiri Baraka Black Arts School/Harold Cruise	1965-1966
Free University/Charles Johnson	1966-1967
Nation Building Classes/RNA Consulate Mtayari Sundiata	1966

Community and Organizing Experience
Hiroshima Maidens, NY [hosted Hiroshima atomic bomb survivors]	1950s
Harlem Parents Committee/Isaiah Robinson	1963-1964
Harlem Women's Group/Mae Mallory	1964-1966
Organization of Afro-American Unity/Malcolm X	1964-1965
Hiroshima/Nagasaki World Peace Study Mission, NY	1964
Asian Americans for Action/Kazu Iijima	1969-1974
Republic of New Africa/Imari Obadeli	1969-Present
Numerous Asian and Third World Coalitions	1969-Present
National Committee for the Defense of Political Prisoners	1971-1977
Japanese American Redress & Reparations Committees	1980s
United Front [against U.S. Terrorism]	2001-Present
Asian Prisoners Support Committee	2003-Present

Movement Experience
Civil Rights [Visited Alabama & Louisiana/63]	1963-1968
Ethnic Studies [With 3rd World Students at CCNY]	1968
Anti-Vietnam War [Spoke at rallies, demonstrations]	1965-1973
Prison struggle	1970-Present
Via NCDPP & numerous defense committees. Corresponded with and visited many inmates in 22 prisons in 6 states	1970-1977
Anti-imperialist struggles/Third World liberation support work	
Anti-Apartheid	1970s-1980s
Native American Indian sovereignty	1970s
Palestine homeland and against all U.S. interventions	1970s
Puerto Rican independence	1970s
Southern Africa support	1970s
Solidarity with Cuba/Venceremos Brigade, 19th Brigade	1987
Legal Defense Committees: Queens 17, Harlem 6, Harlem 5, Panther 21, New York 5, Tombs 7, Rap Brown 4, Carlos Feliciano, Martin Sostre, Assata Shakur, Dhoruba Bin Wahad Shasha Brown,	1967-Present

Sundiata Acoli, New Haven 3, RNA 11, BPP & BLA cases, Puerto Rican Nationalists, Queens 2, New York 3, Chol See Lee, Vincent Chin, Amiri Baraka Defense, New York 8, Mutulu Shakur, Leonard Peltier, Marilyn Buck, D.C. 6, David Wong, Yu Kikumura, Mumia Abu Jamal, Robert Williams, Muhammad Ahmed, Rocky Boice of Carson 10, etc.

Other Community Experience

Advisor [with husband Bill]—Nisei-Sino Service Organization	1950-1960
Writer—*New York Nichibei* (sports & politics)	1960-1980
Contributing Editor—*East Wind* Magazine	1982-1989
Teacher—Riverside Church (English as Second Language)	1983-1992
Volunteer—NYC Churches (soup kitchen & homeless shelters)	1983-1992

Board or Advisory Committee Experience

Malcolm X Commemoration Committee	1965-Present
Third World Media News (Inter-Church Center)	1972-1973
Committee for Puerto Rican Decolonization	1973-1974
Puerto Rican Solidarity Committee	1974-1975
The New Harlem YWCA	1976-1977
Day of Remembrance Committee, NY	1980s-1990s
Women & the Law Conference—Steering Committee	1984-1985
Jeff Adachi Campaign for San Francisco Public Defender	2002
Women's International Network/Marilyn Fowler	2002-Present

International Travel

Cuba—19th Venceremos Brigade [at age 67]	1987
Peru—International Emergency Committee/Abimael Guzman	1993
Philippines & Japan—International Emergency Committee/ Human Rights	1994

Public Speaking and Awards

Delivered speeches at over 100 high schools and colleges in at least 15 states and Canada, including the following colleges and universities: Harvard, Radcliffe, Yale, Princeton, Emory, Temple, University of Massachusetts/Amherst, Oberlin, University of Hawaii, New York University, UC Berkeley, UCLA and others. Topics include: Asian American movement; Malcolm X; cross-cultural relations among Blacks, Asians, and others; U.S. foreign policy; anti-war movements; etc. Taught one semester in the Asian American Studies Department at City College of New York in 1972.

In recent years received numerous awards and honors, including: New York State Governor's Award for Outstanding Asian American (1994); Frederick Douglas Award, from North Star Fund (1994); Dean's Medal, from CUNY School of Law, Queens College (1996); Japanese American of the Biennium in the field of Politics/ Public Affairs/Law, from the Japanese American Citizens League (1996); 100 Most Influential Asian Americans of the Decade, from *A Magazine* (1999); Sisters of Fire Award, from Women of Color Resource Center (2000); University in Exile Award, from the New School University, NYC (Winter graduation 2000); Asian Pacific

American Law Students Association Award (2002); Lifetime Achievement Award, from SUNY Stony Brook (2002); "Long Walk to Freedom" Civil & Human Rights Activists Award, from Community Works, San Francisco (2003); "Harlem Is" Award honoring Harlem Activists, from Community Works, New York (2003); and National Women's History Project Award (2003).

In 1994, received the Charles Bannerman Memorial Fellowship, awarded annually to activists of color. In 1998, served as Visiting Fellow at UCLA under the auspices of the Japanese American Studies Chair Endowment. Also, donated collection of personal papers and archives (primarily related to the Asian American movement and the internment) to the UCLA Asian American Studies Center for the UCLA Library's Special Collections Department, and to the Japanese American National Museum.

Documentary Films

Cool Women. Produced and directed by Debbie Allen. Romance Classics, 2000. [1/2-hour television feature series]
The Long Walk to Freedom: Portraits of Civil Rights Activists Then and Now. Directed, written, edited, and shot by Tom Weidlinger; produced by Ruth Morgan for Community Works/California, 2003. [1 of 12 Bay Area Activists featured]
My America: Honk if You Love Buddha. Directed and produced by Renee Tajima-Peña, 1998.
Yuri Kochiyama: Passion for Justice. Directed and produced by Pat Saunders and Rea Tajiri, 1993.

Selected Articles and Books about or by Yuri Kochiyama

"Yuri Kochiyama: With Justice in Her Heart." Revolutionary Worker, 13 December 1998.
Adachi, Jeff. "Asian American Activist Has Long History of Fighting for Rights," *Asian Week*, 7 May 1993.
Bolling, Deborah. "Recalling a Friend Named Malcolm," *New York Times*, 21 February 1999.
Chang, Carrie. "Yellow and Black," *Monolid Magazine* 2:2 (Summer/Fall 2001), 6-9.
Fujino, Diane C. *Heartbeat of Struggle: The Revolutionary Practice of Yuri Kochiyama.* [Work in progress].
Fujino, Diane C. "Revolution's from the Heart: The Making of an Asian American Woman Activist, Yuri Kochiyama," in *Dragon Ladies: Asian American Feminists Breathe Fire*, Sonia Shah, ed. (Boston: South End Press, 1997), 169-181.
Hung, Melissa. "The Last Revolutionary," *East Bay Express*, 13 March 2002.
Kochiyama, Yuri. "A History of Linkage: African and Asian, African American and Asian American," in "Shades of Power: Newsletter of the Institute for Multi-Racial Justice 1:1 (Spring 1998), 3.
Kochiyama, Yuri. "Preface: Trailblazing in a White World: A Brief History of Asian/Pacific American Women," in *Dragon Ladies: Asian American Feminists Breathe Fire*, Sonia Shah, ed. (Boston: South End Press, 1997), v-viii.
Kochiyama-Ladson, Akemi. "An Activist Life: 15 Minutes with Yuri Kochiyama," *A Magazine* Special edition 1994, 33.

Nakazawa, Mayumi. *The Life and Times of Yuri Kochiyama*. Tokyo: Bungei Shunju, 1999. [in Japanese]

Niiya, Brian. "From San Pedro Schoolgirl to Political Activist: Yuri Kochiyama," *JANM Quarterly*, Autumn 9:3 (1994), 3-4.

Tobier, Arthur. *Fishmerchant's Daughter: Yuri Kochiyama, An Oral History*. Vols. 1 and 2. New York: Community Documentation Workshop, 1981 and 1982.

Personal

Born on May 19, 1921 and raised in San Pedro, California. Spent two years in a concentration camp in Jerome, Arkansas, during World War II (1942-1944); worked at the Aloha USO Center in Hattiesburg, Mississippi (1944-1945). Moved to New York City following the war and married World War II Army veteran Bill Kochiyama (member of all-Japanese American 442nd combat team). Mother of six children; nine grandchildren; four great-grandchildren; and three godchildren. Relocated to Oakland, California in May 1999.

About the Editors–

AUDEE KOCHIYAMA-HOLMAN is the daughter of Yuri Kochiyama. She has been the Development Director for the Asian Law Caucus—a nonprofit agency serving low-income Asian Americans in San Francisco—for over nine years. She also serves on the Board of the EastSide Arts Alliance, which is a grassroots organization of artists and community activists whose programs are dedicated to building bridges between racially and ethnically diverse communities in Oakland.

AKEMI KOCHIYAMA-SARDINHA is the granddaughter of Yuri Kochiyama. She graduated from Spelman College. She is currently in the City University Graduate Center's Ph.D. Program in Cultural Anthropology. She is also a freelance editor and grantwriter, and has worked with Scholastic Press and the Japan Society in New York City for several years. Akemi plans to conduct her field research in Trinidad in Fall 2004.

MARJORIE LEE manages the Reading Room/Library of the UCLA Asian American Studies Center, as well as the processing of special collections of Asian Pacific Americans and the Asian American Movement. Her recent community research activities resulted in DUTY & HONOR: a Tribute to Chinese American World War II Veterans of Southern California, a collaborative work between UCLA and the Chinese Historical Society of Southern California.